I0813098

PREFACE

Klara Geywitz
Federal Minister for Housing, Urban Development and Building

DEAR READER, DEAR ARCHITECTURE ENTHUSIAST,

Be it droughts, torrential rain, or flooding—the consequences of climate change have already reached Europe. Venice, like many coastal cities and island nations around the world, is threatened in its very survival by the constant rise in sea levels.

It therefore seems self-evident that resources and the climate are playing a key role at this year's Venice Architecture Biennale. They are, after all, among the most urgent problems of today. Many people, and not just younger generations, are demanding swift action. Politicians and governments, the building and housing sectors, architects, and planners are likewise increasingly aware of their unique responsibility to achieve an economy and a way of life that are climate-friendly, sustainable, and resource-efficient.

The building industry remains responsible for 40 percent of energy consumption and 36 percent of CO_2 emissions in the European Union. The EU member states plan to reduce their net greenhouse gas emissions to zero by 2050 and uncouple economic growth from resource depletion. Achieving this will necessitate a profound change in the building sector. We need a resource-friendly revolution in architecture.

Building responsibly starts well before the groundbreaking, namely with a few simple, but fundamental questions: Where are we building and for whom? Do we need a new building or would it be more appropriate to convert an existing one? Can we rely on recycled materials to save costs and resources? Questions such as these are the starting point for new ideas, new technologies, and, eventually, a new attitude in the building sector.

OPEN FOR MAINTENANCE

is the motto of this year's German Pavilion at the Architecture Biennale. It reads as the expression of this type of new attitude and as an invitation to discussion.

The decades-old practice of demolishing existing buildings and replacing them with new ones with ever shorter life cycles has, at any rate, proved to be the wrong path. We must learn once again to responsibly use what already exists. By converting and extending buildings and by prolonging the use of materials, we can not only reduce damaging greenhouse gas emissions and land area usage. We also conserve fossil resources and enable more rapid and cost-efficient construction with shorter supply chains.

One key aspect of the resource-friendly revolution in architecture is the idea of sufficiency. By reusing or converting existing buildings, applying methods of circular construction, employing regenerative construction materials, and responsibly using resources we can transform our built environment in a climate-conscious and high-quality manner. The existing building stock can, on the one hand, provide cultural stimuli. On the other, it can function as the material repository for new construction projects. Just as this year the German Pavilion will become the storeroom for the materials from the 2022 Art Biennale. Sustainable construction is a societal task that focuses not only on individual buildings, but on the neighborhood and the entire city. By means of modern urban development policies geared toward the common good we will be able to overcome the major challenges facing our cities and communities. The New Leipzig Charter will act as the strategic compass here, for it underscores the transformative powers of European cities as places of diversity, creativity, and solidarity.

Firmly in keeping with the notion of the laboratory, which underpins this year's Architecture Biennale, titled *The Laboratory of the Future*, ARCH+ / SUMMACUMFEMMER / BÜRO JULIANE GREB have engaged intensely with the conditions for the expansion and/or conversion of existing buildings in a resource-efficient and responsible manner.

In their contribution, which has been funded by the Federal Ministry for Housing, Urban Development and Building, the curators have addressed the ecological and social challenges of today.

By tapping into the notions of care, repair, and maintaining (by squatting), the curatorial team directly references the processes of urban repair and cautious urban regeneration in line with the ethos of the 1984/87 International Building Exhibition (IBA) in Berlin. The German Pavilion at the 18th Architecture Biennale is therefore making an invaluable contribution to our national discussion on construction practices and urban development.

This year, Venice is an invitation to a thought experiment. We are all invited to think and design along—both at the Biennale and beyond.

OPEN FOR MAIN-TENANCE — WEGEN UMBAU GEÖFFNET

Text: Anne Femmer, Franziska Gödicke, Juliane Greb, Christian Hiller, Petter Krag, Melissa Makele, Anh-Linh Ngo, Florian Summa

Open for Maintenance is not an exhibition. It is an action framework for a building culture beyond the prevailing model hinging on the exploitation of resources and humans. The spotlight is put on previously used materials gathered from over 40 national pavilions and exhibitions at the 2022 Art Biennale, as well as on a broad network of Venetian and German activist groups. By carefully working with the existing—in material, social, and urban terms—the German Pavilion renders visible processes of spatial and social care work which are usually kept hidden.

Open for Maintenance squats and maintains the German Pavilion "as found," including Maria Eichhorn's contribution *Relocating a Structure* for the 2022 Art Biennale. In this way, the Art and Architecture Biennales become spatially and programmatically interwoven for the first time. The new architectural interventions are oriented towards local needs and include a ramp for accessibility, an ecological and nondiscriminatory bathroom, a space for meetings, a kitchenette, a material repository, and a workshop. The interventions, made entirely with materials salvaged from the 2022 Art Biennale, address questions of social and spatial inclusion in addition to resource issues.

Open for Maintenance transforms the monumental German Pavilion into a living place of (re)production. Assisting various groups from civil society, university students and crafts apprentices will help to maintain, repair, and care for social infrastructures across Venice as part of the *Maintenance 1:1* workshop program. Designing with the unpredictable—be it the unknown availability of materials or the open-ended participatory processes—generates creative possibilities that spell an optimistic outlook for architecture while simultaneously contributing to its regeneration as a social practice.

THE RAMP

In cooperation with
FORWARD DANCE COMPANY by LOFFT – DAS THEATER + Goethe-Institut / Performing Architecture, Rebiennale / R3B

In 1938, German architect Ernst Haiger remodeled the Bavarian Pavilion, dating from 1909, in accordance with Nazi ideology, turning it into the monumentalist piece of architecture we know it as today. Ever since, four massive fluted Doric columns have adorned its portico, separated from the grounds of the Giardini by five steps. This building is the vector of an architectural ideology proudly affirming its superiority and its claim to power. Anyone who does not conform to its norms is systematically excluded, not only in a political and cultural sense, but in a physical one as well: Classicism, from which this Pavilion inherits its traits, has always been modeled after the *healthy* body—aligned, during national socialism, with a racist ideal hellbent on annihilating other bodies.

Open for Maintenance views repairing the existing built fabric as a chance for a structural and ideological correction centering the needs of marginalized groups and bodies disadvantaged by ableism. The temporary remodeling of the German Pavilion's entrance adds a semicircular access ramp, facilitating access not only to visitors with reduced mobility, but also to cleaning personnel, guards, and technicians with heavy equipment. The ramp frames a new, public podium, which will be activated by the mixed-able FORWARD DANCE COMPANY by LOFFT – DAS THEATER in cooperation with the program partner Goethe-Institut on the occasion of the Pavilion's opening.

THE MATERIAL REPOSITORY

In cooperation with
Rebiennale / R3B, Concular

At the end of each Biennale, and hidden from the visitors' eyes, tons of exhibition materials are transported across Venice by hand, handcart, and boat every year. Only a fraction of these is reused. Not least because storage locations in the city are scarce and logistics costs notoriously sky-high—common problems encountered in circular building—most discarded materials go straight to the nearest landfill or recycling facility. This is where *Open for Maintenance* comes into play: Taking over Maria Eichhorn's contribution *Relocating a Structure* at the 2022 Art Biennale directly following the closing of the exhibition enabled immediate access to the Pavilion and utilizing it as a material repository. Materials gathered from over 40 national pavilions and exhibitions were saved from the landfill and moved to the German Pavilion in a physically demanding process in collaboration with Rebiennale / R3B. These "spolia" from the previous Biennale have become part of the structural interventions at the German Pavilion, all built from the left-behind materials. For the duration of the 2023 Architecture Biennale, and with the help of a new digital database developed in collaboration with Concular, the materials are inventoried and made available for further processing in the *Maintenance 1:1* workshop program.

THE WORKSHOP

In cooperation with
Sto-Foundation, AIT-Dialog, Rebiennale / R3B, universities, apprenticeship providers

The profit-oriented architectural production is geared toward demolition and new construction instead of repairing, toward growth instead of sufficiency and maintenance. This contravenes all sensible environmental and social changes needed in light of contemporary crises. Repairing—the system as well as the built fabric—therefore becomes the inevitable political and architectural code of practice. Already today, more than half of construction projects in Europe are refurbishments and conversions. In the future, practicing architecture will mean, first and foremost, *repairing* that which already exists. But to repair, one needs a set of tools, knowledge, and techniques, which will be at the disposal of all visitors in an openly accessible workshop in the German Pavilion. The central idea is to empower people to maintain their (built) environment. A workshop program with grassroots organizations from various countries, universities, and apprenticeship providers will make these aspirations become a practical reality well beyond the limits of the Biennale itself: Collaborative projects will lead to small repair works across and around Venice. Based on actual interventions, participants will learn that the (re)production of space is inextricably linked to both the social and the ecological issue.

THE BATHROOM

In cooperation with
Project Group Sanitary Revolution (Eawag, finizio – Future Sanitation, KanTe – Kollektiv für angepasste Technik, klo:lektiv, IGZ – Leibniz Institute of Vegetable and Ornamental Crops, urin*all, among others), Agriluska, IDRO Group

The transformation of the German Pavilion into a living site of (re)productive work will encompass the integration of heretofore missing sanitary infrastructure into the building. Beyond an answer to practical concerns, the bathroom also materializes a response to several topical issues surrounding a necessary "sanitary revolution": From an ecological perspective, a water-based sanitary network is increasingly untenable given ever-longer droughts. The matter is an especially pressing one in Venice, where the lack of a sewer system leads to most toilets being directly emptied into the canals. (Only a minority of buildings is equipped with septic tanks.) We need alternative solutions to reduce water usage and close nutrient cycles.

Open for Maintenance features an accessible prototype for a urine-separating dry toilet and a unisex urinal combined with a urine treatment reactor. Working with the organic farm Agriluska in the Veneto region, human waste is composted and then reused as fertilizer (the urine is converted to fertilizer in the on-site reactor). On a sociopolitical level, however, such basic needs as using the toilet and personal hygiene, as well as infrastructures of maintenance and cleaning, are also linked to questions of justice in terms of gender, dis_ability, race, and class. The role of care work is further addressed by the incorporation of tools for changing diapers, washing, and cleaning.

THE KITCHENETTE

In cooperation with
Assemblea Sociale per la Casa, Centro Sociale Rivolta, ConstructLab, Haus der Materialisierung, Institute of Radical Imagination + S.a.L.E. Docks, Kotti & Co, Laboratorio Occupato Morion, Sozialgenossenschaft Bellevue di Monaco

Maintenance is a process, the terms of which need to be negotiated by society. Groups from civil society hold a crucial position in the maintenance of and care for built and social infrastructures. Communicating, supporting each other, and organizing need a range of low-threshold spaces for communication and collective care work. Part of *Open for Maintenance* is a kitchenette which is intended to become such a communicative switchboard. Here, the broad network of organizations and activist groups will be represented with their ecological, social, and urban policy demands. Posters, leaflets, and other communication material gathered in the kitchenette will reflect and promote the work surrounding the social struggles for the right to the city by organizations based in Venice and Germany, such as Assemblea Sociale per la Casa, Centro Sociale Rivolta, Laboratorio Occupato Morion, and Institute of Radical Imagination, as well as Bellevue di Monaco, Haus der Materialisierung, and Kotti & Co.

THE MEETING SPACE

In cooperation with
Haus der Materialisierung, CRCLR House (Concular, Die Zusammenarbeiter, Impact Hub Berlin, LXSY Architekten, TRNSFRM)

Open for Maintenance does not pretend to reveal any groundbreaking information. It is no secret that the construction sector contributes more than 40 percent to global CO_2 emissions; that housing in urban agglomerations is becoming increasingly unaffordable, partly due to touristification, which in the case of Venice is being further exacerbated by the Biennale in particular; that the social and ecological consequences of these developments will be felt by the already vulnerable and marginalized groups who perform (spatial) care work all over the world, maintaining and caring for the building stock. What is crucial is how we deal with this knowledge.

The current crises besetting architecture can only be solved through new forms of collaboration between architects, craftspeople, engineers, artists, researchers, and civil society. The meeting space in the German Pavilion creates an opportunity for that kind of exchange. Here, however, visitors can also playfully engage with what they have seen and experienced. They can create bags from materials left over from the 2022 Art Biennale using patterns created by Haus der Materialisierung, or they can play the board game *Trivial Circuit* developed by LXSY Architekten in cooperation with Impact Hub Berlin and Concular, which helps to understand the complex reorganization of the planning processes involved in circular construction, questioning the conventional construction phases and focusing on ecological and social aspects.

Using the medium of architecture, the German Pavilion makes maintenance work—on the built fabric, on society, and on the discipline itself—tangible. The explicit reference to the concept of *maintenance* in the contribution's title places it in the footsteps of a feminist artistic practice that emphasizes the importance of everyday reproductive care work for the preservation of societies. The curatorial concept translates maintenance into the architectural practices of *Caring*, *Repairing*, and *Maintaining (Through Squatting)*, aimed at reappropriating and consolidating preexisting material and social networks through their upkeep, reinforcement, and transformation.

Demonstrating the need for a "double consciousness," as demanded by Lesley Lokko in her concept *The Laboratory of the Future* for the 2023 Architecture Biennale, the contribution consciously engages with Venice as the Biennale's host city. Architecture must always consider the local challenges for and global implications of its actions. One example: Venice's population has been dwindling steadily because a growing number of people cannot afford to live in the city. This problem of displacement is linked to the commodification of urban space by mass tourism, Biennales, and the events industry. Alongside the residents, daily life and the networks of social and material maintenance which do not generate a profit are increasingly disappearing from the city. At the same time, a multitude of activist groups are forming to genuinely address these problems. One of these is Assemblea Sociale per la Casa (ASC). Despite the dynamics of displacement, more than 2,200 publicly owned housing units stand empty and are left to decay. ASC squats those apartments and renovates them with materials left over from the Biennales before allocating them to people in need of housing. Their work mends the urban fabric and stabilizes social relations in the tradition of historical practices of maintenance through squatting like the *Instandbesetzung* movement operating in 1980s Berlin. This practice, whose name combines the German words "Instandsetzung" (maintaining) and "Besetzung" (squatting), was formally recognized and institutionalized in Berlin's 1984–87 International Building Exhibition and greatly contributed to the preservation of the urban fabric and historically grown communities. Local activist groups like ASC will use the German Pavilion as a platform of allyship. And yet, the collaborative interventions at the Pavilion and within the city are not limited to a critique of the Biennale as a format and of architecture as a discipline. Rather, the practically minded approach sheds light on the myriad possibilities for action in converting and designing inclusive and socioecological cities and architectures while emphasizing the chances and potentials that lie in this much-needed work. At the center of the German contribution lies the joy of working away at these challenges with like-minded people.

ACKNOWLEDGEMENTS

The German contribution to the 18th Architecture Biennale has evolved into an international project involving over 100 people. Without their trust and commitment, *Open for Maintenance* would never have seen the light of day. This is why we want to thank everyone who supported and contributed to this project. They are too numerous to be highlighted individually here; the complete list can be found at the end of this publication. But without the fantastic teams at ARCH+, SUMMACUMFEMMER, and BÜRO JULIANE GREB, this project would not exist: Elke Doppelbauer, Nora Dünser, Mirko Gatti, Anna Hugot, Sascha Kellermann, Beatrice Koch, Daniel Kuhnert, Arno Löbbecke, Victor Lortie, Vittorio Romieri, Barbara Schindler, and Finn Steffens deserve our special thanks.

PERFORMING
ARCHITECTURE
Eine Veranstaltungsreihe des Goethe-Instituts als Programmpartner
des Deutschen Pavillons auf der 18. Internationalen Architekturausstellung
La Biennale di Venezia
A series of events run by the Goethe-Institut as program partner
of the German Pavilion at the 18th International Architecture Exhibition
La Biennale di Venezia
Programm / program
www.goethe.de/performingarchitecture
GOETHE
INSTITUT
Sprache. Kultur. Deutschland.

ARCH+ team for this issue:
Nora Dünser (managing editor), Mirko Gatti, Franziska Gödicke *(FG)*, Christian Hiller, Markus Krieger, Daniel Kuhnert *(DK)*, Victor Lortie, Melissa Makele (project lead), Alex Nehmer, Anh-Linh Ngo (editor-in-chief), Finn Steffens

In cooperation with:
BÜRO JULIANE GREB:
Juliane Greb, Petter Krag
SUMMACUMFEMMER:
Anne Femmer, Florian Summa

ARCH+ features 117
Open for Maintenance – Wegen Umbau geöffnet
Anne Femmer, Franziska Gödicke, Juliane Greb, Christian Hiller, Petter Krag, Melissa Makele, Anh-Linh Ngo, Florian Summa

Squatting and Maintaining the German Pavilion
Juliane Greb and Petter Krag (BÜRO JULIANE GREB) & Anne Femmer and Florian Summa (SUMMACUMFEMMER)

CULTURE

#VWGroupCulture

We support museums, exhibitions and concerts. We facilitate the dialog between visual art, music, science and technology. We help to put culture at the heart of society.

FOR ALL.

VOLKSWAGEN
AKTIENGESELLSCHAFT

vwgroupculture
volkswagengroup_culture

Recycling and circularity in focus

The LS 990, LS CUBE, AS 500, A 550, A FLOW and A CREATION series and ranges from JUNG have been awarded the Cradle to Cradle (C2C) certificate and the C2C Material Health certificate following an elaborate testing process.

Over 50 individual products, including rocker switches, push-buttons, frames, inserts, classic sockets, sockets with USB connections and Safety+ inserts, covers and entire modules have received the coveted Cradle to Cradle Certified® (Bronze) distinction. One particular challenge was the certification of the complete KNX modules, such as the push-button sensor module and the room controller module with their small-sized technology. The Bronze certification of the JUNG KNX sensor technology and the KNX motion detector is a significant step forward for the industry, and JUNG is currently the only manufacturer in the world to have secured it.

Squatting and Maintaining the German Pavillion at the 18th International Architecture Exhibition – La Biennale di Venezia

The German contribution to this year's Venice Biennale practises the resource-conserving but labour-intensive principles of reuse and circularity, involving along the way many civil society actors, researchers and creative artists. Under the title Open for Maintenance – Wegen Umbau geöffnet, curated by ARCH+ / SUMMACUMFEMMER / BÜRO JULIANE GREB, the German contribution is dedicated to the topics of care, repair and maintenance – viewed from both an architectural and social perspective. JUNG is delighted to be a corporate partner supporting this creative approach to some of the most pressing issues of our time.

JUNG is aware of its responsibility as a manufacturer and employer for the environment and people, and wants to contribute to the preservation of living spaces today, tomorrow and for future generations. To this end, it is publishing the JUNG Sustainability Report 2021 / 2022, in which the company transparently discloses its ESG strategy. It will be used to assess sustainability in the three areas of Environment, Social affairs and Governance (ESG).

JUNG.DE/C2C follow us on @junglovesarchitecture

JUNG | 111 YEARS

CERTIFIED
cradle to cradle
BRONZE

EQUITONE

Let's explore
circular building together

After over a century of designing light-weight fibre-cement cladding that lasts a lifetime, we are shifting our focus to 'What Lies Beyond'. We are determined to push the boundaries of our industry and close the loop on our materials. We are targeting zero waste to landfill by 2030.

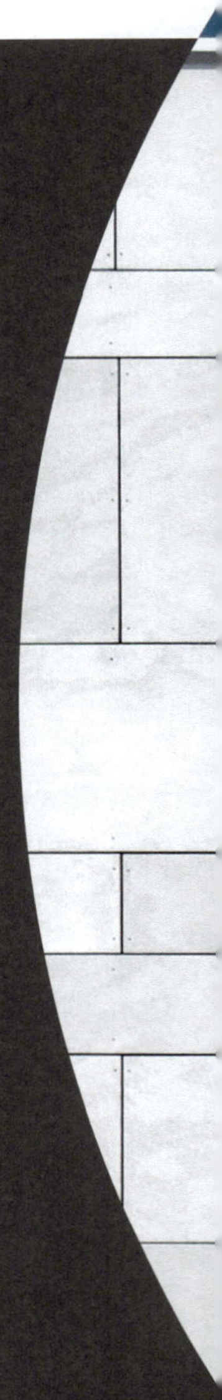

Certifiably sustainable

All EQUITONE fiber cement façade materials are Cradle to Cradle Certified®. Widely regarded throughout the building industry as a preferred sustainability standard, it gives architects fact-based, at-a-glance assurance that EQUITONE's façade materials meet some of the world's most rigorous sustainability standards.

Discover now: **www.equitone.com**

Do you believe
in the afterlife?
etex
inspiring ways
of living

RE-THINKING VALUE

Goal of the *Hand schafft Wert* initiative: To focus on the value of craftsmanship. By so doing, we are expressly supporting the concept of the German Pavilion at the 18th Architecture Biennale "Open for Maintenance" and bringing working processes in construction out of the shadows.

Creating value

When challenges become greater and resources scarcer, a new way of thinking is required. And this new thinking is applied best where change is visible most rapidly: in value. Value is changing and being radically renegotiated. Value is becoming more multidimensional and interdisciplinary. This is nowhere more noticeable than in the construction and energy sector.

The value of a building has always had an economic, a spatial and a temporal dimension. This is manifested in the moment someone is willing to pay the quantified equivalent value for property X in location Y. However, there is a lot more to this value than the sum of the raw and building materials.

So now, as living space, energy and materials become scarce, first of all the pure equivalent value increases. Aesthetic value and functional value must not be disregarded, but rather re-thought. Planning and execution trades have always worked hand in hand to achieve both. But their work does not end – or no longer ends – with the initial valorisation. Architecture that wants to conserve and reuse resources must take an integral approach to the preservation of value over time. Those who want to do justice to their social responsibility as a reality-shaping discipline must therefore open up and overcome boundaries: limits of trades or responsibilities, but also limits of a valuation of the inventory or a warranty for second-hand values.

Preserving value

Craftsman trades have always had the task of maintaining and servicing technical building equipment. This is why concepts that focus on value preservation are actually nothing new for the trade sector. Skilled craftsmanship, however, is the scarcest resource of the 21st century, alongside physical raw and building materials. The dimensions are no longer felt only personally while waiting for an appointment with a craftsperson. This is because, at the moment, an entire society is waiting for the solutions that are so urgently needed for the energy transition to actually be installed. So if installation skills become the limiting factor for progress and the cost factor for the national economy, the value of craftsmanship must also be strengthened. This can be demanded or encouraged. One is more of a political reflex. The other is a cooperative principle that spreads confidence. In all conceivable constellations between industry, architecture or planning and execution, craftsman trades play a decisive role.

This role can best be fulfilled if digitalisation, market concentration or even a shortage of skilled workers are not seen as a threat, but rather as an opportunity. As an opportunity to shape the future with new, courageous cooperation agreements.

Encourage

The *Hand schafft Wert* (Hand Creates Value) initiative is campaigning for more appreciation and value creation in the skilled crafts and trades. And for the free thinking of new ideas. Many such value-preserving and resource-saving ideas are still too often developed without input from the skilled crafts, or not quite thought through to the end. Unresolved warranty issues often block implementation in practice. It is precisely this pragmatism that is more in demand than ever in many places, on both a large and small scale. Providing all the trades involved in construction with a sense of security not only facilitates the successful search of joint solutions, but also raises the cooperation between architecture and skilled crafts to a new, valuable level.

— Why do groundbreaking designs still fail because no craftsman can be found who dares to actually implement them?

— Why are promising large-scale geothermal projects in the Münsterland region threatened with delays only because no craftsman is willing to

Excellent example of continued use and value retention: the Nakasone House, Mexico City/Mexico by Escobedo Soliz, Grand Prix Winner in the Erich Mendelsohn Prize 2020. "Here, a wonderful home was conjured up in an existing building with the simplest of means and materials."

The jury explicitly acknowledges the value and importance of craftsmanship in the implementation of sustainable concepts and trend-setting visions: "Drawing on local materials and the tradition of local craftsmanship, the concept succeeds in (...) reinterpreting modesty in a new and refined way."

install the heat pumps provided by the building contractor – or is unable to do so because he lacks the necessary number of skilled workers?

— Or why does the 5-year guarantee on a completely overhauled designer fitting from a brand manufacturer only apply if it is installed by a specialist tradesman?

Building for value

The fact that a new type of insurance product can provide answers to these questions may sound surprising. Or maybe obvious. Thus, the ideas of *Hand schafft Wert* close gaps in the warranty at crucial points. And overcome hurdles in availability.

The first product solution, Craft Care, is a guarantee insurance for materials provided by the customer that takes effect even before installation. This provides a whole new promise of security in terms of craftsmanship. In the BtoB context, Craft Care Pro finally provides clarity over questions of liability for materials provided by the customer. Both solutions are available in a completely digital process with maximum simplicity via the web portal: handschafftwert.de

The value of a novel solution is measured in its application. Understood in this way, "Open for Maintenance" is an explicit invitation to all construction-related trades to explore possible applications in all phases of construction and service. To think further about novel or circular building concepts in their own projects. With the skilled craft sector as an enabler for sustainability, value creation and value preservation. For joint re-thinking and further development in science, industry and above all in building practice.

HAND SCHAFFT WERT.

As a practical start-up, the *Hand schafft Wert* initiative is working hard for more appreciation and value creation in the skilled crafts and trades and thinks of solutions in terms of cooperation between all construction-related trades.

×

VHV VERSICHERUNGEN

As Germany's leading specialist construction insurer, VHV Versicherungen is a strategic partner of *Hand schafft Wert* and a risk carrier for innovative product solutions.

↓

hsw-x.de

NEW TENDENCY

NEWTENDENCY.COM

LION: A NEW SERIES

BERLIN-KAULSDORF
LION-FEUCHTWANGER-STRASSE
COMPLETION: Q4 2023

- 124 FLEXIBLE APARTMENTS
- 20 FLOOR PLAN VARIATIONS
- COMMUNAL GARDEN AND SHARED SPACES FOR ALL RESIDENTS

LION.EUROBODEN.DE

EUROBODEN X FAR

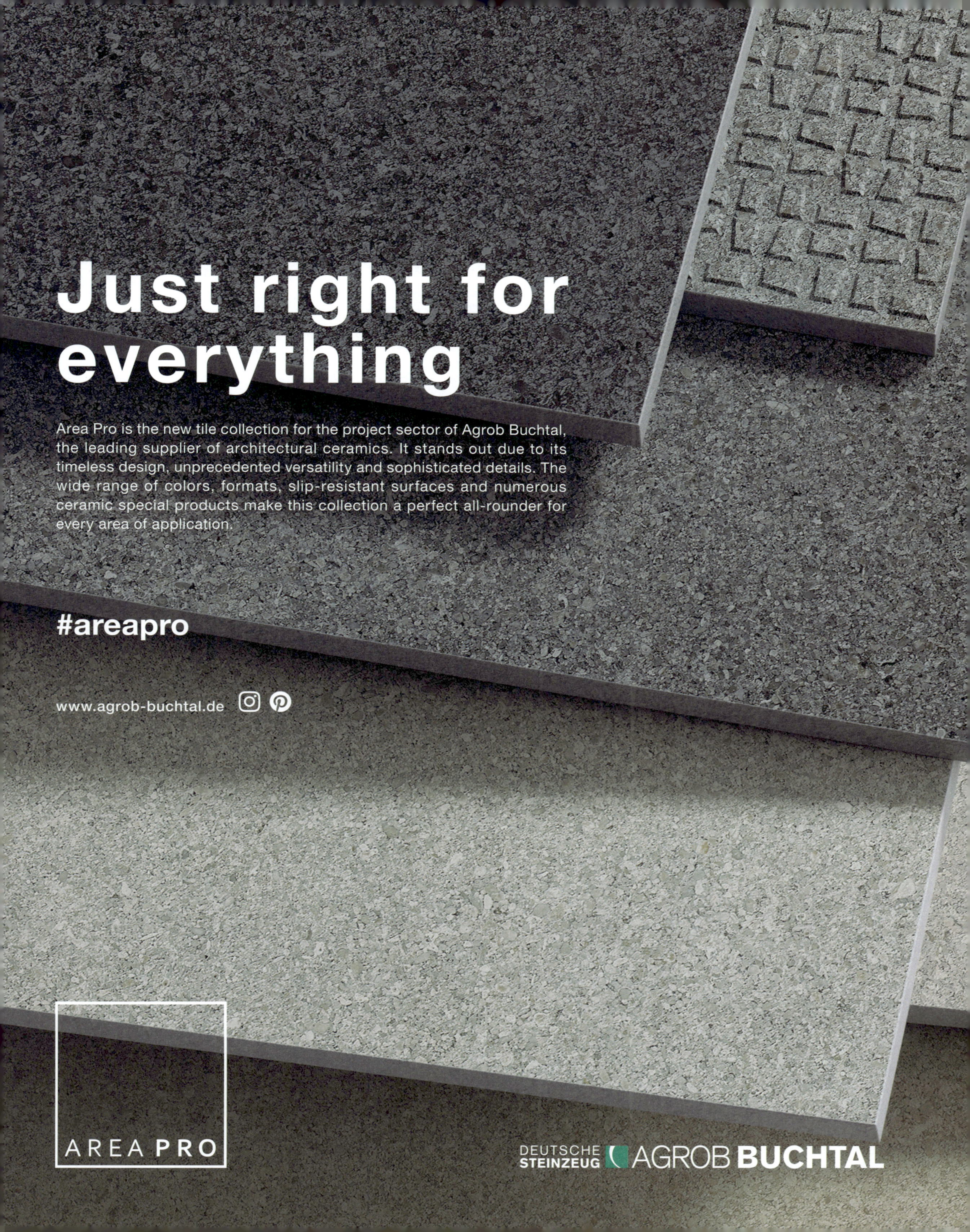
Just right for everything
Area Pro is the new tile collection for the project sector of Agrob Buchtal, the leading supplier of architectural ceramics. It stands out due to its timeless design, unprecedented versatility and sophisticated details. The wide range of colors, formats, slip-resistant surfaces and numerous ceramic special products make this collection a perfect all-rounder for every area of application.
#areapro
www.agrob-buchtal.de
AREA PRO
DEUTSCHE STEINZEUG AGROB BUCHTAL

ILBAGNOALESSI
DESIGN STEFANO GIOVANNONI
LAUFEN.COM

LAUFEN

MAINTENANCE

AND

REMODELING

MOTTOS FOR MAINTE-NANCE AS CARE WORK

A Short Reflection Inspired by Shannon Mattern's Foundational Essay "Maintenance and Care" (2018)

Text:
Hélène Frichot

"Maintenance at any particular site, or on any particular body or object, requires the maintenance of an entire ecology: attending to supply chains, instruments, protocols, social infrastructures, and environmental conditions.… If we wish to better support the critical work performed by the world's maintainers, we must recognize that maintenance encompasses a world of standards, tools, practices, and wisdom. Sometimes it deploys machine learning; other times, a mop."[1]
Shannon Mattern, *Maintenance and Care* (2018)

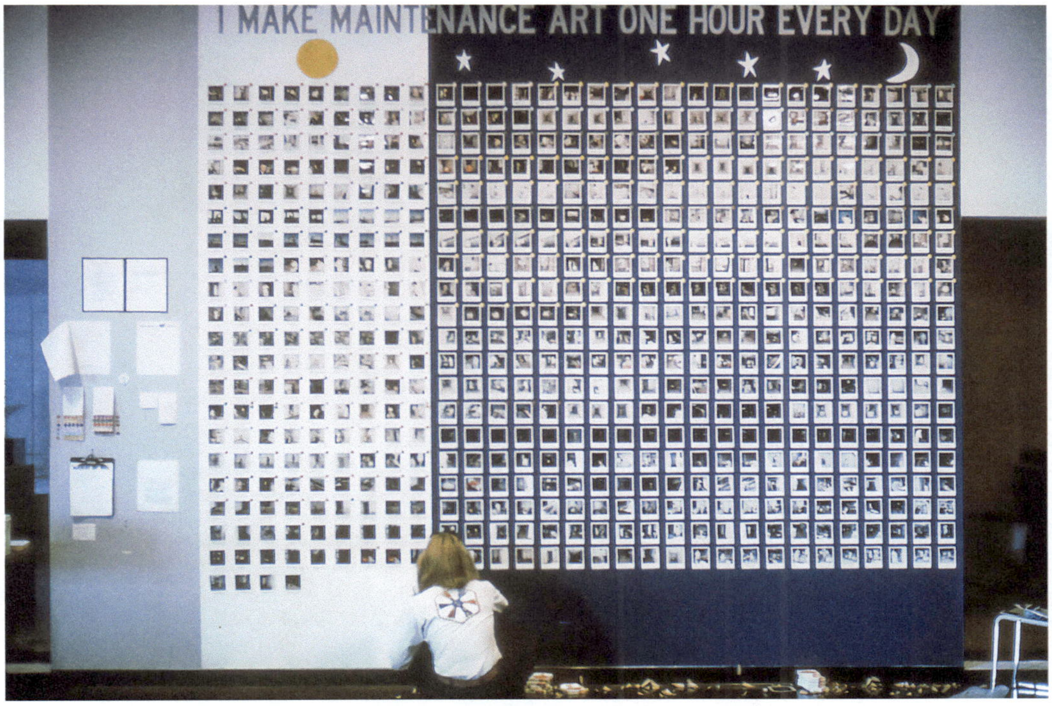

FIG. 1
Mierle Laderman Ukeles, *I Make Maintenance Art One Hour Every Day,*
September 16 – October 20, 1976

Performance with 300 maintenance employees during their day and night shifts over the course of five weeks at 55 Water Street, New York
Installation and performance commissioned for *ART ⇄ WORLD* exhibition at Whitney Museum Downtown at 55 Water Street

720 Polaroid photographs mounted on paper; two kinds of printed labels to be attached to the bottom of each polaroid: one saying MAINTENANCE ART, the other saying MAINTENANCE WORK; color-coded stickers; seven handwritten and typewritten texts; clipboard; custom-made buttons, one for each participating worker; 12 × 15 ft (overall)
Acquired for the permanent collection of The Whitney Museum of American Art, New York, 2017

During the exhibition's five-week run time, Mierle Laderman Ukeles photographed the maintenance employees working in the 3.5 million square feet skyscraper, having previously asked them to consider an hour of each day's work as art. Showing them the Polaroids, she asked them to define whether this was *Maintenance Work* or *Maintenance Art* and labeled the photographs accordingly.

Covering a vast territory from machine learning to mops, Shannon Mattern's near-exhaustive 2018 essay *Maintenance and Care* demonstrates how environment-worlds[2] are held together. Rather than heroic acts of construction and infrastructural connection, ribbon-cutting and expressions of rude wealth inscribed into facades rising dizzyingly high, it's the minor, everyday acts of maintenance, repair, and making do that matter. Rusting infrastructures, dust that must be cleaned away, cracks that need to be fixed, a link lost, a format that has become obsolete thwarting the archivist's attempts at keeping safe past forms of digitized knowledge … these are but a few of the circumstances where a leap of imagination is badly needed for new creative practices of maintenance and repair to emerge. Connections can be made across infrastructural scales and rhythms that combine acts of maintenance and repair in relation to registers of cognitive, embodied, and reproductive labor. As we look at the broken, exhausted world around us, we are provoked to ask ourselves material questions: Can maintenance constitute a project in its own right, one of world-mending as distinct from world-building? How do we know when to repair, and when not to repair? Our response to such questions affects how we frame our design pedagogies and how we reimagine practice.

The literature calling on us to pay attention to—and shift—our habits of world-making compiles long lists enumerating the extraction of materials, labor, and life. The hubris of human

FIG. 2
Ila Bêka and Louise Lemoine, *Koolhaas Houselife,* 2008, film still

The film's central protagonist is Guadalupe Acedo, the housekeeper of the iconic Maison à Bordeaux (1994–98), which OMA designed for wheelchair-bound newspaper publisher Jean-François Lemoîne. The camera follows Acedo during her daily work in the house, which is significantly complicated by the building's maintenance-intensive architecture and mode of operation—contrasting with the outward image of effortlessly living in tidy, barrier-free architecture.

FIG. 3
Suzanne Lacy with Meg Parnell, *Cleaning Conditions,* 2013, performance, Manchester Art Gallery

Artist Suzanne Lacy, together with Meg Parnell, developed this two-week cleaning performance, which, through accompanying public discussions and employee meetings in the Manchester Art Gallery, addressed the political dimensions of care and cleaning work at the intersection of migration, unpaid care work, precarious working conditions, as well as the role of women in the global care and cleaning industries.

power and hopelessness fuse. It is certainly difficult not to be overwhelmed, to be struck preemptively with exhaustion by the question, the challenge: What is to be done? In Mattern's own words, "What we really need to study is how the world gets put back together."[3] On this account, I'd like to propose a semantic experiment: It is curious indeed that the lament is often structured as a long list, even a litany. Rather than taking the list as overwhelming, it might instead be represented as a to-do list; a schedule of tasks to be undertaken. A list might be revised as a manifesto, or reframed as a series of mottos to motivate action. What follows are mottos I have extrapolated from Mattern's text in an attempt to reflect upon what can be done rather than what has gone wrong.

"LABOR IS ESSENTIAL TO MAIN-TENANCE"

We cannot speak of maintenance without extending due respect to the work of artist Mierle Laderman Ukeles, who, as a young wife and mother, turned her domestic space into a laboratory of care, subsequently extending her experiments outward from this undervalued domain of reproductive labor into the world. Ukeles identifies two conflicting human instincts in her *Maintenance Art Manifesto*. The "Death Instinct" leads us down a self-interested, self-aggrandizing path: "separation, individuality, Avant-Garde par excellence; to follow one's own path to death."[4] At the opposite end of a vast spectrum of care, the "Life Instinct"—which Ukeles calls maintenance—unifies us, speaks to the eternal return: "Maintenance is a drag; it takes all the fucking time!" The life instinct embraces the perpetual work of maintenance required to sustain no less than the continuation of the species.[5] *"Maintaining life*—that's a big job."[6] Indeed, Mattern places Ukeles's performance events and typewritten scores alongside the work of feminist activist and scholar Silvia Federici. In her book *Revolution at Point Zero: Housework, Reproduction, and Feminist Struggle,* Federici discusses the post-Second World War period as a brief moment in time where women had become sick of performing their reproductive labor to prop up productive economies and churn out yet more workers and soldiers.[7] Federici argues that the enclosure of the commons, alongside a general devaluation of women's labor and the gradual proscription of women from practicing crafts, accessing inheritance, and maintaining control of their bodies, rendered them extremely vulnerable and dependent on men. Emancipation eventually went to die in suburban cul-de-sacs, where family life turned nuclear. Following Dolores Hayden's magnificent *The Grand Domestic Revolution* and her recovery of the program of action of the materialist feminists, we must remember that the radical revaluation of domestic labor once promised more collective social relationships of care. Hayden argues that the socialization of housework and child care entails "a complete transformation of spatial and material culture" and a concentration on "economic and spatial issues as the basis of material life."[8] This pragmatic utopian vision, still so relevant today, reclassifies reproductive labor as a collective endeavor rather than as a merely individual affair circumscribed by a domestic sphere.

"WHO DOESN'T CARE FOR CARE?"

Who is it who knows no act, small or large, of care? They are the ones who have the least intimate knowledge of designed living environments. The proud image of the housekeeper Guadalupe Acedo attending to Rem Koolhaas' Maison à Bordeaux to the tune of Johann Strauss Jr.'s "Accelerations" waltz—as seen in Ila Bêka and Louise Lemoine's acclaimed film *Koolhaas Houselife* (2008)—is a compelling reminder that expertise can be humbly learnt, and greater acknowledgement is owed to those who care. If you claim any expertise whatsoever in design and construction, then this knowledge must intersect with a capacity to care for the minutiae, for the mundane. As we go through a list of mundane activities compiled by architectural scholar Catherina Gabrielsson, "cleaning, polishing, dusting, airing, ripping, pairing, drilling, aching, leaking, breathing, sweating, panting …"[9] we hear and feel how housework combines body and building; the sweat of the maintainer with the inevitable entropy of a structure perpetually falling into disrepair. We know this list is an open-ended one, composed as a rhythm of repetition and difference. Mattern cites a similar list drawn from Evelyn Nakano Glenn: "Purchasing household goods, preparing and serving food, laundering and repairing clothing, maintaining furnishings and appliances, socializing children, providing care and emotional support for adults, and maintaining kin and community ties,"[10] to which she adds the kinds of digital care required today in raising kids, like tech support, digital filtering, and screen time allowances. "Housework is ethics," I once scrawled across a notebook page in an attempt to make a connection between the daily Sisyphean grind of attending to domestic duties and the role practical ethics play in the maintenance of equitable and fair social relations. Gabrielsson argues that housework, "points to an ethics of care that is fundamentally at odds with capitalist

FIG. 4
The Nest Collective, *Return to Sender* (detail), 2022

In their work *Return to Sender*, made of used textiles and electronic garbage, presented at documenta fifteen (2022), the multidisciplinary Nest Collective from Nairobi make globally unequal material flows and politics of waste disposal perceptible through a confrontational inversion. Bales of old clothes tied up for shipping, which are usually imported to Kenya from the Global North—and 40 percent of which end up in local landfills—were installed as expansive structures on a meadow in front of the Kassel Orangerie.

This deliberate irritation addressed the existing relations of how industrialized countries' ways of life and consumption co-produce precarious ecological and economic realities of waste and final disposal in the Global South.

accumulation."[11] She adds, furthermore, that the omission of housework from architectural discourse, "exposes the fragile, yet enduring imaginations of authorship, progress and control that structure the discipline." It is hard to glorify maintenance, let alone document its achievements or its impact. And yet …

"CARE, LIKE MAINTENANCE, IS EASILY ROMANTICIZED"

We must be wary of romanticizing performances of care, too often undertaken by minorities: Black and brown bodies, disadvantaged women, children, and migrants; the unpaid, underpaid, and the devalued. The bare life of the worker has been stripped to the bone; it is a battle for mere survival, hand to mouth. "Sometimes, it seems, repair entails complicity with capitalism and colonialism," Mattern warns us. She continues: "around the world, many formal infrastructures are products of colonialism, and imperial legacies persist through global financing."[12] There is the risk that by maintaining such infrastructures, we maintain the status quo. Sometimes, repair and intended improvement only make things worse. In *Colonial Lives of Property: Law, Land and Racial Regimes of Property*, legal scholar Brenna Bhandar discusses the implications of an "ideology of improvement" that has been used to justify colonial expansion.[13] She explains that this ideology defines land use in a narrow way, one that privileges Western practices of land management under concepts of cultivation and settlement. Determined through calculation and measurement, this ideology not only seizes control over land through mapping and surveying, but quantifies the labor of people as well, reducing them to mere units of value: "The 18th century witnesses both the criminalization of groups of people not tethered or fixed geographically to regular work, as well as the rise in statistical forms of knowledge aimed at the governance of these (and other) populations."[14] Traditional practices and Indigenous practices that do not fit into such categories are disregarded, destroying people's livelihoods. The right to exist in the face of inhumanity is bought with hard work: patriarchy, capitalism, and the continuum of colonization hold immense power. To resist, to reclaim access to basic rights, is "a never-ending struggle, revolution as daily work," as Françoise Vergès insists, calling this unromantic, daily, political toil, "decolonial feminism."[15] This work, she asserts, is undertaken in a "transversal and intersectional way," paying specific respect to the women of the Global South upon whose backs colonizing nations have been built.

"MAINTENANCE TRAVERSES SCALES"

We know all too well that we live on a damaged planet, a broken planet, and that this ramshackle, run-down state of affairs is due to the furious industrial activities of a privileged few whose projects of colonization and capitalist accumulation have laid waste to worlds. This makes an orientation toward maintenance and repair all the more urgent. Environmental storytelling grounds us and asks us to consider specific environments, the cross-species contagions that take hold, the admixtures of societies and technologies, natures and cultures. A great deal is heard about the devastations that have been wrought, and how we must collaboratively work in—and from—the midst of these. The labor required to repair the world is a repeated one and does not arrive at a moment of conclusion: Once you have finished painting the bridge that crosses the river joining one territory with another, you must start all over again; once the bathrooms have been scrubbed down, the surfaces dusted and wiped, the floors mopped, it is time to recommence: housework is an endless task. It is a ritual, holding embodied knowledge extending way beyond the domain of the home. Housework must be understood at different scales, from the domestic interior to the urban block, to practices of cultivation and land use, all the way to the entire planet. The necessity of mundane tasks demands that we pay attention to the minutiae supporting everyday living environments. Care and how it situates us is fundamental to the functioning of a democratic society. In its *Care Manifesto*, published 2020 in the midst of the Covid-19 pandemic, the Care Collective urged us to imagine multiple dimensions of care in addition to its myriad scales: caring politics, caring kinships, caring communities, caring states, caring economies, caring for the world, or planetary care.[16] Care across these fields of action is mobilized to counter the carelessness we witness all around us.

"TO STUDY MAINTENANCE IS ITSELF AN ACT OF MAINTENANCE …

… to fill in the gaps in this literature, to draw connections among different disciplines, is an act of repair or, simply, of taking care—connecting threads, mending holes, amplifying quiet voices,"[17] writes Mattern. On this note, I would like to mention Silvia Federici's account of the witch hunts—a cruel crusade that progressed from the Old World to the New World from the 16th to the 18th century. Federici claims that the witch hunts largely contributed to the gradual transformation of women from active participants in society to docile subjects. She writes that during the witch hunts, so-called witches were often simply elderly women of little means. Deprived of social and economic status, these women would have no choice but to go from house to house asking for food. When turned away, if they were heard to mutter something to themselves, it would be assumed that the muttering must be a spell.[18] Motto comes from the latin *muttum*, or muttering. What we mutter to ourselves as we bend over our work, whether in joy or frustration, with a sense of humor or indignation, can keep us going. A motto, like a slogan, helps us to express a purpose. It has also been taken to be the incantation of witches, placing women who make a fuss at great risk. Mottos, or slogans, can be appropriated from the thinkers who inspire us to practice differently, with attention and awareness: *Slow down! Stay with the Trouble! Reclaim the commons! Pay attention!* Mottos for maintenance as care work are what we are in great need of today.

1 Shannon Mattern, "Maintenance and Care," *Places Journal* (November 2018), accessed February 10th, 2023, doi.org/10.22269/181120.
2 Appropriation of the term "Umwelt" [literally "surrounding world"], which in German means both the environment and one's immediate surroundings, inextricably linking the different scales and dimensions of human action.
3 Ibid.
4 Mierle Laderman Ukeles, *Maintenance Art Manifesto 1969!*, 1969.
5 Ibid.
6 Mattern, "Maintenance and Care" (see note 1).
7 Silvia Federici, *Revolution at Point Zero: Housework, Reproduction, and Feminist Struggle* (Oakland: PM Press, 2012).
8 Dolores Hayden, *The Grand Domestic Revolution* (Cambridge: MIT Press, 1982), 3.
9 Catharina Gabrielsson, "The Critical Potential of Housework," in *Architecture and Feminisms: Ecologies, Economies, Technologies*, eds. Hélène Frichot et al. (Abingdon: Routledge, 2018), 246.
10 Evelyn Nakano Glenn, "From Servitude to Service Work: Historical Continuities in the Racial Division of Paid Reproductive Labor," *Signs: Journal of Women in Culture and Society* 18, no. 1 (1992), 1–43.
11 Gabrielsson, "Housework" (see note 9), 251.
12 Mattern, "Maintenance and Care" (see note 1).
13 Brenna Bhandar, *Colonial Lives of Property: Law, Land and Racial Regimes of Property* (Durham and London: Duke University Press, 2018).
14 Ibid., 36.
15 Françoise Vergès, *Decolonial Feminism* (London: Pluto Press, 2021), 5.
16 The Care Collective: *The Care Manifesto: The Politics of Interdependence* (London: Verso Books, 2020).
17 Mattern, "Maintenance and Care" (see note 1).
18 Federici, *Caliban and the Witch: Women, The Body and Primitive Accumulation* (2004. Reprint, New York: Autonomedia, 2014).

"All Buildings Are Beautiful; Stop Building More"

The Winding Road Toward a Culture of Conversion

Text:
Christoph Grafe, Tim Rieniets

In December 1967, Oswald Mathias Ungers, at the time Dean of the Faculty of Architecture at TU Berlin, hosted a conference simply called *Architecture Theory*. It was meant to be the largest convention the faculty had organized since the end of the Second World War, and boasted a befittingly distinguished and contrasting guestlist: Sigfried Giedion, Reyner Banham, Colin Rowe, and Kenneth Frampton all attended. Julius Posener and Lucius Burckhardt were likewise among the participants. It had not escaped Ungers's attention that architecture theory was on the verge of completely diverging from actual building activities and that it urgently needed new stimuli. Ungers hoped that the conference would provide an off-ramp to this development.

German publisher Wolf Jobst Siedler had, in 1964, penned the controversial *Die gemordete Stadt* [The Murdered City], which attacked the destructive force of modernist urban planning.[1] *Die Unwirtlichkeit unserer Städte* [The Inhospitability of our Cities], authored by renowned psychoanalyst Alexander Mitscherlich, had likewise already caused quite a stir.[2] However, architects and architecture theorists in academia had kept suspiciously silent, much to the annoyance of students. Instead of finally attempting to tackle the urgent questions of the day, most of the contributions to the conference ducked the issues the audience was interested in.[3] The convention ended in a fiasco, not because of the lectures but because of a banner that students unfurled in front of the dais. It read: *Alle Häuser sind schön, hört auf zu bauen* [All Buildings Are Beautiful; Stop Building More]. Uproar ensued; Sigfried Giedion, vexed, left the hall; the conference was prematurely terminated, having reached no conclusive findings.

"Stop building more." A protest against politics and the real estate business—which, outside the university lecture hall, were busy creating a *fait accompli*—as well as against the blithely oblivious lecturers inside. The students demanded a different, more careful approach to architecture and the city. Their demands were by no means only academic in nature; while Ungers was busy hosting a conference, the large-scale postwar razing of historical urban structures, which, in German, is euphemistically referred to as *Flächensanierung* [area redevelopment], was already well underway in the Berlin districts of Kreuzberg, Schöneberg, and Wedding, and elsewhere in the Federal Republic. West Germany was hurtling toward the apex of a building boom fueled by postwar reconstruction efforts and the ordoliberalist "economic miracle." Only a few years after the momentous conference at TU Berlin, the number of

FIG. 1
Designed by Juliaan Lampens in the 1960s, the Onze-Lieve-Vrouw pilgrimage chapel with its concrete cantilevered roof in Kerselare, Belgium, has been a listed building since 2009. In 2012, yellow girder trusses were installed to support the roof, which had been damaged by concrete degradation.

housing units destroyed annually passed the 30,000 mark, while 700,000 were being built each year—numbers unheard of before or since. It is exactly these buildings that form by far the largest proportion of today's building stock in all industrialized countries and most especially in Germany, where close to 38 percent of all existing buildings were erected between 1949 and 1979—not an exceptional share in Western Europe. As a result, most people's biographies in this part of the continent are tied to this type of architecture in one way or another. Many baby boomers took their first breaths in a newly built hospital and grew up in a room somewhere in a sprawling new housing development or perhaps in one of the modernist bungalows typical of West Germany. The school, the municipal swimming pool, the department store, or the theme park where kids of that generation spent their summer holidays were most probably built around that time.

Presumably, the moments spent in buildings of the postwar era were not among the worst, because it is during that period and in those buildings that many people in Western Europe experienced a historically unique social and economic upturn: They were able to spend more, enjoy better healthcare, pursue a more advanced education, and benefit from more spacious housing. It is therefore all the more astonishing that these buildings trigger few emotions or memories. It is almost as if society were suffering from collective amnesia. These buildings are now torn down without afterthought as if it were impossible to imagine a future for and with these buildings. Yet, it is necessary to start thinking about their fate, as all these buildings are now (more or less simultaneously) reaching the end of the economically determined "life expectancy" (i.e., their service life) sanctioned by their owners. Although only a few decades old, buildings from this construction period tend more frequently to be the object of demolition than others,[4] mostly without any concerns from authorities for the protection of historic buildings. And that is just the beginning, as millions of other buildings will follow in the foreseeable future. Neither the waste management industry nor the construction industry will be up to the historically unique task of demolition and replacement of such a large number of buildings. It is already facing unbearable strain under the current political targets set for housing construction; how then would it be able to offset the additional loss of (usually cost-effective and therefore urgently needed) living space? Besides, the demolition of these buildings would entail a loss in cultural and material resources that would defy all sustainability goals. That is why it is essential to fundamentally question the construction industry's values and working methods.

FIG. 2
Spolia in the Tomb of Caecilia Metella on the Via Appia Antica in Rome

FIG. 3
Gordon Matta-Clark, *Conical Intersect*, 1975

For his contribution to the 1975 Paris Biennale, Gordon Matta-Clark cut large holes into the floor and facade of two vacant 17th-century Parisian residential buildings in Les Halles. This neighborhood affected by demolition and urban clearing was in the immediate vicinity of the Centre Georges-Pompidou, which was under construction at the time.

FOUNDATIONS OF A REASSESSMENT

If today, against the backdrop of the climate emergency, large sections of the general public feel increasingly uneasy about the untenable practice of demolition and rebuilding, this awareness is by no means new. The spirit behind the inevitable resource-friendly revolution in architecture can be traced back to a culture of repairing houses and cities prevalent in preindustrial Europe out of economic necessity, for the materials, labor power, and time tied up in each building were invaluable. The impulse to preserve the existing can be traced to decidedly different origins, ideological legitimations, and traditions of thought. Even the pragmatic reuse of materials and construction elements, as was self-evident in preindustrial times, was not always free of explicitly political or cultural ambitions, as testified to by the use of spolia in early Christian churches. The presence of reclaimed construction elements and the visibility of historically antecedent buildings can be read as the conscious reliance on traditions or as a reference to continuities of power and legitimacy.[5]

Isolated examples of a rediscovery of organic urban structures in postwar reconstruction efforts—initially mostly in Italy, then from the 1970s onward in other countries as well—led to a revaluation of premodernist architecture and subsequently to a new appreciation of repair and conversion of 19th-century neighbourhoods, although the change in attitude was once again for a wide range of reasons. Cultural conservatism permeates the period's various organizations for the rescue of the unprotected urban fabric and architectural legacy. For example, the Victorian Society, founded in 1958, took its cues from the Georgian Group, which dated back to 1937 and whose founding members were, without exception, members of the British upper and upper-middle classes. The resistance to the demolition of neighborhoods and individual buildings in the USA (Jane Jacobs's opposition to buildings being torn down in Manhattan's Greenwich Village to build a highway springs to mind), in the UK, or, later, in the Westend district of Frankfurt, was often a battle for interpretative hegemony between a cultural middle class and investors. Coalitions between the insistent middle-class rejection of inner city demolitions and the new social movements of the 1970s thus also formed the seedbed for new political formations. The year 1979 saw a party with an ecological platform, the Green Party, elected to a German State parliament for the first time, in Bremen, after campaigning against the demolition of buildings in the city's Ostertor district, whose structural and intellectual resemblance to Berlin's Kreuzberg district—one of the few other leftist

FIG. 4
Between 2014 and 2018, the listed Victorian former bathhouse in south London's New Cross area was converted and extended by the architecture collective Assemble. Today it houses the Goldsmiths Centre for Contemporary Art. Assemble's design approach reflects the building's history and usage, and creates a distinctive identity for its new function as a cultural center.

countercultural centers in West Germany at the time—was certainly no coincidence.

Just how strongly the attitude toward the existing built environment has changed can best be gauged from the debate around the preservation of landmark industrial buildings. Once a battle waged by a small number of individual heritage protection experts, the cause has, since the 1980s, become a generally accepted consensus. Former factories and warehouses have become such an integral part of the nostalgic landscape of a post-industrial society that the tough struggle for their preservation is often overlooked. That battle obviously required fierce opposition to demolition, but also economic and financial concepts for their preservation, as well as a collective process of acculturation. The *Architectural Review* pioneered the cause as early as 1957 with a special issue entitled "The Functional Tradition," exploring the inherent architectural intelligence and the aesthetic potential of warehouses, port buildings, factories, breweries, and railway buildings.[6] In the context of the British discourse on the protecting of architectural heritage, the term *industrial archaeology* had already been introduced in 1955.[7] Outside the UK, specifically in Germany, at least another two decades would lapse until abandoned industrial buildings were granted anything remotely resembling amnesty. Heritage preservation experts like Roland Günter and Axel Föhl, who advocated for the preservation of the Ruhr's "dying" monumental mines and workers' housing estates, pleaded for new uses to be found for them, but made no headway at all for many years.[8] Traditional heritage preservation, not to mention the broad general public, needed to be painstakingly convinced of the value of the gigantic industrial structures—even if the state government of North Rhine-Westphalia had committed to the preservation of technical monuments as early as 1975.[9]

Moreover, aesthetic appropriation strategies in New York or London in the late 1950s and early 1960s—as part of daily survival and artists' quests for spaces to work and live in—demonstrated for the very first time that the abandoned relics of industrialization still had value.[10] Accepting the unfinished, the ruined, the long-since derelict, as well as intentionally leaving visible traces of past works: All of these would have been inconceivable without the intellectual and creative trailblazing and embodied artistic practice of Donald Judd and Gordon Matta-Clark, not to mention the investigation of everyday culture and strategies of the *as found* by artists and architects, first and foremost among which Alison and Peter Smithson of the informal Independent Group emerging in London at the time. The focus was always also on the examination of spaces and spatial images that resisted consumer society's faith in a notion of progress.

FIG. 5

As part of the renovation of Bordeaux's Cité du Grand Parc, large housing estates from the 1960s were remodeled by the Parisian architecture office Lacaton & Vassal. More than 500 apartments were equipped with new sunrooms. This enhanced the units' lighting and enlarged the apartments' footprint. The project embodies the architects' protest against the common French housing policy of demolishing social housing estates from the 1960s and 1970s and replacing them with expensive new builds with fewer apartments.

FROM HERITAGE PRESERVATION TO URBAN REPAIR

In West Germany, the above-mentioned actions of young architects-in-the-making, such as the protest at Ungers's conference in Berlin, were prescient of the political mood that would break out fiercely the following year in the shape of the students protests in Berlin, Paris, and other cities. These marked the beginning of a gradual rethinking in West Berlin's policies on urban development, which, as in Amsterdam, ultimately closed the chapter of large-scale urban redevelopments. However, the path leading to that goal proved long and full of conflict. Citizens and civic activist groups took to the metaphorical barricades, occupied buildings threatened by demolition, and polemically attacked the construction policies and the real estate industry of the day in exhibitions[11] and pamphlets.[12]

An attempt at building bridges between civic opposition and the officials in charge of construction policy was made with the European Architectural Heritage Year 1975. Initiated by the Council of Europe, it called on national governments to actively champion the preservation of their architectural heritage. One of the Heritage Year's merits lies in the expansion of the rigid academic definition of monuments to include everyday architectures. Special attention was forthwith to be paid not only to historical churches and prestigious monuments, but also to industrial buildings, apartment blocks, and even backyards. With the discourse opened up in this way, supported by public relations efforts that overtly challenged the established policy of simply tearing things down ("A Future for Our Past," "Your Home Is Dying House by House"), public opinion was emphatically swayed in the new direction.[13] In Berlin, the modernization of Block 118 in the Charlottenburg-Klausenerplatz urban renewal area garnered special attention. Here, for the first time, a turn-of-the-century block was to be modernized in a way that largely retained its internal structure and avoided the otherwise customary resettlement of the inhabitants. Lead architect for this pilot project, made possible only after substantial public pressure had been exerted on the city's administration and the public housing agency in charge of the modernization, was Hardt-Waltherr Hämer, who had already gained experience in modernizing properties in a socially responsible manner.[14]

In Berlin's Kreuzberg district, the protests against demolition and the clearance of entire areas intensified and eventually culminated in the occupation of countless buildings, backed by broad support among parts of civil society.

A change in the overall policy on construction became inevitable. Civil society no longer had confidence in the willingness of politicians and administrations to change direction, and as a result a new institution was created that could operate parallel to the administration: the IBA International Building Exhibition of 1984 (it received the suffix "87," by which it is known today, only years later after its prolongation). The plan was for the IBA to kick off a new era, based on two guiding principles. First, the practice of *Kritische Rekonstruktion* [critical reconstruction] was intended to emerge as an alternative to modernist urban planning, and relied on the reestablishment of the historical urban footprint by repairing perimeter blocks and supplementing destroyed urban structures with new buildings where necessary. The second vision was dubbed *Behutsame Stadterneuerung* [careful urban regeneration], and focused on testing new tools for a redevelopment approach that relied on the principles of preservation and a social responsibility. Two architects were appointed as directors of the International Building Exhibition, both of whom had already made their mark during the protests of the 1970s: Josef Paul Kleihues, who was to take the helm of the so-called *IBA Neu* [IBA New] section and provide prime examples of critical reconstruction, and Hardt-Waltherr Hämer, who had come to attention with his modernization project in Berlin-Charlottenburg, and was to drive the careful urban regeneration in the context of *IBA Alt* [IBA Old].[15]

The projects launched by Hämer's IBA Alt were smaller in proportion and more discreet; today, they remain hardly noticeable in the urban fabric. That is the success and the unique quality of this part of the IBA in Berlin: Contrary to modernism's obsession with renewal—many examples of which can be found in projects developed under IBA Neu—Hämer emphasized continuity in the architectural and social fabric. Accordingly, the new was relegated to the back bench, leaving space for methods of preserving, repairing, and improving what already existed in the built environment. The innovations of IBA Alt were less about architecture in and of itself, and more a matter of experiments with civic participation, alternative types of financing, new forms of housing, and other topics that tend to have less direct impacts on architecture. Aspects of ecological construction were also underlined, although these were not yet formulated as a critique of the environmentally unsustainable production processes in the building industry, but rather sought to create a healthy living environment in tune with nature.

It was not until 2012 that the topic of preserving the existing was more closely linked to the discourse on climate protection and sustainability—by then already a megatrend. With his contribution to the German Pavilion at the 13th Architecture Biennale, it was Muck Petzet who provided one of the key stimuli in Germany, Austria, and Switzerland. As a title, he chose the succinct "Reduce, Reuse, Recycle," which he adopted from the waste management industry. Petzet's transliteration not only pointed to alternative strategies in the way existing buildings are treated, but also alluded to the problem of waste in the building industry. Moreover, the highly effective presentation of architectural environments from a selection of conversion projects underscored how reuse could stimulate architectural innovation—not, or at least not primarily, as the result of technical fixes to problems. In this context, especially buildings from the postwar period, the *Trente Glorieuses*, seemed to appear in a new light.

Conditions for a New Culture of Conversion

"Stop building more." This simple sentence contained all the pent-up dissatisfaction and annoyance—not just among students in Berlin—regarding the thoughtless postwar construction policies. The opposition to the demolition frenzy of the postwar period that had arisen both there and elsewhere was driven by decidedly differing viewpoints and motivations. But at heart, all these movements centered on the same themes. First, there were the issues of heritage protection that focused on addressing the mass loss of historical buildings and the destruction of cityscapes that had evolved over time. Second, the critique addressed the social consequences of the bulldozing policies that destroyed local urban fabric and cultures. Only later, after the shock provoked by the Oil Crisis, and once the environmental cause gained traction, did ecologically relevant topics (among which the issue of energy conservation was central) start to come into the crosshairs of policymakers concerned with building regulations. For a long time, it seemed as if the construction industry could fulfill its environmental responsibilities simply by equipping buildings with heat insulation and modern heating systems—a practice fueled with increasingly ambitious legislation on energy efficiency. Yet, these costly measures only had limited effects on total energy consumption by private households, as the savings achieved by insulation and HVAC technology have been continuously offset by the rising size of the average home. Simultaneously, public awareness arose about what had been obvious all along: The constant raze-and-replace practice consumes immense amounts of raw materials. The building industry is the most important sector of the economy when it comes to the consumption of non-renewable raw materials and the generation of waste. Only gradually did this knowledge transpire into the insight that an ecological transformation of the building sector is imperative—and that this goal cannot be achieved by heat insulation and installing new heating systems alone. Instead, the thinking has to be far more comprehensive. The culture of conversion will thus also have to include a critical reassessment of the technology-dominated strategies defining many of the current political efforts aimed at an ecological transformation, from the level of the individual German federate states all the way to the European Commission's Green Deal.

Given this information, the claim that, "All buildings are beautiful," as students at the TU Berlin proclaimed in 1967, should today no longer be read as a provocation, but as a specific call to action for everyone who plays a role in shaping the built world of tomorrow. All buildings are beautiful. And if not, then they simply have to be *made* beautiful. Unconditionally maintaining existing buildings (most importantly those that are not listed as historically significant) instead of just declaring them to be irrecoverably moribund—using them as a resource for the future architecture of our cities—that would be the logical path forward. It would be the coherent answer to the worsening conditions in a world in which raw materials are getting scarce, while ever larger volumes of such resources are being tied up in buildings, streets, and other built structures. The figures clearly show the extent to which the built environment has long been a gigantic stockpile of raw materials and energy. What we cannot quantify, by contrast, is the immaterial values stored therein—be it memories, meanings, or traces of the past. The critical and dedicated appreciation of that which exists as testimony to a shared history literally set in stone—this is perhaps as important to a society increasingly aware of the problem of planned obsolescence and the threat to its own survival than the sensible use of raw materials. After all, people will eventually want to be able to keep and recognize the cities and countrysides in which they live today. Existing buildings—and this includes more than just a few listed monuments—can act as points of reference toward that end. Whatever the arguments advanced to justify the need for conversion, they all entail a fundamental change in the definition of and preconditions for today's understanding of architecture; this change relates at once to the object of preoccupation and to the understanding of the profession as a whole. Viennese architect Hermann Czech already recognized this in the 1970s, when he pointed out that the act of conversion displays exactly how every design decision is influenced by past ones—decisions sometimes

FIG. 6
After years of vacancy, this former postage stamp printing workshop in northern Brussels was converted to a studio, workshop, and event space for Zinneke, a nonprofit organization, between 2016 and 2020. Ouest Architecture and Rotor, a design firm specializing in building conversions, focused on reusing building components and materials.

FIG. 7

In line with their pedagogical approach, Zinneke moved into the building during construction and involved their employees in various stages of the building's conversion. For instance, a training program for metalworking was part of the process.

made by other architects. Czech believed that everything is a matter of conversion, even new buildings inserted into an existing city or countryside.

To this day, preservation and conversion tend to be considered as alternatives: Such is the case with turn-of-the-century apartment blocks that constitute a strongly culturally connotated segment of the housing market; or as visually defining unique selling points for cultural institutions. Such projects can, however, hardly be compared with the many situations in which the argument for conversion first needs to be made—and where different degrees of inventiveness are required. This is particularly true for the architecture of everyday life, chief among which is the large surviving postwar building stock. Thousands of old apartments, vacant commercial lots, trade buildings, schools, churches, administrative and office buildings—structures that are considered to be either technologically outdated, insufficiently impressive, or bereft of their original purpose. In other words: buildings for whose upkeep there are seemingly no arguments, let alone advocates.

FIG. 8
A soccer pitch in the old production hall

After its closure in the 1970s, the old velvet weaving mill in the German city of Krefeld housed the city administration's offices. Between 2014 and 2017, Böll Architects converted it into 37 partly publicly funded rental flats. Initiated and funded by the nonprofit Montag Stiftung Urbane Räume, local residents participated in the decision over how to use the adjacent 3,500 square meter manufacturing floor. After completion, residents, commercial tenants, and committed people from the neighborhood founded the *NachbarschaftStiftung Samtweberviertel Krefeld* [Neighbourhood Foundation Samtweberviertel Krefeld] to carry on the community work.

In addition, once influential opinions still hold sway. For example, the view that conversions entail greater planning risks than building anew. While such knowledge, derived from experience, may partly be true, it cannot be an obstacle forever. Since the establishment of the first fire insurance company in Hamburg in 1676, the insurance industry has not found a single event against which it cannot offer a suitable product. So why not insure against the planning risks of conversion work in the future?

Construction laws remain the second roadblock, because it does not in any way distinguish between new projects and conversions, instead setting the same requirements for all buildings. While these standards can be factored in from the outset in a new project (accessibility, noise and heat insulation, parking spaces, etc.), they cannot always be straightforwardly met in the case of a conversion without substantial additional costs. Given the need to intensify reliance on existing buildings, this policy needs to be revised. Why must housing that has proved to be sturdy for many decades need to be structurally *strengthened* beyond recognition? And why must a vacant church, which originally did not need to prove adequate parking spaces, suddenly have to do so when converted into housing? There are countless examples of conversion projects sacrificed on the altar of current legislation. That is why a simplification of building regulations and possible compensation arrangements are a necessary step toward making the economic advantages of conversions over new projects clear.[16] In particular, the laws on energy conservation must be amended, as meeting them at present is not only very costly but leads to characteristic facades disappearing forever behind layers of insulation frequently made from anything-but-sustainable materials. Compensation arrangements would meet the task, not just for economic reasons but also for environmental and urbanistic ones. One could, for example, add to the calculus the energy embodied in the building and already saved by its preservation.

For architecture, conversion means nothing less than a paradigmatic shift. It also involves a redefinition of architecture. John Ruskin, who had gained a reputation as a dyed-in-the-wool sentimentalist for his opposition to the reconstruction of medieval cathedrals and to the construction frenzy of his contemporaries, wrote: "Watch an old building with an anxious care; guard it as best you may, and at any cost, from every influence of dilapidation. Count its stones as you would jewels of a crown; set watches about it as if at the gates of a besieged city; bind it together with iron where it loosens; stay it with timber where it declines; do not care about the unsightliness of the aid: better a crutch than a lost limb."[17] In an age in which repairing the existing should be prioritized, these words are imparted with urgent and essential meaning. Architects must reinvent themselves as *bricoleurs*, as tinkerers, or simply as experts who understand repair. Not only will cutting-edge technology come to bear, but also ancient knowledge. "I may use an electric drill, but I also use a hammer," wrote Bruno Latour, striking at the heart of a long-repressed truth about building.[18] Moreover, activating various forms of crafts expertise is also an important act of self-empowerment by urban societies. The inclusion of long-established and newly arriving citizens in caring for and converting the city makes sense, and not just from an economic viewpoint: It also offers the prospect of social and cultural participation. *Co*-building is the best step to appropriating the city for yourself.[19]

As regards the repair of the city and its buildings, the turn to conversion offers options for fundamentally new urban scenarios, including a socially balanced modernization and the process-driven development of neighborhoods and existing structures. Reanimating crafts trades and design cultures is a key precondition for intelligent and successful strategies of adaptation and reuse. This will have to rely on urban knowledge networks of craftspeople, architects, and members of civil society working together with a profound understanding of the material and immaterial heritage—specifically regarding new opportunities for experimentation, innovation, and sustainable improvements. Such networks consider the city as a rich repository of existing building typologies, materials, and practices, which then become the source of new forms of urban mining by reusing and modifying what already exists on the ground and also by devising new, adaptable buildings with components designed with their recyclability in mind. Cities are never finished; their architectures aren't either.

The history of the struggle against the demolition of buildings and entire neighborhoods is also a history of new beginnings: of artistic site-specific ways of working, of new ideas on how we can live together, of social discourses that manifested themselves in the practices of everyday life. Those key moments for broad social changes were labeled as part of an *alternative culture* for a long time. Against the backdrop of the climate emergency, there is *no alternative* to turning our backs on the raze-and-replace building cycles, just as there is *no alternative* to expanding access to renewable energies and sustainable mobility concepts that go beyond simply setting up new charging stations for electric vehicles. To this end, in Germany, the recent push for a moratorium on demolitions[20] needs to be flanked by a manifesto to restrict unfettered soil sealing. Sustainable strategies for human settlements and the repair of existing buildings are flip sides of the same coin: a comprehensive turn in the building industry. There is no alternative to this turn, but that does not spell the end of the tradition of the architectural discipline. On the contrary: The necessity to build with what already exists provides space for new possibilities in architectural design—opportunities long lost in the conception of new buildings. What will remain is a resource—for the future of architecture, it is a gift.

1 See Wolf Jobst Siedler et al., *Die gemordete Stadt: Abgesang auf Putte und Straße, Platz und Baum* (1964. Reprint, Munich: Siedler, 1993), 5. Siedler himself was a controversial figure and later contributed significantly to Albert Speer's rehabilitation with his biased and whitewashing publishing work.

2 See Alexander Mitscherlich, *Die Unwirtlichkeit unserer Städte: Anstiftung zum Unfrieden* (Frankfurt a. M.: Suhrkamp, 1965).

3 See Hartmut Frank, "Alle Häuser sind schön, hört auf zu bauen," *Bauwelt* 48 / *Stadtbauwelt* 80 (1983): 354–58.

4 See *Neue Umbaukultur: Baukulturbericht 2022/23*, ed. Bundesstiftung Baukultur (2021), 23.

5 See Christoph Grafe and Bie Plevoets, "The Iconography of Spolia: Meanings of Material Reuse in Contemporary Architecture," *Trace: Notes on Adaptive Reuse*, no. 4 (2023), 26; see also Tim Rieniets, "Umbauen: Zur ökologischen und symbolischen Bedeutung des Gebrauchten," *Forum Stadt* 4/2022, 229–40.

6 See James Maude Richard, "The Functional Tradition," *The Architectural Review* 122, no. 726 (July 1957): 6.

7 See Andreas Rossmann and Marita Pfeiffer, *Weil es zur Industrienation dazugehört. Und zur Kulturnation auch. Ein Gespräch mit Axel Föhl*, ed. Stiftung Industriedenkmalpflege und Geschichtskultur (Dortmund, 2022), 5.

8 Axel Föhl, "Die Thematik (der Industriearchäologie oder -denkmalpflege) war für alle Beteiligten in diesen Ämtern neu. … Es gab sogar eine Phase am Anfang, wo meine Gegenspieler im Amt selber saßen," ibid., 6.

9 See ibid., 8.

10 See Sharon Zukin, *Loft Living: Culture and Capital in Urban Change* (1982. Reprint, New Brunswick: Rutgers University Press, 1989), 58.

11 See Josef Lehmbrock and Wend Fischer, *Profitopolis oder: Der Mensch braucht eine andere Stadt* (Munich: Neue Sammlung Staatliches Museum für Angewandte Kunst, 1971).

12 See Rolf Keller, *Bauen als Umweltzerstörung: Alarmbilder einer Un-Architektur der Gegenwart* (Zurich: Artemis, 1973); see also Hugo Kükelhaus, *Unmenschliche Architektur: Von der Tierfabrik zur Lernanstalt* (Cologne: Gaia-Verlag, 1973).

13 See *Das Europäische Denkmalschutzjahr 1975: Bruchstücke zu seiner Entstehung*, ed. Deutsches Nationalkomitee für Denkmalschutz, July 24, 2014, accessed February 13, 2023, www.dnk.de/fokus/das-europaeische-denkmalschutzjahr-1975-bruchstuecke-zu-seiner-entstehung.

14 See Hardt-Waltherr Hämer and Jürgen Rosemann, "Stadterneuerung ohne Veränderung: Ein Versuch," *ARCH+* 29 (January 1976), 2–12.

15 See Harald Bodenschatz et al., *Learning from IBA: die IBA 1987 in Berlin*, ed. Senatsverwaltung für Stadtentwicklung (Berlin, 2010), 9–29.

16 For more information on the overall conditions under building laws and their possible amendment, see *Neue Umbaukultur* (see footnote 4), 94.

17 John Ruskin, *The Complete Works: Library Edition*, vol. 8, *The Seven Lamps of Architecture* (London: George Allen, 1903), 244–45.

18 Bruno Latour, *We Have Never Been Modern*, trans. Catherine Porter (1991. Reprint, Cambridge: Harvard University Press, 1993), 81.

19 See Tim Rieniets, "Umbauen als Weltaneignung," in *Umbaukultur: Für eine Architektur des Veränderns*, eds. Christoph Grafe and Tim Rieniets (Dortmund: Kettler, 2022), 112–19.

20 "Offener Brief an die Bundesministerin für Wohnen, Stadtentwicklung und Bauwesen," accessed February 13, 2023, abrissmoratorium.de/Offener-Brief.

THE SOCIAL DIMENSION OF MAINTENANCE:

Ecological and economical sustainability are indivisible from a third, social dimension. Achieving a sustainable future for all will require transforming user behavior and readjusting the social relations between all participants involved in spatial production—including the care workers tending to and maintaining the built fabric. To this end, architects will have to pay special attention to the heretofore neglected spaces and infrastructures enabling access to the most vulnerable groups in society. But they will also have to bolster the value of the mostly hidden yet indispensable care work maintaining communities and institutions by centering the secluded spaces—from storage rooms for cleaning supplies to workshops, from material repositories to bathrooms to infrastructures for the maintenance of the urban fabric—as design challenges to be solved with care and attention.

CARING

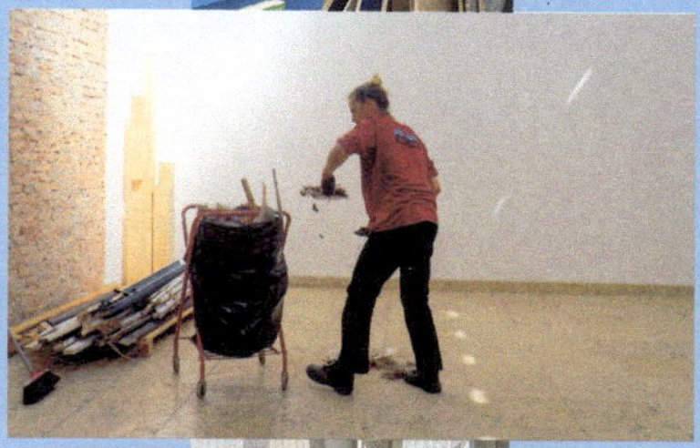

MAIN-TAINING VENICE

Photo essay by Giovanna Silva, from her series *Veritas (on Venice)*, 2022

In the early morning hours, architect, photographer, and artist Giovanna Silva documents an often unnoticed reality of the city of Venice. The usually prevalent depictions of the lagoonal city with its prestigious memorials, monuments, canals, bridges, and squares give way to an unglamorous image of Venice focusing on the infrastructure of its daily maintenance: storage facilities and utility rooms, access corridors and transit spaces, construction sites and barriers. Due to its particular location, surrounded by water, the city not only requires special care, but also demands different tools, media, speeds, as well as extraordinary bodily effort for its maintenance and preservation. Goods and waste have to be transported, squares and canals cleaned, facades and flooded floors repaired. Silva's images draw attention to this necessary everyday work and all the craftspeople and construction workers, handlers, and cleaning personnel who keep the city alive. *FG*

FIG. 1
Every day after it closes at noon, the Mercato di Rialto, a fish and vegetable market dating back to the 9th century, is thoroughly cleaned and rid of debris to prevent pests.

FIG. 2
Unlike most large cities, Venice does not have fire hydrants or other subsurface systems for firefighters, street cleaners, or public utilities to use, so the appropriate infrastructure must be transported on site by hand.

FIG.3

Venice's buildings rest on a multitude of wooden piles driven into the solid clay soil (*caranto*). In turn, the buildings' foundations themselves lie on a kind of floating platform made of two layers of larch planks fixed with bricks (*zattaron*). Many foundations have been undercut by water due to the the dredging of deeper fairways for cruise ships. Regular flooding and the tidal movements also stress the buildings' foundations, so that entire canals must be drained regularly in order to repair them.

FIG. 4
The scaffolded dome of the Basilica di Santa Maria della Salute

The church's marble cladding and metal roofing require repair and maintenance in regular intervals.

FIG. 5
The Modulo Sperimentale Elettromeccanico (MOSE) storm surge barrier was the city of Venice's response to the 1966 flood, when the water level rose to 194 centimeters above sea level. After decades of planning and 17 years of construction (2003–20), with a cost of 6 billion euros, regular operations began in 2021. The expected annual maintenance costs amount to about 20 million euros.

FIGS.6–7
In the lagoon city, everything that cannot be transported by boat must be delivered by foot. For this reason, supermarkets, hotels, and restaurants bundle their deliveries into packages that fit onto handcarts.

Venezia Garibaldi
Venezia Garibaldi
coop
coop

FIGS. 8–9
Only very few of the 30 million tourists who visit Venice every year stay overnight. Nevertheless, even during the off-season, the waterways are filled in the early morning hours with boats transporting dirty hotel laundry to the mainland for industrial cleaning.

FIG. 10
In Venice, approximately 7,000 households have septic tanks in the basement, where the (toilet) wastewater is filtered and regularly drained using septic boats. All other households are directly connected to the canals via the *gatoli* (masonry sewage retention basins), through which unfiltered sewage is flushed out of the lagoon into the open sea twice a day by the tides.

FIG. 11

The septic boats are equipped with pumps that generate a vacuum to drain the content of the houses' stationary tanks into the mobile tanks on board.

VENICE — A HISTORY OF MAIN-TENANCE

Text:
Ludovico Centis

BETWEEN PERMANENCE AND UTOPIA

Venice maintains an ontological relationship with water. Yet, this relationship is not without conflict. From its origins, it is thanks to a centuries-old history of technological development and planning that the fragile, sometimes hostile, and insalubrious territory of the Venice lagoon has been made habitable. In this process, its rationales of economic development have always had to be reconciled with those of environmental protection.[1] The lagoon is in a perpetual battle against its transitional geographical condition, whose natural destiny teeters between being engulfed by the sea or silted up as an extension of the mainland. For almost one and a half millennia, to oppose this fate, humans have changed the course of rivers, drained and reclaimed entire stretches of land, pumped water, consolidated mud, built embankments, canals, levees, dams, and bridges. By its own nature a mutable space, the Venice lagoon requires constant maintenance work, from the great engineering efforts of the Republic to the small-scale interventions of fishermen, millers, and farmers who have supported the subsistence of the city's population for centuries.[2]

The myth of the lagoon's naturality has created many opposing visions about the territorial developments of the Republic of Venice. Among these, an intellectual clash that occurred in the 16th century is paradigmatic: the one between the notorious head engineer of the Venetian water management authority *Magistrato alle Acque* [Magistrate of Waters] Cristoforo Sabbadino and the wealthy landowner Alvise Cornaro.[3]

Sabbadino saw technology as a conservative force: a tool for maintaining the existing hydraulic equilibrium of the lagoon. To this end, he envisioned spectacularly vast hydraulic works across the Venetian mainland, strenuously

FIG. 1
Laying of the main water pipe connecting Venice to the mainland, 1882

Inaugurated two years later, the modern aqueduct steadily supplies Venice with fresh water from the rivers Brenta and Seriola. Previously, the city relied on thousands of public and private rainwater cisterns, whose poor state of maintenance was one of the main causes of frequent outbreaks of cholera.

advocating for changing the course of entire rivers to stop sediments from accumulating and burying the lagoon. In Sabbadino's eyes, the lagoon was the most important defensive wall for Venice—the less visually "finished," the safer.[4]

Alvise Cornaro instead saw technology as a transformative force. A nobleman who experimented with land reclamation techniques in his family estate near Chioggia at the southern end of the lagoon, Cornaro illegally erected dams in the area, which were demolished by order of the Magistrato alle Acque. It is from the stubborn defense of his embankments that Cornaro began to gradually formulate a utopian vision for a new lagoon, complete with a floating theater and a *vago monticello* [a vague mountain] to be realized on reclaimed land in the middle of Saint Mark's Basin, right in front of the Doge's Palace.[5] Cornaro's utopian vision mirrored that of another 16th-century city: Tenochtitlán, the capital of the Aztec Empire, whose powerful imaginary featured in the 1528 *Isolario* [Book of Islands] compiled by Venetian cartographer Benedetto Bordone.[6] Tenochtitlán was built in the middle of Lake Texcoco, which was later drained by the Spanish colonizers to accommodate the newly conceived Mexico City. In a similar fashion to Tenochtitlán, and opposing Sabbadino, Cornaro proposed to enclose the whole lagoon within a sharp edge defined by an embankment that would clearly separate land and water, keeping open just one of the inlets that put the lagoon in direct communication with the Adriatic Sea. The almost entirely closed new lagoon as envisioned by Cornaro would be, in his view, healthier, richer, safer, and more beautiful.[7] The potential effect of his vision on the nature of Venice's relationship to its surrounding water is most clearly pronounced in Cornaro's use of a new term, influenced by Bordone's map: the lagoon as a "holy lake."[8]

Most Venetians, however, would be aware of how such a vision infringed on the ontological relationship between the city and its lagoon—not least because, to this day, Venice has no modern sewage system. The city still largely depends on the daily rise of brackish water into the *gatoli* (old masonry cavities below the pavements) to clear wastewater out into the canals and further out into the open sea.

BETWEEN NORMALIZATION AND TRANSFORMATION

The opposing visions of Sabbadino and Cornaro reflect a pivotal change in the collective understanding of Venice. Up until the 14th century, the Venetian model of urban expansion was defined by cycles of aggregation, whereby the limits of the city were still seen as dynamic, transitional, and unstable. Between 1530 and 1550, this approach came into question, also as a result of the popularization of Bordone's influential depiction of Venice, placed in the middle of a perfectly oval, idealized lagoon.[9] Propelled by this iconographic turn, the 16th century saw the idea of fixing a perpetual relationship between developed surface and water gain traction. In 1557, Sabbadino laid out an overall program of expansion and normalization of the edge of the city, leading to urban renewal operations such as the construction of the Fondamenta Nuove.

Simultaneously, the Republic of Venice was becoming less and less maritime due to its gradual loss of significance as a seafaring power. This development came as a result of the establishment of new trade routes at the end of the 15th century, such as the "discovery" of America in 1492 and of the sea route to India by Vasco da Gama in 1498, accompanied by the rise of new maritime powers in Europe. In search of a new political and economic balance, the city increasingly turned its attention to the mainland.[10] After many hydraulic interventions carried out during the 17th century—most of which had already been proposed by Sabbadino around 1550—the future of the lagoon was considered to be protected from the sediments carried by the rivers that once directly fed into it. From then on, every push toward a physical expansion of the city would be approached by the Venetian government with a conservative attitude aimed at limiting all possible modifications to the existing hydraulic regime. The magistrates of the Republic began to engage solely in what might be considered works of ordinary maintenance. This process culminated in the last decade of the 18th century with the formalization of the *Conterminazione Lagunare*—the boundary defining the jurisdiction of the Magistrato alle Acque—and the placement of stone markers that largely define it to this day.[11] The city's newly constructed permanence implied that henceforth, in Venice, one could now only intervene by means of preservation, improvement, or adaptation.[12]

Today, it is impossible to know how the magistrates would have behaved had the Venice Republic not fallen to Napoleon in 1797. What can be accurately stated, however, is that the lagoon's lack of maintenance and subsequent slow decay started at the end of the 18th century, with French—and later Austrian—functionaries lacking the environmental sensibility and culture developed by Venetian hydraulic engineers over centuries. The millenary insularity of Venice was abruptly ended by the Austrians in 1846 with the inauguration of the trans-lagoon railway bridge. Things did not improve much after Venice was annexed to the Kingdom of Italy in 1866. Under Italian rule, many canals were filled and large swaths of the urban fabric demolished. By then, it had also become clear that the permanent state of sanitary emergency caused by decades of poor maintenance of the traditional rainwater cisterns serving the city had to be addressed. A modern aqueduct was inaugurated in 1884, which did not only put an end to Venice's thirst for fresh water, but also to the career of the obstinate chief engineer of the municipality, Giuseppe Bianco, who, between 1857 and 1858, had carried out the ambitious task of drawing up a detailed census of thousands of public and private rainwater cisterns. It is said that the prospect of the aqueduct and the simultaneous abandonment of the cisterns exacerbated the mental illness of Bianco to such an extent that he was admitted to the psychiatric hospital on the island of San Servolo.[13]

The anecdote reads as a warning that every major innovation in Venice must inevitably accommodate the idiosyncrasy of the city's unique urban condition. Today, the publicly owned shareholder company Insula S.p.A carries out the maintenance of the city in its wider sense, from public housing to urban mobility infrastructures to the dredging of canals.[14]

BETWEEN DISASTER AND LEGISLATION

As Northern Italian industry flourished in the early 20th century, the Venetian mainland went through a series of further radical changes, including vast new land reclamations that would have made Sabbadino turn in his grave. In 1920, works began for the creation of the first industrial zone—the core of what is now known as Porto Marghera—later expanded with the development of a second industrial zone. In 1924, 2,300 hectares of lagoon were filled in for agricultural use and an automobile bridge parallel to the railway was completed in 1933. Between 1961 and 1969, the Malamocco-Marghera Canal, also known by its nickname *Canale dei Petroli* [petroleum canal], was dredged in the shallow lagoon for oil tankers to reach the refineries in the port of Marghera from the inlet at the port of Malamocco. The material resulting from the excavations was used to create artificial islands intended to accommodate a projected third industrial zone, abandoned in the wake of the 1973 oil crisis. The booming tourism industry also played a role in this new process of land reclamations: starting in 1960, a large salt marsh was filled on the northern edge of the lagoon to accommodate the Marco Polo International Airport. Lastly, the historically delicate equilibrium between protecting the lagoon as an ecosystem and the traditional extensive aquaculture, which both relied on fish naturally migrating into the lagoon, has been severely compromised by the establishment of about 100 square kilometers of closed retention basins, which now shield off more than one-sixth of the lagoon's total surface area.

FIG. 2
Venetian hydrographic network today

As rivers move through the delta, they take increasingly sinuous courses, either into artificial bypass canals that lead directly to the Adriatic Sea, or into *ghebi*, the typical marshland streams that characterize the lagoon's landscape. Channeled into underwater ramifications, tidal currents drive brackish water in and out of the lagoon twice a day through the three inlets of Chioggia, Malamocco, and Lido.

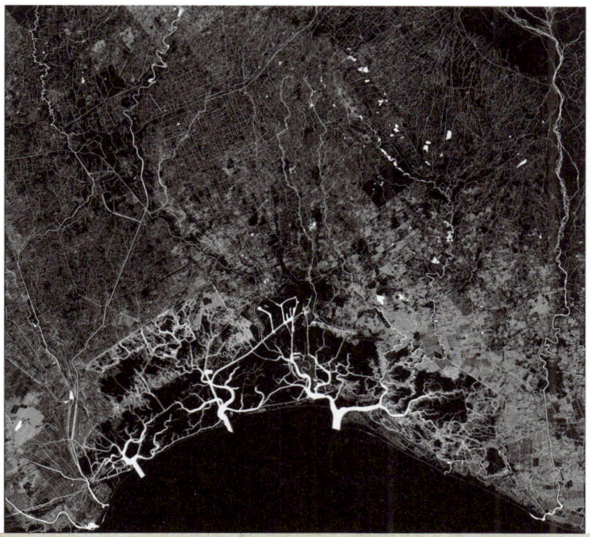

FIG. 3
Antonio Vestri's map of the hydrographic network of the Venetian lagoon and its hinterland, 1709

The map depicts the status quo after centuries of hydraulic works had been undertaken to deviate the courses of all main rivers away from the lagoon in order to avoid it being buried under their sediment.

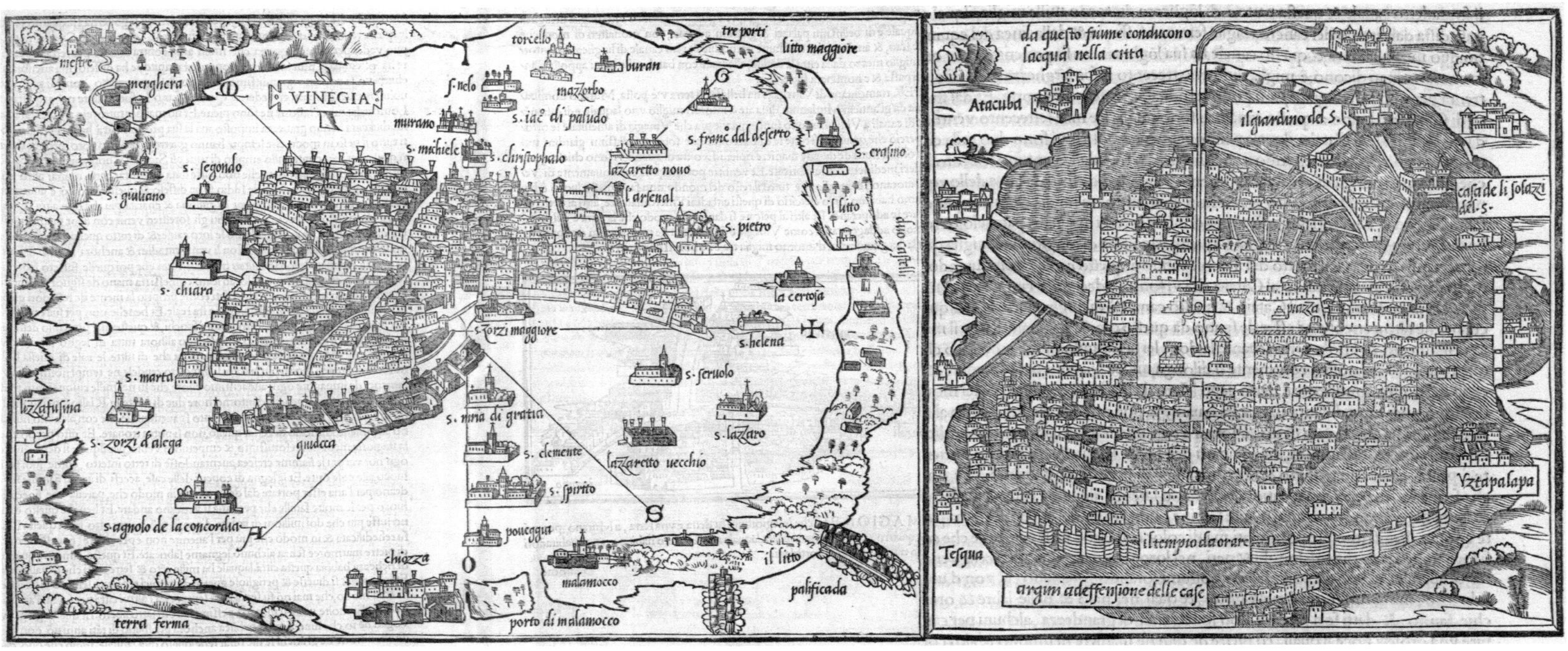

FIG. 4
Illustrations of Venice (left) and Tenochtitlán (right), from Benedetto Bordone's 1528 *Isolario*

Tenochtitlán was the capital of the Aztec Empire. It rose in the middle of the lake Texcoco, which was later drained out by the Spanish colonizers to make space for Mexico City. Laying at the center of a perfectly oval, idealized lagoon, Bordone's depiction of Venice—like that of Tenochtitlán—was widely influential in shaping a new collective understanding of a fixed boundary for the city.

However, an ecological disaster abruptly marked the end of this phase of large-scale infrastructural transformation: the great flood of 1966, which submerged Venice in almost two meters of water above average and exposed the city's alarming state of disrepair. The tragic event sparked a vehement political and social debate on a diverse set of issues affecting not only the city center but the whole metropolitan area. These include the depopulation of the historic city, the lack of maintenance of the old sea defense works called *Murazzi*, the abandonment of minor islands, and the reckless excavation of increasingly deeper industrial canals to enable the transit of bigger ships. All these factors led to the widespread belief that a law dedicated to the environmental and socio-economic protection of the city was needed. Ironically, a national law had been passed three years earlier but was never implemented.[15]

Only in 1973 did a special law establish that the city held a preeminent status of national interest, thus giving the Italian state special authority on issues like the safeguarding of the lagoon's environment and its hydraulic and hydrogeological equilibrium, as well as the regulation of watercourses and sea tides.[16] In 1984, another special law invested the state with the power to design, experiment, and execute works aimed at reestablishing the hydrogeological balance of the lagoon, inverting the process of degradation, and protecting the city's urban islands and settlements from high tides.[17] An agreement was signed granting a controversial unitary concession to the *Consorzio Venezia Nuova*, a consortium composed of 26 companies with expertise in hydraulic and civil engineering. Instead of coordinating this consortium, the Magistrato alle Acque was reduced to performing secretarial functions on its behalf—as a mere bureaucratic-administrative body rather than the planning-operational one it had been for centuries.

A third special law, passed in 1992, indicated the need to adjust and reinforce the three lagoon inlets of Lido, Malamocco, and Chioggia.[18] In the following three decades, this mission resulted in what is now known as MOSE (an acronym for Experimental Electromechanical Module)—a hugely controversial, multi-part technological endeavor, whose aim is to stem the exceptionally high tides that threaten the historical city with the installation of a series of floodgates at the inlets. Activated only in the event of *acqua alta* (an exceptionally high tide), the system would still allow water to flow in and out of the lagoon to preserve the functioning of its delicate ecosystem, as well as that of the city's peculiar wastewater drainage. Although not fully completed, MOSE is already operational and has proven successful in protecting Venice from high tides. Its success, however, has come at the cost of dissolving the institution of the Magistrato alle Acque, abolished in 2014 in the wake of several embezzlement and corruption scandals that involved not only powerful stakeholders in the project, but also members of the regional and national government.

EPILOGUE

Before the construction of the aqueduct, which alledgedly took its toll on the Venetian chief engineer Giuseppe Bianco's mental health, rainwater had often not been sufficient to satisfy the city's demand. Large tankers called *burchi* had to be sent to the mainland to load fresh water and bring it to Venice. These days, the problem is not supplying the city with drinking water, but disposing of its wastewater: septic boats are regularly called to clean tanks, cesspools, and drains. The use of septic tanks—of which there are only an estimated 7,000 in the city—helps Venice contain the environmental damage caused by the lack of a modern sewage system. But since MOSE became operational in 2020, a small leap of imagination is all it takes to picture a scenario in which, following a global rise of sea levels, the floodgates must be increasingly lifted up to the point of their definitive closure. This would effectively realize Cornaro's vision, turning Venice into a modern Tenochtitlán.[19] Caught up in this tragic scenario, Venice would find itself quite literally drowning in shit. As for the building of the aqueduct 150 years ago, the public administration would then have no choice but to undertake the titanic task of finally equipping Venice with a modern sewage system: an operation which would elevate the yellow sluice gates of MOSE—by then permanently separating the Adriatic Sea from the "holy lake" of Venice—to the status of a new involuntary monument[20] celebrating the maintenance of Venice and of its lagoon.

FIG. 5
The sluice gates of MOSE in operation at the lagoon inlet of Lido

MOSE is designed to stem exceptionally high tides that threaten the historical city, while still allowing water to flow in and out during regular tides in order to preserve the functioning of the lagoon's delicate ecosystem.

1 See Élisabeth Crouzet-Pavan, "La conquista e l'organizzazione dello spazio urbano," in *Storia di Venezia*, vol. 2: *L'età del Comune*, eds. Giorgio Cracco and Gherardo Ortalli (Rome: Istituto per l'Enciclopedia Italiana, 1995), 550.
2 See Salvatore Ciriacono, *Venice, Holland, and the Construction of the European Landscape in Early Modern Times* (New York: Berghahn, 2006), 101.
3 See Manfredo Tafuri, *Venice and the Renaissance*, trans. Jessica Levine, 1st English ed. (Cambridge: MIT, 1995), 139–58.
4 See Manfredo Tafuri, "'Sapienza di stato' e 'atti mancati': architettura e tecnica urbana nella Venezia del '500," in *Architettura e Utopia nella Venezia del Cinquecento: Venezia, Palazzo Ducale, Luglio-Ottobre 1980*, ed. Lionello Puppi (Milan: Electa, 1980), 32.
5 See ibid., 118.
6 See Girolamo Fracastoro, *Lettera di Girolamo Fracastoro sulle lagune di Venezia, ora per la prima volta pubblicata ed illustrata*, ed. Sergio Stratico (Venice: Tipografia di Alvisopoli, 1815), 9–10.
7 See Alvise Cornaro, "Trattato di acque" (1566), in *Antichi Scrittori d'idraulica Veneta,* vol. 2, pt. 2: *Scritture Sopra La Laguna Di Alvise Cornaro e di Cristoforo Sabbadino,* ed. Roberto Cessi, 1st ed. (Venice: Ferrari, 1941), 60–69.
8 See ibid.; David Y. Kim, "Uneasy reflections: Images of Venice and Tenochtitlan in Benedetto Bordone's 'Isolario,'" in *RES: Anthropology and Aesthetics*, vol. 49–50 (Spring–Autumn 2006): 88.
9 See André Corboz, "L'immagine di Venezia nella cultura figurativa del '500," in *Architettura e Utopia* (see note 4), 63.
10 See Salvatore Ciriacono, "Scrittori d'idraulica e politica delle acque," in *Storia della cultura veneta,* vol. 3, pt. 2: *Dal primo Quattrocento al Concilio di Trento*, eds. Girolamo Arnaldi and Manlio Pastori Stocchi (Vicenza: Neri Pozza, 1980), 192.
11 See Giovanni Caniato, "La conterminazione della laguna di Venezia," in *I cento cippi di conterminazione lagunare*, eds. Emanuele Armani et al. (Venezia: Istituto Veneto di Scienze, Lettere ed Arti, 1991), 11–52.
12 See Ennio Concina, "Venezia, 'tra due elementi sospesa,'" in Laura Anglani et al., *"Tra due elementi sospesa": Venezia, Costruzione di un paesaggio urbano* (Venezia: Marsilio, 2000), 46.
13 See Giorgio Gianighian, "Una cisterna interna d'una casa doppia a Venezia (1555)," in *Archeologia e tecnica dei pozzi per acqua dalla pre-protostoria all'età moderna*, eds. Silvia Cipriano and Elena Pettenò (Trieste: Editreg, 2011), 175.
14 Insula S.p.A., *Venezia manutenzione urbana: Insula: 10 anni di lavori per la città* (Ponzano Veneto: Vianello, 2007).
15 *Nuove norme relative alle lagune di Venezia e di Marano-Grado* [New Norms Relating to the Lagoons of Venice and Marano-Grado], L. n. 366, Italy 1963.
16 *Interventi per la salvaguardia di Venezia* [Interventions for the Protection of Venice], L. n. 141, Italy 1973.
17 *Nuovi interventi per la salvaguardia di Venezia* [New Interventions for the Protection of Venice], L. n. 798, Italy 1984.
18 *Interventi per la salvaguardia di Venezia e della sua laguna* [Interventions for the Protection of Venice and its Lagoon], L. n. 139, Italy 1992.
19 See Lorenzo Fabian and Ludovico Centis, *The Lake of Venice: A Scenario for Venice and its Lagoon* (Conegliano: Anteferma, 2022).
20 For the term "involuntary monument," see Alois Riegl, *Der moderne Denkmalkultus: Sein Wesen und seine Entstehung* (Vienna: Braumueller, 1903), 6.

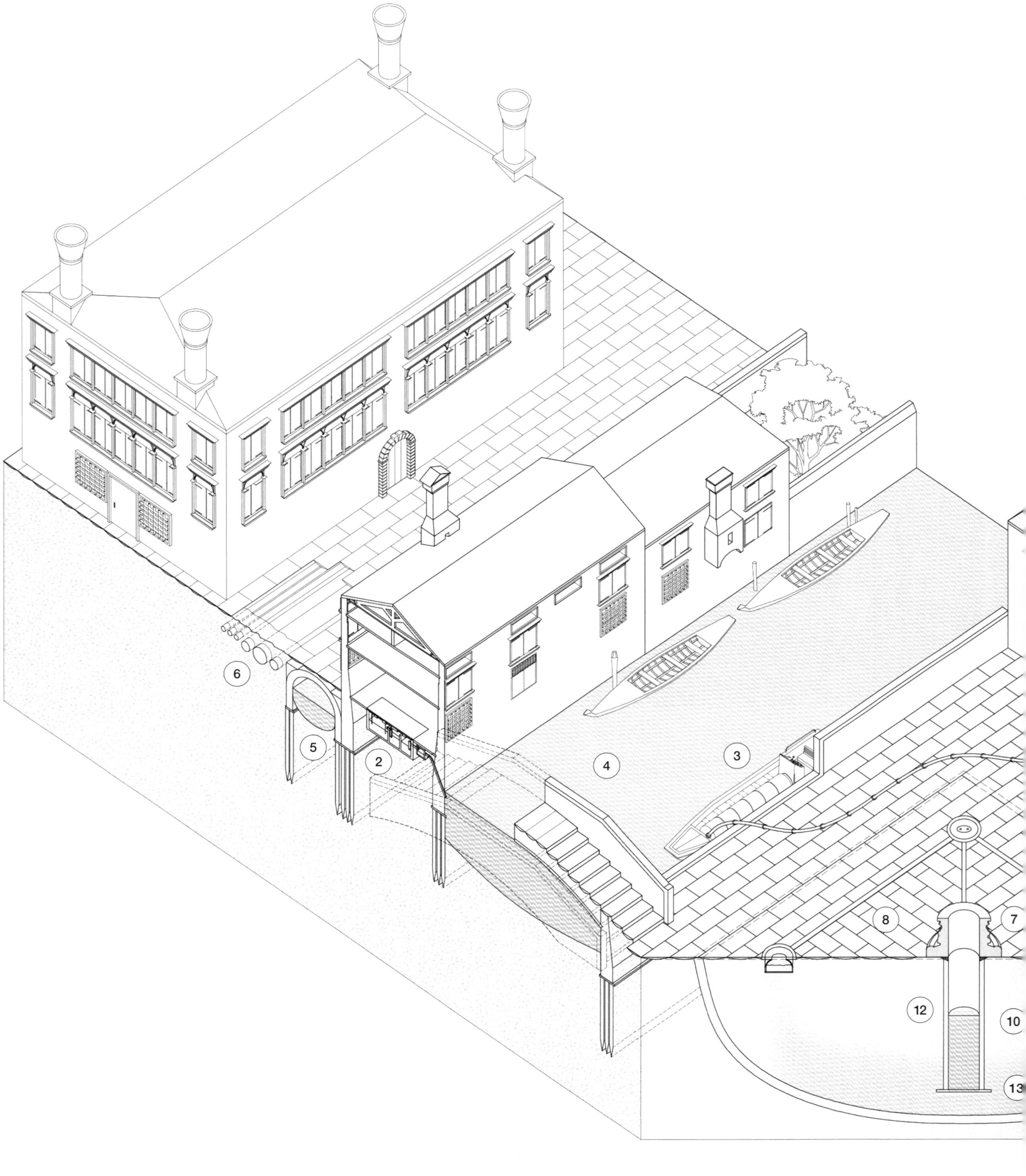
6
5
2
4
3
8
7
12
10
13

FIG.6
Elements of the Venetian water infrastructure

1 *Gatolo* (masonry sewer)
Traditionally, domestic wastewaters (including human waste) are collected in cavities below the pavements. Twice a day, tidal currents push brackish water into the cavities, clearing waste into the canals and further out into the open sea. Because Venice is not equipped with a modern sewage system, the majority of private households still relies on the old *gatoli*.
2 Septic tank
Today, upon renovations, landlords are legally encouraged to install septic tanks to filter wastewater before it is discharged in the canals. But due to the city's exceptional historical condition, this is often impossible to enforce, especially for private households. As of today, it is estimated that there are only about 7,000 septic tanks installed in the city.
3 Septic boat
To avoid clogging, septic tanks require regular maintenance. For this reason, a large number of private companies offer septic tank purging services carried out by special cistern boats.
4 Canal
5 *Rio terà* (filled canal)
6 Public utilities ducts—for electricity, streetlights, telephone, fiber-optic lines, water, and gas—run under stone embankments and pavements, and cross over the canals under the bridges' flooring.
7 Traditional stone water cistern
Before the completion of a modern aqueduct in 1884, fresh water supply relied on thousands of public and private rainwater cisterns.
8 The trachyte stone traditionally used to clad Venetian *campi* (squares) is laid in a gentle inwards slope, leading rainwater towards strategically positioned drains.
9 Stone drains
10 Below the pavement, rainwater is filtered through a deep layer of sand.
11 A curved impermeable layer of clay holds water in.
12 Masonry well barrel
13 Impermeable stone slab

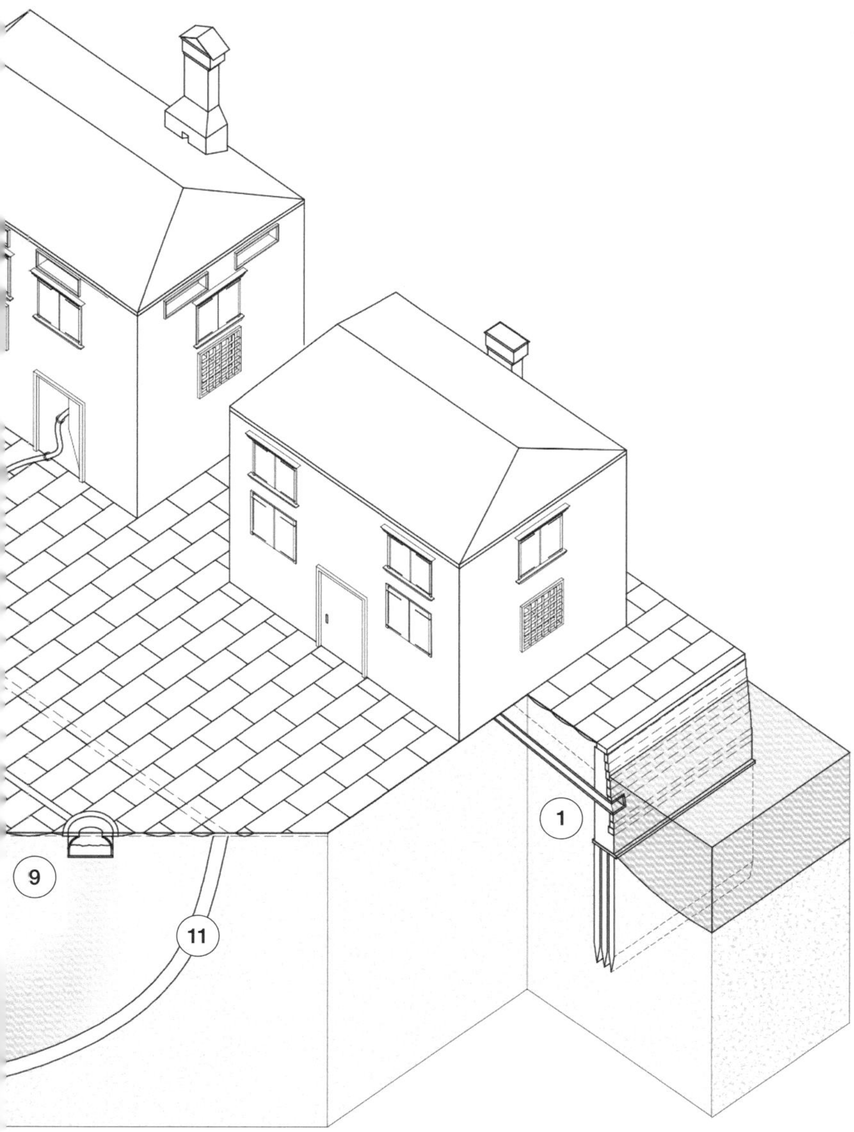

This text as well as the drawing on this double-page spread were produced by the author in conjunction with the iNEST research project Spoke 8 – Maritime, Marine and Inland Water Technologies, funded by NextGenerationEU.

NOTES FROM A PERFORMATIVE INVESTIGATION

Text:
Marco Baravalle

The Institute of Radical Imagination (IRI), founded in 2018, is a network of artists, academics, and curators working at the intersection of art and the commons. Their project Art for Universal Basic Income (Art for UBI)—consisting of a manifesto, a campaign, and a book—advocates for an unconditional universal basic income (UBI) above the poverty threshold and focuses on the role of art worker struggles in the transition to post-capitalist forms of social organization. The project also includes a performance, which will premiere on the occasion of the German Pavilion's opening on May 19, 2023, in the context of the 18th International Architecture Exhibition—La Biennale di Venezia, and will draw on the experiences of cultural workers in Venice and beyond. Ahead of the performance, its coordinator, Marco Baravalle, a founding member of the IRI and Art for UBI, writes about the origins of the project and the structures and assumptions underlying the Venetian cultural scene.

ART FOR UBI

The driving force behind our campaign is *Art for UBI (manifesto)*, a collectively written text developed in online public assemblies convened alongside art worker protests during the Covid-19 pandemic.[1] Published in 2021, the manifesto consists of 14 articles on the benefits of an unconditional universal basic income for art workers, as well as for workers more generally. It highlights the benefits not only in the realm of pay and artistic production, but also in the battle for transfeminism, decolonialism, and climate justice. Its drafting started from the premise that a systemic solution is needed to address the fragmentation of artistic labor and the by now normalized idea that everyone should be an "entrepreneur of himself."[2] Such a solution should be firmly opposed to the micro-corporatisms and competition typical of the neoliberal model, which blocks the formation of united battle fronts.

In Italy, the lockdowns of 2020 and 2021 were tough times for workers in the cultural and entertainment sectors, who had to fight for professional recognition in the form of the so-called quarantine pay. But if the halt imposed by the pandemic dramatically highlighted the importance of having access to reliable forms of income, it did so by exacerbating a structural feature of artistic work: that of discontinuity. In the realm of cultural production, discontinuity is the byproduct of the necessary preparation, bureaucracy, autodidactics, and constant filling out of funding applications, but also of sexism, the erosion of rights, and blackmail directed at these professionals for whom precarity is so often an unavoidable part of the job. *Art for UBI (manifesto)* makes the case for a publicly granted income as a means to pay art workers for their enormous amounts of invisible labor and to give them the option of saying no to shit jobs and abuse.

In 2021, Art for UBI helped organize a protest in Venice against the neoliberalization of museums and the city's cultural policies, a process which hinges on the precarization of labor. The protest was initiated by the S.a.L.E. Docks collective—which I am part of—along with the cultural sector workers network Mi Riconosci? [Do You Recognize Me?]. In Rome, Art for UBI joined performing arts workers in the temporary occupation of the Globe Theater. That same year, in Madrid, Art for UBI was turned into a performance titled *Una Renta Muchos Mundos / One Income Many Worlds,* which was shown in the Museo Reina Sofía and various community spaces around the city. In October 2022, a new Art for UBI performance was shown at the *Le Alleanze dei Corpi* festival in Milan, this time with the title *Incondizionatamente* [Unconditionally]. In this way, Art for UBI has transformed from a platform into a fundamentally hybrid assemblage challenging the separation between art and politics.

A PERFORMATIVE INVESTIGATION

The following notes are taken from a "self-investigation" carried out by S.a.L.E. Docks in 2017. The goal was to cast light on the working conditions of those laboring in the giant culture factory of Venice. I refer to it as a "self-investigation" not only because of its relatively small scale (16 interviewees and around 50 questionnaires), but also because the sample of interviewees was structurally very similar to the composition of S.a.L.E. Docks: aged between 25 and 40, white, majority women, many with a university degree. This is the typical profile of the cultural precariat that sustains the Biennale and its many spin-off businesses.

When I say "investigation," I do not mean it in the traditional journalistic or sociological sense. I am thinking instead of the militant political tradition of the Italian workerists in the 1960s—those of the *Quaderni Rossi* journal, which was followed by *Classe Operaia*. The workerists broke away from traditional Marxism and, in part, from the Italian workers' movement more generally. This was due, first and foremost, to an epistemological shift, intended to free revolutionary knowledge from its ideological shackles and put it to the test of reality by centering on a critique of labor. This did not lead to the end of dogma or blind trust in Marxist "sacred texts," but rather to a rereading of these texts in light of how they played out on the ground—or, in the 1960s context, on the factory floor in the industrial centers of northern Italy. The so-called *Conricerca* [Co-research]—a research methodology put forward, in particular, by Romano Alquati[3]—was not a quest for knowledge *on* the subjects but *with* the subjects, implying an end to the distinction between the theoretical and the political. It offered a way to interpret the process of knowledge production not as a single moment prior to a transformation in the status quo, but as a participant in the transformation itself.

The S.a.L.E. Docks initiative of self-investigation continues, although it has taken on the hybrid form of a performance within the assemblage of Art for UBI. Through performance, Art for UBI is able to create a space of radical autonomy. According to philosopher Jacques Rancière, such autonomy is one of the oppositions that characterizes art, and also a sign of art's radical nature.[4] Rancière sees art as defined by its ability to construct an elsewhere in respect to the social context in which it is produced, with its miseries and violence, and to function as a force for the "distribution of the sensible," pointing to potential new forms of communal living.[5] In today's era of neoliberal art, however, the condition of this autonomy is not—as classical aesthetics and common sense would have it—the astronomical distance between art and life, but rather the distance, yet to be created, between art and capital: an inherently social issue which Art for UBI needs to tackle head-on.

It goes without saying that carrying out an investigation of workers today is not the same as during the 1960s. The main arena of class struggle, at least in Europe, is no longer the Fordist factory. Furthermore, it must be said that while the workerists correctly identified the points at which the broadest class ruptures would occur—the *mass worker* (*operaio massa*) first and the *social worker* (*operaio sociale*) later[6]—our goal here is much less ambitious; realistically, perhaps our investigation/performance can make a little headway in an analysis of the subjectivity of the artistic precariat. As such, certain questions have come to form the basis for our work: Is it possible to do an investigation through a performance? Is it possible to do so in a way that does not result both in a subpar investigation and a subpar performance? What even is a performative investigation? Is it simply a study with a performance as its output? What type of knowledge does it generate? Is staging an investigation into a particular segment of cultural work a gesture that begins and ends with the staging itself, or is it an action capable of forging alliances, further actions, and routes to community building and collective action? Can a performance help us advance the struggle for rights and fair pay? Is it possible to make the performance an autonomous space without feeding into the apparatus of capture that is the neoliberal dispositive of art?

To hint at least at some of the responses to these complex questions, we can look to the results of the S.a.L.E. Docks self-investigation, which highlights some of the thornier issues—issues that, at this point, I will leave it to our interlocutors to voice.

THE CULTURE INDUSTRY'S GLOBAL SUPPLY CHAIN

"MAY I SWITCH TO ENGLISH?"

This phrase, says Antonia, was the exit strategy of choice for her US temporary employer whenever they wanted to avoid sensitive topics such as contracts, back pay, or work trips. Antonia is a university student in Venice and she attends a few training courses run by nonprofit cultural organizations. As a first job, she worked off the books for one of the big Venetian events companies with strong ties to the Biennale. For five months, she regularly worked over eight hours a day, having been left in charge of running ten exhibitions—alone, and in spite of her lack of experience. Her duties included handling press, hooking up internet in the exhibition spaces, managing staff, writing daily reports on the condition of displayed works, and everything in between. All of this for two or three hundred euros a month, paid in cash. We are not talking about a start-up here, but about companies managing dozens of properties in Venice; during the Biennale, the rent for these places runs to hundreds of thousands of euros, ensuring healthy profit margins. Understandably dissatisfied with this situation, Antonia decided to leave. She wanted to strike out on her own and set up a business with friends and classmates. She registered for a VAT number but soon realized that being a freelancer was not really a suitable option, the fiscal regime being too rigid for someone with a low and inconsistent income like hers. In the absence of any financial safety net, she quit. But now that she had cut her teeth in the field, she was contacted by the head of another small company working in cultural events. It was an international company based in a European capital, with links to Venice on account of the Biennale and its international showcasing opportunities. Antonia's first conversation with them was brief: "Hi Antonia, I need a personal assistant."—"When?"—"Can you move here by Monday?" She accepted the role, but it was the same tune. Her boss was late in providing her with a work contract, the pay was insufficient, the hours long. She started to receive requests from the company manager unrelated to work. Nobody helped her make professional connections. In fact, Antonia found herself systematically excluded from social events and, eventually, decided to move back to Venice and re-enroll in university. She says she needed to remind herself why she had chosen the artistic field in the first place. So much of her experience is typical of work in the cultural sector, in which the chain of exploitation, defined by informality and working off the books, begins at university and then extends to a global scale.

LABOR MARKET DISTORTIONS

"THERE HAS TO BE A THIRD WAY IN BETWEEN ALL THE YOUNG PEOPLE WORKING FOR REDUCED RATES AND THE BIG COMPANIES FORMING OLIGOPOLIES TO INFLATE PRICES"

Giorgio has been running a nonprofit contemporary art space through a cultural association in Venice since 2010. He did not take his first salary until 2016 and he is still waiting to earn back the 20,000 euros he put down as an initial investment. His comment—reported above—touches on two issues that kept coming up during our conversations with art workers. The first is the difficulty of operating as a legal enterprise in a market where newcomers work for next to nothing in exchange for building a portfolio, thereby undercutting those small businesses that demand larger investments in hopes of securing fair pay for themselves and their collaborators. It must be emphasized, however, that newcomers are certainly not the biggest culprits in this regard. On the contrary, the worst offenders come when we move up the chain from self-employment and small businesses to the multi-million-dollar business of contracting out cultural services—so-called "outsourcing." Big firms that share the market for these services at a national level are undoubtedly the ones profiting most from underpaid workers. At the other end of the spectrum is the second issue, which is very specific to Venice and its prosperous industry cultural events. Here, a handful of wealthy companies are in charge of an enormous quantity of real estate, including palazzi and other prime locations. They rent these out to the highest bidder, paying little or no attention to the nature of the project at hand. These companies have come to function as the "landlords" of culture,

FIGS. 1–3
Art for UBI: Incondizionatamente. Vita Reddito Amore, performance, Milan, September 2022

turning the extraction of profit into a culture in itself. This is not artistic production; it is an artistic rental market. In an emptied-out city, the rental companies are custodians of the emptiness. Art is the perfect decoy, enabling them to spin profit from a void. It may seem different, but it is exactly the same logic that drives the market for short-term holiday rentals. Art is simply the latest agent of touristification in a city already on its knees.

THE DIFFERENCE BETWEEN BUSINESSES AND ASSOCIATIONS

"ENTREPRENEURS MAKE MONEY FROM PRODUCTS. ASSOCIATIONS, ON THE OTHER HAND, HAVE TO FIND MONEY TO MAKE A PRODUCT THAT DOESN'T GENERATE ANY PROFIT OF ITSELF"

Most event organizers in Venice are *associazioni culturali*, or cultural associations. Simona is a member of one that focuses on live art and experimental music. She lived in Venice for 17 years before being forced to return to the mainland. Her job in the cultural sector had ceased to be financially viable, and she was no longer willing to supplement it by working as a cleaner for a tourist rental agency. For her, it is clear that the solution to the endemic precarity of art work is not everyone becoming an entrepreneur of themselves. She rejects the idea that we should always expect cultural production to conform to the logic of business. "Instead," she says, "culture should be financed through a legal structure such as that of the association, which is formally bound to prioritize content over profits." In our current legal context, however, this alone is often not enough. For obvious reasons of conflict of interest, members of an association do not take a share of the profits; instead, we need guidelines regarding how to pay them and any potential collaborators for their work. More public funding programs should be open to associations, rather than exclusively to cultural businesses. Associations, unlike businesses, are inherently concerned with the social development of the place where they carry out their activities, but the social cohesion they bring has yet to be deemed valuable in economic or political terms. Talking to Simona raised a crucial point: There is a whole world of young professionals out there who do not want hand-outs from the state, but simply to be in the position to put their talents to use and have their work recognized. Entrepreneurial individualism is often the professional reality for cultural workers, but associations offer the possibility of a collective alternative. An example? For several months, Simona's association has been holding open meetings with similar organizations operating in Venice. It is still early days, but the first three meetings led to the idea of building an online platform listing everyone's services and finding a physical space in which they can share skills and technical equipment.

THE MISUNDERSTANDING OF WELFARE AS PRIVILEGE

"I'VE NEVER REALLY THOUGHT ABOUT A UNIVERSAL BASIC INCOME … WELFARE IS GOOD, BUT FOR EVERYONE, NOT JUST FOR CULTURAL WORKERS"

Roberto's opinion was one that came up a lot in the interviews. Many people did not have much of an opinion about an unconditional universal basic income. Others, in keeping with the neoliberal discourse, maintained that competition is the only route to professional validation, as well as an incentive to make high-quality content. Regardless, almost everyone was pro-social welfare, so long as "it's for all jobs, not just a few." The different rationales for this radically anti-corporate position—a position shared by Art for UBI—are interesting. While a minority of cases had political motives, the vast majority of interviewees seemed to have a general feeling of guilt and embarrassment at being paid in a form other than wages or invoices. There was a widely shared perception that welfare is a privilege, not a right. This ambiguity around rights and privileges is a constant in the field of cultural work. The idea of having rights makes workers uncomfortable. The concept that their invisible, unpaid labor should, and could, be financially compensated seems largely alien to them. For many young people, the few salaried positions that have survived the relentless outsourcing of the culture industries are the privilege of a group of "untouchables"—older workers with permanent contracts, who are now demotivated and resistant to change. It is worth noting that, of all the interviewees, only one mentioned—correctly—that a universal basic income differs from traditional welfare, in that it constitutes a structural way to value life according to the terms of the current system of production. Most interviewees acknowledged, at least in part, this value system: They know they are creating value when they organize an event, transform an apartment into a cultural center, or share original content online, yet it rarely seemed to occur to anyone that this labor should be financially compensated.

THE CREATIVE BOHEMIAN

"I'VE REALIZED THAT, IN THIS CITY, VOLUNTEERING IS IMPORTANT"

This is another quote from Roberto, who collaborates every so often with one of the city's small cultural spaces. The space is run on a nonprofit basis by a group of young people who use it to host events such as concerts, book launches, workshops, small exhibitions, and meetings. I have to admit Roberto's comment surprised me. It echoes those of several other interviewees who have found ways to integrate informal cultural projects into their lives. Roberto had never considered that the space could be a fertile ground for developing his own artistic work. This is partly because it does not have all the technical equipment he needs, but mainly because he sees his presence there as something he does to volunteer and show support to his friends who run it. In this sense, there seems to be a clear division between the independent cultural scene, where one volunteers, and formalized working arrangements, where one makes serious art.

Nicoletta expressed a largely similar view, commenting on the phenomenon of turning private apartments into temporary spaces for small-scale cultural activities. She told me, "It's not so much about the specifics of the show or the concert. It's more that, in a city that's so completely overrun, it's truly fulfilling to have somewhere just to be with friends, to share a drink … no one's there talking about careers." No career talk, thankfully. But what we could call Venice's "independent scene" is clearly perceived as a refuge, as an interruption to the stretched-out time dedicated to performing labor. It is not that conviviality and building relationships cannot themselves serve the function of aesthetic variables, but this is not the point. The point is that this apparent pause in the cycle of value production, characterized by informality, is in reality one of the classic tools of neoliberal urban transformation, which exploits "the creative bohemian." In Venice these initiatives luckily function more as ways to reclaim and decommodify for-profit spaces, rather than as bridgeheads for the gentrification that has been ravaging the city for years leading to the exodus of its inhabitants. Still, the lack of self-reflection within the independent scene, and its reduction to a space of conviviality, serves to keep it subaltern to the city's institutional landscape and the dominance of the industry of cultural events.

CONCLUSION

In 1971, Danilo Montaldi published his *Militanti politici di base* [Grassroots Political Activists], a collection of testimonials from activists based in the lower Po valley, gathered through conversations and interviews.[7] The book retains the spoken syntax of these interactions, including the use of dialect. This is a history from below, presenting the lived reality of the political struggle of the late 19th century, to the years of antifascist resistance, to the struggles of the 1960s. In the introduction, Montaldi writes of the conflicting character of some of these voices: "In addition to the life forms, worldviews, and ideologies that endure and accompany contemporary man, and not just in his moments of weakness … are others that come to establish themselves, suitable for and in keeping with the changing times but which are also clearly anticipatory; a premise. It may seem odd to talk of anticipation and 'memories' in the same breath, but, as you will see, the animating force for these various subjectivities is always a certain conflict with historical time, which extends from political reasonings to all of life's norms and customs."[8] Times have changed, along with contexts and methods, but it is worth taking note and keeping this passage in mind as we set forth on our Venetian campaign—because art and militant investigations have at least one thing in common: When they insist on having the last word, they end up becoming a gravestone for the possible; but when they succeed in embracing what is yet to come, they retain the radical character of a premise.

1 See Institute of Radical Imagination, *Art for UBI (manifesto)*, eds. Marco Baravalle et al. (Venice: Bruno, 2022), accessed March 14, 2023, instituteofradicalimagination.org/the-school-of-mutation-2020/som-iterations/art-for-ubi/.

2 Michel Foucault, *The Birth of Biopolitics: Lectures at the Collège de France*, trans. Graham Burchell (London: Palgrave Macmillan 2004), 226.

3 See Romano Alquati, *Per fare conricerca* (Rome: Derive Approdi, 2012).

4 See Jacques Rancière, *Aesthetics and Its Discontents*, trans. Stephen Corcoran (Cambridge: Polity, 2009) 43–44.

5 "What we must therefore recognize both in the linear scenario of modernity and postmodernity, and in the academic opposition between art for art's sake and engaged art, is an originary and persistent tension between the two great politics of aesthetics: the politics of the becoming-life of art and the politics of the resistant form. The first identifies the forms of aesthetic experience with the forms of another life. The finality it ascribes to art is to construct new forms of life in common, and hence to eliminate itself as a separate reality. The second, by contrast, encloses the political promise of aesthetic experience in art's very separation, in the resistance of its form to every transformation into a form of life." Ibid.

6 *Operaio massa* and *operaio sociale* are two different subjectivities formulated by the Italian workerists. *Operaio massa* is understood as the typical assembly line worker who is only responsible for a very small task within an automated process of production and, as a result, becomes disqualified as an "unskilled" worker. *Operaio sociale* is a worker who identifies with the working class, although they are not necessarily subjected to the classic Fordist relationships of production which traditionally take place inside the factory, but more generally to capitalist relations of production that extend into all economic sectors. See Antonio Negri, "Proletari e Stato: Per una discussione su autonomia operaia e compromesso storico" in *Libri del rogo* (1976, reprint, Rome: Derive Approdi, 2006), 144–45.

7 See Danilo Montaldi, *Militanti politici di base* (Turin: Einaudi, 1971).

8 Ibid., XI.

CAPITAL-OCENE, WASTE, RACE, AND GENDER

Text:
Françoise Vergès

INTRO (2023)

When I published the essay "Capitalocene, Waste, Race, and Gender" in 2019, I had not yet measured the extent to which racial capitalism had built an uninhabitable and unbreathable world for billions of Black, Brown, and Indigenous people, although the signs were already there. Covid-19 revealed even more glaringly the entrenched colonial/racial division between lives that matter and lives that do not. We have witnessed a higher mortality rate in racialized and poor communities due at once to their insufficient access to health services and to graver courses of diseases, themselves a result of precarious living conditions. The latter already led to countless premature deaths before Covid-19 due to polluted air, polluted water, polluted food, contaminated soil, xenophobia, imperialism, authoritarianism, and a permanent state of war. Wasted lands, wasted lives.

But how can we inhabit this world differently, care for it differently? We need to go beyond denunciation and engage with the tasks of cleaning, maintaining, and genuinely caring to work toward a collective imaginary that is not based on capitalist destruction, over-exploitation, and endless suffering.

White, bourgeois feminism criticized cleaning and other housework as a burden and restriction to the freedom of (white) women that had to be overcome. Instead of negotiating politics of care that acknowledge the social value of this labor and consequently reorganizing it on a societal level, white, bourgeois feminism naturalized the racial divide of these low-paid jobs by externalizing them to mostly racialized or migrant women. But an antiracist, decolonial, anticapitalist feminism needs to go further and ask: What might daily practices of maintenance that care for the planet and its human and non-human lives, are *not* gendered and racialized, and do *not* rest on extraction, dispossession, contamination, and exploitation look like?

For we cannot externalize/eliminate this work. We cannot avoid it: We will always have to clean and maintain this world. Cleaning *is* caring. Examples of collective care work elaborated and nurtured by Black, Brown, and Indigenous communities will contribute to future politics of maintenance.

Using a dish towel printed with a Confederate battle flag motif, the artist, Sonya Clark, cleans the exhibition floor of the Fabric Workshop and Museum in Philadelphia of dust collected from various historical sites in Philadelphia that reflect the US history of racism and Civil War. This performance reveals an inscription on the gallery's floor, taken from the preamble to the Declaration of Independence. Clark wears a reproduction of the dress worn by Ella Watson, who worked for decades as a housekeeper for the US Administration in Washington, in *Washington, D.C. Government Charwoman (American Gothic)*, the iconic photograph by Gordon Parks.

FIG. 1
Sonya Clark, in collaboration with
The Fabric Workshop and Museum, Philadelphia,
Reversals, March 30, 2019

RACE AND GENDER AS CONDITIONS OF THE EXTRACTIVE SYSTEM

Every day, in every urban center of the world, thousands of Black and Brown women, invisible, are "opening" the city. They clean the spaces necessary for capitalism to function. They are doing dangerous work: They inhale toxic chemical products and push or carry heavy loads. They have usually traveled long hours in the early morning or late at night, and their work is underpaid and considered to be unskilled. A second group, which shares with the first an intersection of class, race, and gender, go to middle-class homes to cook, clean, and take care of children and the elderly, so that those who employ them can go to work in the places that the former group of women have cleaned. Meanwhile, in the same early hours of the morning, in the same big metropoles of the world, we can see women and men running through the streets, rushing to the nearest gym or yoga center. They follow the mandate of late capitalism to maintain healthy and clean bodies in order to perform; they usually follow their run or workout with a shower, an avocado toast, and a detox drink before heading to their clean offices. When they arrive, the cleaners have already left. On the way home, the latter try to find a seat on public transit for their exhausted bodies. They doze off as soon as they sit, their fatigue visible to those who care to see it.

The working body that is *made visible* is the concern of an ever-growing industry dedicated to the cleanliness and healthiness of body and mind. The other working body is *made invisible* even though it performs a necessary function for the first: to clean spaces in which the "clean" ones circulate, work, eat, sleep, have sex, and perform parenting.

Without the work of Women of Color, which is necessary but must remain invisible—literally and in valuative terms—neoliberal and patriarchal capitalism would not function.

FIG. 2
Gordon Parks, *Washington, D.C. Government Charwoman (American Gothic)*, 1942

The portrait alludes to the eponymous 1930 painting by Grant Wood. The young African American photographer and journalist Gordon Parks, who would later become a celebrated filmmaker, depicts Ella Watson in her work as housekeeper in the White House. The iconic image was the result of an exchange between Parks and Watson and marked the first in a series showing Watson not only as a worker and housekeeper, but also as a mother and member of her Black community.

Her exhaustion is the consequence of the historical logic of extractivism that built primitive accumulation and capital—extracting labor from racialized bodies.

FEMINIST THEORIES OF CLEANING / CARING

In Europe, domestic work was traditionally done by young white women, and European literature abounds with the figure of the abused, raped, naive, or cunning domestic. At the beginning of the twentieth century in France, this figure was caricatured in the comic strip *Bécassine*; the title character was a stereotyped young Breton housemaid, stupid and slow, in contrast to the more refined women of Paris. In the 1960s, cleaning/caring became racialized in France and other European countries as governments organized the migration of Women of Color from their former colonies (this type of work had long been racialized in the colonies themselves). As European women were entering paid jobs, societies were becoming wealthier, and domestic work looked more and more disconnected from the image of the modern woman promoted by western societies.

In the 1970s, as white feminists denounced the boredom and invisibility of unpaid housework, the recruiting of racialized women for cleaning and caring jobs accelerated. White feminists asked for greater sharing of domestic tasks between women and men, ignoring the racial dimension of housework. Adam Smith's remark that "menial tasks and services … generally perish in the instant of their performance and seldom leave any trace or value behind them" weighed on the question of the place and role of cleaning/caring.[1] Being modern meant abandoning tasks that were associated with a backwards femininity and fighting for "valued" work positions. The "invisible hand" of Black women would do the unvalued jobs. Marxist feminists offered a trenchant critique, as Rada Katsarova summarizes, identifying "social reproduction as a field of productive, generative activity. For them, patriarchal relationships and the subordination of women in the home appeared as a precondition to capitalist exploitation."[2] Marxist and socialist feminists demonstrated the central role that social reproduction played in capitalism. Yet, it was the pioneering work of Black feminists, first articulated in Claudia Jones's seminal 1949 essay "An End to the Neglect of the Problems of the Negro Woman!," which was deeply revolutionary, that showed the triple oppression of working-class Black women.[3] Jones demonstrated that Black women had never been confined to the "domestic" sphere alone. Hazel Carby, Angela Davis, and so many others followed suit, challenging various dominant white/heteronormative feminisms that criticized the subjugation of domestic (white) women while ignoring how race and colonialism have been implicated in these histories.[4] Black women understood very well what was at stake, and the first union of domestic workers in the world was created in the United States by Black women.[5] This critique is still very much relevant today; when some women are freed from cleaning/caring work, other women—primarily Women of Color—will have to do the job.

Today, according to the International Labor Organization (ILO), women are still responsible for 75 percent of all unpaid domestic work, spending up to three hours more per day doing such work than men; this calculation includes fetching water, caring for children and the elderly, and doing housework.[6] Unpaid care and domestic work is worth 10 to 39 percent of a given country's gross domestic product. The ILO says that there are at least 67 million domestic workers worldwide, 80 percent of whom are women. Everywhere, domestic work is situated at the lower end of the care economy. Though commercial cleaning is currently the largest cleaning service market, residential cleaning is expected to grow rapidly. Leading companies in the industry, aware of the negative image of the exploited cleaning worker, insist on legal protections for workers and promote their health and safety.

The neoliberal euphemism "service providers" is often used to describe cleaning/caring workers. But these workers have cut through this vocabulary, laying bare the violence hidden behind such expressions. For her book *The New Maids: Transnational Women and the Care Economy*, Helma Lutz interviewed both cleaners and employers to demonstrate why this expression has been useful for women who employ Women of Color: "Employers … like to see their domestic workers as service providers; … it is largely a form of exculpatory rhetoric which conveniently diverts the debate away from relations of power and dependence, since the (academically) educated upper-middle-class clients will usually know that they are not party to a legally safeguarded service-provider contract."[7]

Today, cleaning/caring female Workers of Color are politicizing their field, showing how and why they are performing indispensable work. They push us to go further in our analysis of that work. Their struggle for better pay and the right to unionize and be protected from abuse is now global.[8] Women of Color are showing what a decolonial feminism can be, one that brings together many intersecting issues: migration, the economy of exhaustion, visibility/invisibility, race, gender, class, capitalism, and violence against women.

The photomontages of CAUTION warning signs were created as part of activist protests organized by the Goldsmiths University and College Union (UCU) in the context of the grand opening of Goldsmiths Centre for Contemporary Art (Goldsmiths CCA) in 2018. With the slogan "Justice for Cleaners," the movement successfully demanded that housekeeping staff no longer be employed through the multinational facilities management company ISS, which had been in the headlines for its unscrupulous treatment of workers, and instead be given direct employment by the CCA.

FIG. 3
Justice for Cleaners Goldsmiths, Flyer (detail), 2018

CAPITALISM IS WASTE

The word "waste" usually refers to rubbish, but it is important also to consider the phrase "laying waste." Slavery, colonialism, and capitalism have laid waste to lands and people. Instead of answering human needs, slavery, colonialism, and capitalism have constructed desires for things that we do not need while obstructing access to things we do need, like clean water, clean air, clean food, clean cities.

Waste, as Fred Magdoff and Chris Williams have argued, "is a sign of capitalism's success."[9] In 1966, economist Joseph Phillips demonstrated that in the US, the economic surplus—the portion of things produced that serve no socially useful purpose—averaged over half of gross national product. In 2015, advertising, packaging for brand promotion, and e-commerce orders led to the production of 35 million tons of cardboard. In 2016, a thousand ships were dragged onto beaches in the Global South, cut into pieces, and sold for scrap metal (the world's biggest ship scrapyard is on India's western coast, at Alang).[10]

According to the World Bank, 11 million tons of solid waste are produced every day in the world. In 2016, the world's cities generated 2.01 billion tons of solid waste. By 2050, annual waste generation is expected to increase by 70 percent from 2016 levels, to 3.4 billion tons. Although they only account for 16 percent of the world's population, high-income countries collectively generate more than a third (34 percent) of the world's waste. East Asia and the Pacific region are responsible for generating close to a quarter (23 percent) of all waste. By 2050, waste generation in Sub-Saharan Africa is expected to more than triple from current levels, while South Asia will more than double its waste stream. Moreover, region-specific data masks the fact that waste circulates (air and water do not know borders). In other words, waste generated by Western imperialism ends up being dumped on racialized people, either at home in impoverished racialized neighborhoods, or in the countries of the Global South.

"The racialization of the world," Nikhil Pal Singh has written, "has helped to create and re-create 'caesuras' in human populations at both the national and global scales that have been crucial to the political management of populations." He adds: "We need to recognize the technology of race as something more than skin color or biophysical essence, but precisely as those historic repertoires and cultural, spatial, and signifying systems that stigmatize and depreciate one form of humanity for the purposes of another's health, development, safety, profit, and pleasure."[11] Geographer Ruth Wilson Gilmore has called this "the state-sanctioned or extralegal production and exploitation of group-differentiated vulnerability to premature death."[12] Racialization is created by white supremacy to make its world clean while destroying other worlds. White supremacy creates a clean/dirty divide that posits a clean/civilized Europe against a dirty/uncivilized world, even though archives testify to the fact that non-European peoples were aghast at the uncleanliness of whites, at their disregard for personal hygiene. By the nineteenth century, building on ideologies of race developed under slavery and colonization, Europeans drew a strong contrast between, on the one hand, a clean Europe and clean European bodies, and on the other, dirty indigenous dwellings, bodies, and sexuality.

In the current reworking of the geopolitics of cleanliness/dirtiness, the *invisibility* of the cleaning jobs of Women of Color creates the *visibility* of clean homes and public spaces. Furthermore, representations of cleanliness/dirtiness in the world construct a racial spatialization. Images of mountains of garbage, of *dirty* streets, *dirty* rivers, *dirty* beaches, *dirty* neighborhoods, of plastic covering fields, of people—women, children, men—searching through garbage or pushing carts filled with refuse, of children swimming in polluted water, all this in the Global South—such images contribute to the creation of a naturalized division between dirty and clean. Added to this proliferation of images are reports on efforts by government agencies and NGOs to teach hygiene to "these" people, and reports on the alarming levels of plastic and pollution in "these" countries. But the root causes of all this remain hidden: the legacies of colonialism, of colonial urbanization and the racial restructuring of the landscape; structural adjustment programs that require governments to reduce public expenses; the externalization of polluting industries.

The geopolitics of clean/dirty draws a line between areas of dirtiness—characterized by disease, "unsustainable" birth rates, violence against women, crime, and gangs—and areas of cleanliness, which are heavily policed and where children can safely play, women can walk freely at night, and streets are occasionally closed to traffic to allow shopping, dining, and other leisure activities. The clean/dirty division is connected to the militarization and gentrification of cities, with poor People of Color blamed for their innate dirtiness and driven out of their neighborhoods in order to make the city "clean."

FIG. 4
Thalamuthu, *Revathy*, 2018

This bust of a train station platform cleaner, shown in the exhibition *Archiving Labour,* was subsequently installed at the Chennai Central Station as a monument of acknowledgement and respect to invisible and undervalued (cleaning) work.

DECOLONIZING CLEANING / CARING AND THE POLITICS OF SOLIDARITY

In her essay "We Have Always Been Post-Anthropocene: The Anthropocene Counterfactual," Claire Colebrook writes that the Anthropocene concerns two clashing temporalities: one that opens humans to the scale of geological time, and another that draws them back to the scale of human agency and human historical forces.[13] But are these the only temporalities we can think of? If we look beyond the temporalities imposed on indigenous and racialized communities—who have their own conceptions of time—what do we see? Let me try to trace some other temporalities: The time needed to clean the world, to repair what has been broken by slavery and colonialism. The time taken by Women of Color to care for their own families, to clean and cook for their own families, and then to commute to the homes of middle-class families and clean their houses, care for their world. The time taken for the production of capitalist goods, and the temporality that this production imposes on the bodies of Women of Color (working long hours in polluted factories, barely eating, having no time to go to the bathroom or take care of themselves during menstruation). The time to bring the waste produced by the Global North to the Global South. The fact that none of this work is ever really finished because somewhere, something is being broken, damaged, wounded.

The time for decolonial caring/cleaning (for reparation), for caring and cleaning what has been laid to waste in the past, clashes with the accelerated time of neoliberalism.

As we repair the past we must simultaneously repair the current damage that increases the vulnerability to death of millions of people in the Global South. The past is our present, and it is within this mixed temporality that futurity can be imagined. The long history of laying waste is racialized, as Kathryn Yusoff has remarked in her book *A Billion Black Anthropocenes or None*: "If the Anthropocene proclaims a sudden concern with the exposures of environmental harm to white liberal communities, it does so in the wake of histories in which these harms have been knowingly exported to Black and Brown communities under the rubric of civilization, progress, modernization and capitalism. The Anthropocene might seem to offer a dystopic future that laments the end of the world, but imperialism and ongoing (settler) colonialisms have been ending worlds for as long as they have been in existence."[14]

How do we put our solidarity with care workers and cleaning workers into practice? In March 2018 in Chennai, Dalit curator Krishnapriya opened her exhibition *Archiving Labour,* whose commissioner, the College of Fine Arts, was originally a colonial technical school. In this exciting exhibition of 33 young art students, one particular installation caught my eye because it dealt with cleaning work. It consisted of multiple portraits of the women who clean the Chennai train stations and of their activities, in which they are seen, for instance, removing human excrement from the rails and trains. A young artist added three notebook pages on which he handwrote the following words: "Cleaning feces is not a normal thing. With his bare hands, my grandfather cleaned human feces to the point that it filled the lines on his hands, like blood on blood." He concluded, "This woman should stop cleaning human excrement; everyone should clean their own excrement. We should join this woman in cleaning human excrement, that way, this woman would become our equal, and she would become our equal concretely, not just in words."[15]

This essay is a shortened and slightly revised version of a text originally published in May 2019 in e-flux Journal *(Issue #100), www.e-flux.com/journal/100/269165/capitalocene-waste-race-and-gender/. It has been supplemented with a new introduction. Reproduced with kind permission of the author and* e-flux.

1 Adam Smith, *An Inquiry into the Nature and Causes of the Wealth of Nations*, vol. 2 (Homewood: Irwin, 1963), 255. Editor's note and correction: Adam Smith's understanding of value concerns the possibility of work to "fix or realize itself in any permanent subject, or vendible commodity, which endures after the labour is past, and for which an equal quantity of labour could afterwards be procured." He is referring to the possibility of exchanging/selling one good for another after its production/completion. Ibid.

2 Rada Katsarova, "Repression and Resistance on the Terrain of Social Reproduction: Historical Trajectories, Contemporary Openings," *Viewpoint Magazine*, October 31, 2015, accessed January 26, 2023, viewpointmag.com/2015/10/31/repression-and-resistance-on-the-terrain-of-social-reproduction-historical-trajectories-contemporary-openings.

3 Claudia Jones, "An End to the Neglect of the Problems of the Negro Woman!," *Political Affairs,* June 1949, accessed January 26, 2023, abolitionnotes.org/claudia-jones/neglect.

4 See for example Angela Davis, "The Approaching Obsolescence of Housework: A Working-Class Perspective," in *Women, Race, and Class* (New York: Vintage Books, 1981), 230; Hazel Carby, "White Woman Listen!" in *Black British Feminism: A Reader*, ed. Heidi Safia Mirza (London: Routledge, 1997), 46; Selma James, "Wageless of the World," in *Sex, Race, and Class: The Perspective on Winning. A Selection of Writings, 1952–2011* (Oakland: PM Press, 2012), 104.

5 See Premilla Nadasen, *Household Workers Unite: The Untold Story of African-American Women Who Built a Movement* (Boston: Beacon Press, 2015). The author describes the birth of the movement in the 1930s and tells the story of what Ella Baker and Marvel Cooke called "slave markets"—the street corners in New York City where African American women waited to be hired for a day of work.

6 International Labour Organization (ILO), *World Employment Social Outlook: Trends for Women 2018,* accessed January 26, 2023, www.ilo.org/wcmsp5/groups/public/---dgreports/---dcomm/---publ/documents/publication/wcms_619577.pdf.

7 Helma Lutz, *The New Maids: Transnational Women and the Care Economy* (London: Zed Books, 2011), 32.

8 See, for instance, Women in Informal Employment: Globalizing and Organizing (since 1997), Domestic Workers United (since 2000), and International Domestic Workers Federation (since 2013).

9 Fred Magdoff and Chris Williams, "Capitalist Economies Create Waste, Not Social Value," *Truthout*, August 17, 2017, accessed January 26, 2023, truthout.org/articles/capitalist-economies-create-waste-not-social-value.

10 Costas Paris, "Economic Slump Sends Big Ships to Scrap Heap," *Wall Street Journal*, August 14, 2016, accessed January 26, 2023, www.wsj.com/articles/economic-slump-sends-big-ships-to-scrap-heap-1471192256.

11 Cited in Daniel Nemser, *Infrastructures of Race: Concentration and Biopolitics in Colonial Mexico* (Austin: University of Texas Press, 2017), 11.

12 Ruth Wilson Gilmore, *Golden Gulag: Prisons, Surplus, Crisis, and Opposition in Globalizing California* (Berkeley: University of California Press, 2007), 28.

13 Claire Colebrook, "We Have Always Been Post-Anthropocene: The Anthropocene Counterfactual," in *Anthropocene Feminism*, ed. Richard Grusin (Minneapolis: University of Minnesota Press, 2017), 1–20.

14 Kathryn Yusoff, *A Billion Black Anthropocenes or None* (Minneapolis: University of Minnesota Press, 2019), xiii.

15 The last paragraph on the exhibition on *Archiving Labour* by Krishnapriya C. P. is taken from the updated revision of the book *Un féminisme décolonial* (2019) by Françoise Vergès; Françoise Vergès, *A decolonial feminism*, trans. Ashley J. Bohrer (London: Pluto Press, 2012), 81–82.

FIG. 5
Rasheedah Phillips (Black Quantum Futurism), *There Are New Suns in Allensworth (Educators of the Black Time Belt)*, from the project *Mmere Dane–Black Time Belt*, 2021
Digital collage utilizing the photograph *Teachers at Allensworth*, courtesy of California State Parks, and an image of a CERN experiment from Rasheedah Philips's residency there

Combining insights from quantum physics with the histories and practices of Black cultural traditions, the interdisciplinary feminist art collective Black Quantum Futurism charts alternative futures through speculative compressions of space and time. The project *Mmere Dane: Black Time Belt* maps several historic all-Black towns in America, almost all of which have been wiped out by displacement, land speculation, and racial violence. The subject of this collage is Allensworth, the first Black self-governing town in California.

INC-LOO*SIVE

FIG. 1
In the 1960s in California, public toilets were subject to a charge, whereas urinals were free. In a performative protest, March Fong Eu, a member of the California State Assembly who would later be elected Secretary of State of California, used a sledgehammer to smash a ceramic toilet in front of the State Capitol in Sacramento in 1969. This form of gendered discrimination is still perceptible in the insufficient equipment and accessibility of public toilets and sanitary infrastructures for women to this day.

ARCHI-TECTURE

Text:
Author collective Rosa Loo

**"To talk about architecture without talking about toilets is to operate in denial of a whole array of sexual, psychological, and moral economies. For all the endless apparent talk about the body in architecture, architects don't really want to talk about it. Architectural discourse is a deodorizer."
Beatriz Colomina and Mark Wigley, "Toilet Architecture: An Essay about the Most Psychosexually Charged Room in a Building" (2017–18).[1]**

Peeing* is political![2] Sanitary facilities are an essential infrastructural part of everyday life. They provide the opportunity to fulfill the basic sanitary needs of urinating and defecating, have an influence on the kind, quality, and radius of activities people can undertake, and constitute a precondition for participating in both private and public life. However, they are often taken for granted and their importance is only registered when they are unusable, unavailable, or inaccessible. When planning and managing buildings and public spaces, sanitary facilities are rarely considered as core infrastructure to be designed for and by society.[3] For example, many local authorities not only lack the monetary and human resources, but also the knowledge about and expertise on inclusive sanitary infrastructures. However, such expertise is essential, as toilets involve a range of structural social marginalizations and discriminations relating not only to the acts of urinating, defecating, and menstruating, but also to all practices regulating access to and use of toilets. "The bathroom—or the lack of a bathroom—generates all kinds of questions about safety, accessibility, gender, sexuality, class, homelessness, race and more," writes geographer and feminist urban researcher Leslie Kern in *Feminist City*.[4] Sanitary facilities and the related infrastructures, practices, and discourses (re-)produce segregation, mechanisms of exclusion, and restrictions that must be critically questioned and revised.[5] Today, the major social challenges of climate change and global access to drinking water raise another urgent question: How can current sanitary systems, which account for a massive share of water consumption and pollution, be converted in an ecologically sound and climate-neutral manner in the future.

THE HUMAN RIGHT TO WATER AND SANITATION

In 2010, the human right to water and sanitation was firmly enshrined in the United Nations Charter. The year 2015 saw the United Nations declare their aim to "ensure availability and sustainable management of water and sanitation for all" as one of their Sustainable Development Goals (SDGs).[6] What has become obvious, however, is that the abstract universalism of human rights does not automatically lead to the reduction of myriad forms of exclusion from urban and social infrastructures. In Germany, the supply and quality of existing public toilet facilities is constantly criticized by actors from civil society; yet, little has been done on the political, legal, and urban planning levels to provide and operate adequate public sanitation infrastructure. Indeed, this can be traced back to a lack of authority, as providing public toilets does not fall under the jurisdiction of local authorities in Germany. In other words, there is no legal obligation for municipalities and local authorities to make any public toilets available at all.

However, a number of regulations exist for bathrooms in private homes and publicly accessible businesses, regarding the number, size, equipment, and accessibility of the facilities. Private spaces are therefore also embedded in public infrastructure systems: The German industrial norm DIN 18040 became part of German building regulations in 2017 and outlines the technical requirements for accessibility in buildings. The aim is to promote inclusion by guaranteeing equal access to the built environment for people with dis_abilities. To this end, the existing barriers between the private and public spaces need to be reduced. For only if the sequence of transportation and movement—from the street to the private or public toilet—is continuously identifiable, usable, and accessible can people's radius of activity be expanded. At the same time, this approach often remains insufficient. Inclusion, in contrast to integration (i.e., assimilation), requires an expansion of the existing systems of thought and infrastructure to do justice to both personal and universal needs.

DE/POLITICIZING THE PRIVATE AND THE PUBLIC

Since Classical antiquity, the division between the private and the public realms has played a key role for the de/politicization (or: de/tabooing) of entire fields of action. What is part of the public realm (agora/forum) is considered political and can be politicized, whereas what is considered private (oikos/domus) cannot. All intimate things, including fundamental bodily functions, are hidden. Once the body evacuates what it does not need, we are rid of it. Everything else is a "private matter." That makes it all the harder for socially marginalized and statistically disregarded groups to achieve political leverage for their concerns and to ensure their most fundamental needs are met, especially without being permanently exposed to and dependent on the good will of others, on support in everyday life, on lucky coincidences. Instead, they should be structurally considered and given a say. Regarding questions of infrastructure, the focus must be

on factoring in needs in a way that facilitates a system benefitting all—not just society but the entire ecosystem. Capitalist structures of governance and logics of valorization, however, produce exclusion, i.e., socially constructed divisions of spheres established as norms and arbitrarily categorizing and ranking beings, bodies, and their properties, such as: human or animal, man or woman, local or foreign, able or unable, useful or harmful? Ultimately: us or the others? Who gets the right to exercise power; who is entitled to act politically? Who and what is/becomes visible when we plan/convert our core infrastructures to master the social and ecological challenges and secure the basis of our lives in the future?

BINARITY AND PATRIARCHAL DESIGN

Socio-spatial power mechanisms are expressed in terms of both bathrooms' accessibility and their labeling, equipment, and design. One of the most obvious power mechanisms is based on the assumption that there are only two genders. This manifests itself in the spatial allocation and binary separation of toilets for *men*, on the one hand, and for *women*, on the other. Those who do not identify with either of these or are perceived by others as not belonging in a restroom ascribed to a certain gender face challenges. Due to the forced designations, those affected often feel discomfort, and repeatedly experience verbal and/or physical violence. For people who align with the binary gender norm, access to and use of public restrooms is easier and has fewer negative connotations. Cis men in particular are advantaged ("potty privilege") by the higher number of "men's rooms" and the presence of standing urinals in urban space. This structure hinging on gender separation goes hand in hand with a cultural coding both of behavioral roles and of design principles for the facilities. For example, body postures when urinating and defecating are historically and culturally determined. In the everyday public mindset, however, they are still naturalized and justified entirely in physiognomic terms. While defecation is primarily structured as a sitting activity, irrespective of gender, the stance for micturition, meaning the posture when emptying the bladder, is linked to genital anatomy (man/penis/standing vs. woman/vulva/seated). In line with this idea, men are offered both sitting toilets and urinals, while sanitary facilities for women only feature sitting toilets. Since sitting toilets, as a general rule, are planned inside cubicles, they require more space than urinals. This often translates to fewer toilets available to women than there are to men.[7] To counter this bias, the newly amended version of the German engineering association VDI's guidelines on restroom design recommends

FIG. 2
The *Urin*all* is a gender-neutral urinal that facilitates contactless urination by different sexes. In the design process, the industrial designers Leonie Roth and Luisa Tschumi conducted extensive ergonomic experiments to enable easy usability for as many people and micturition postures as possible.

that in the future, gender-inclusive toilets (shared by everyone irrespective of their gender) be taken as the new standard for public buildings. This not only aims to raise the number of toilets for all genders, but also simplifies the placement of infrastructure elements such as baby changing tables. The latter, in binarily separated toilets as we encounter them to date, have been placed in women's or barrier-free restrooms, thereby reproducing the gendered division of (child)care work.

TOILETS FOR EVERYONE?!

How can we reclaim (urban) space and the right to pee* by addressing flawed and discriminating infrastructure? According to cultural theorist Lauren Berlant, a possible solution lies in a repair of the commons by the excluded.[8] This would render precisely those goods and infrastructures accessible to the people who are marginalized for their deviation from a socially constructed norm, and often experience an even greater need to access them as a result.

Gender-neutral urinals, which enable all people regardless of their genitals to urinate in a non-seated position, are unfortunately still a rare, albeit simple, measure with far-reaching impacts. Alongside technological devices, we also see low-threshold practices adopted out of solidarity and resistance, such as relabeling toilets with stickers, which eliminate the binary division (men/women) of restrooms.[9] Such a form of repair results in the expanded usability of sanitary infrastructures and can be understood as an intimate, everyday political practice of appropriating identification, access, and participation. Moreover, this form of appropriation shifts our understanding of infrastructure to include the human body, which, instead of being a simple extension of the former, becomes infrastructural itself.[10]

ABLEIST DESIGN: BARRIER-FREE VS. LOW-BARRIER

Toilet infrastructures are highly standardized spaces based on a uniform Western body norm in regards to equipment, as well as measurements and dimensions, as becomes evident from the example of the aforementioned VDI guidelines. Most restrooms' designs are based on adults without dis_abilities and a body weight within the so-called "'normal weight'-range" of the Body Mass Index. This, however, impedes access to these bathrooms—or makes their use altogether impossible—for anyone who does not correspond to these norms.[11] Certain "deviations" from these standards, such as for wheelchair users, are increasingly

FIG. 3
Currently, the *Urin*all* is being developed for serial production in cooperation with a company specializing in waterless urinals. In the German Pavilion at the 18th Architecture Biennale in Venice, a functioning prototype will be available to use for visitors and staff as part of the living lab for circular sanitary systems.

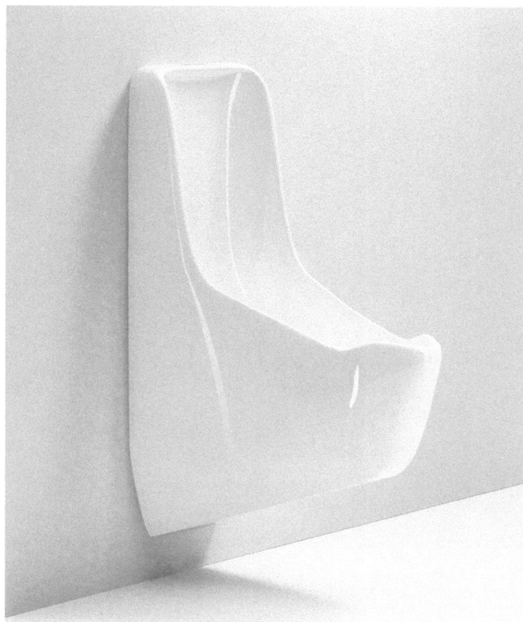

being taken into account when planning accessible public buildings (as mandated by DIN 18040). These efforts usually result in separate wheelchair-accessible bathrooms, marked as exceptions both in terms of architecture and use, and colloquially referred to as "disabled bathrooms" or "barrier-free WCs." In the private realm, many people only recognize the importance of barrier-freedom once their own needs make them necessary. Additionally, the term "barrier-free" is itself controversial. For people with severe or multiple dis_abilities, barrier-free access refers to far more than just level access or the presence of ramps. In its project titled *Toiletten für alle* [Toilets for Everyone], the foundation Stiftung Leben pur [Pure Living Foundation] calls for all barrier-free toilets to include height-adjustable care stretchers as well as disposal amenities for medical products such as catheters, urine bags, or needles. If one applies this standard, "barrier-free" sanitary facilities, the way they are commonly understood today, are merely "low-barrier." Although changes surely cannot be driven by the concerns of a white baby-boomer generation alone, the contexts of an increasingly aging population and age-related incontinence have broadened the calls for restrooms that cater to a wider spectrum of needs, providing the necessary change in perspective—from physical "disability" to the inadequacies of the space itself.[12]

COLONIALIST AND CAPITALIST DESIGN

Alongside the social discrimination on the basis of gender and dis_ability, structural racism has strongly influenced the design of bathrooms and the acceptability of certain sanitary practices. As a result, many Western societies consider water-flushed sitting toilets and the use of toilet paper as the worldwide, normatively set and desirable standard. This assumption becomes clearest in development aid, travel guides, and travel accounts.[13] In the process, not only ecological, but also anatomical and health aspects are ignored: Many people crouch to defecate, which makes it easier to completely evacuate the bowels, while a seated position makes excretion harder.[14] Moreover, flushing toilets and toilet paper waste invaluable resources. The same is true of sanitary products customarily used during menstruation. Disposable single-use products stand for progress and cleanliness, while alternatives, such as reusable sanitary pads, menstrual sponges, and organic materials like natural fibers or plant leaves, are considered primitive and unhygienic. A critical look at the historical development of today's Western bathrooms reveals that the water-flushed private sitting toilet is not only a hygienic achievement in combating pandemics and boosting comfort, but also first and foremost a status symbol. Soon after their invention in the 19th century, ownership of private flushing toilets—or the absence thereof, or even their shared use in stairwells of apartment blocks—began to constitute a segregating infrastructure that divided different socio-economic classes. Likewise, designated sanitary practices reproduce and stabilize social power relations by not only standardizing Western practices but furthermore linking these to certain (consumer) goods. The social inequalities produced in capitalism as regards race, class, and gender reflected in the Global North do not stop at the management and maintenance of bathrooms. Cleaning, particularly of sanitary installations, is socially looked down upon, poorly paid, rendered invisible, and often externalized to racialized people, and above all women. The "throne" therefore manifests multiple, interlinked socio-spatial power mechanisms, ranging from its design, positioning, and type of equipment, to sanitary

practices constituted by the West, to the labor policy aspects of its management and maintenance. A complex analysis of these mechanisms will be required to create future socio-spatial justice in the context of sanitary infrastructure.

FLUSHING TOILETS AND RESOURCE CONSUMPTION

Sanitation facilities as a network of flush toilets connected to a sewerage system and wastewater treatment plants are commonplace in many countries today, especially in the Global North. The system is easy to use, is considered progressive and—purportedly—hygienic or more hygienic than other systems. However, the existing system relies on "linear" exploitation, meaning one that consumes invaluable resources such as water and introduces nutrients and toxic materials into the ecological material cycle without subsequently extracting and/or recycling them. The current sanitary system, for all the ease of use it offers, therefore entails profound ecological disadvantages.

FIG. 4
In the German city of Eberswalde, the startup company Finizio has been running a pilot plant for recycling the contents of dry, urine-diverting, and composting toilets since 2018. In cooperation with other companies leading the sanitary revolution, Finizio is lobbying for the legal framework necessary to use the recycled fertilizer it produces on a commercial scale.

In Europe, the average person flushes about 15,000 liters of processed drinking water down the toilet every year. Given the global water crisis, flush toilets and the use of drinking water to transport human feces warrant scrutiny going forward. Furthermore, combined sewage systems blend reusable materials such as nutrients (e.g., phosphorus, nitrogen, and potassium) and carbon with harmful substances like heavy metals, microplastics, and prescription drugs, while also strongly diluting it with large volumes of water from human use and urban runoff. This dilution makes the retrieval of nutrients and exfiltration of contaminants challenging for wastewater treatment facilities. Centralized sewage systems do not have convincing purification and recycling capacities; instead, they can rightfully be regarded as "nutrient destruction plants"[15] whose emissions are a burden on ecosystems.

The circular use of nutrients is important for two reasons. First, nutrients such as nitrogen, phosphorus, and potassium are indispensable for vegetal growth. Nutrients are food for our food, which we then excrete once digested. But instead of using nutrients circularly, we have built one-way streets for resource depletion. In Germany, each year, 2.5 million tons of reactive nitrogen are extracted from the air using energy-intensive processes to manufacture nitrogen-based fertilizers.[16] The reliance on cheap energy and natural gas for this process resulted in fertilizer factories facing closure throughout Europe in 2022 due to rising operating costs.[17] Phosphorus, for its part, is obtained from open pit mines and imported to Europe. The finite reserves are spread across few locations, including the USA, China, and northwestern Africa.[18] The mining practices in the Moroccan-occupied territory of Western Sahara, which contains the world's largest reserves, are responsible for devastating ecological and health damage to the local population.[19] Moreover, despite modern "purification," far too many nutrients from sewage plants still find their way into rivers, lakes, or coastal waters, where they lead to eutrophication: excessive algae growth, lack of oxygen, and finally the death of fish and the destruction of entire ecosystems.[20] Furthermore, microplastics and diluted residues of prescription drugs find their way into open water, damaging ecosystems. In particular regarding the global material flows of nitrogen and phosphorus, as well as new chemical substances and plastic, we have already crossed the upper limit of the "safe operating space," set by the extent to which the ecosystem can be put under pressure, and are now in a high-risk zone for the planet's habitability.[21] In short, we are poisoning our environment in a way that lastingly endangers the regenerative ability of natural material cycles. Bathrooms are part of this problem. However, they could also be part of the solution if we turn what is now effectively a straight line back into a circle. The idea being that wastewater should no longer be viewed as some dirty slurry that has to be begrudgingly disposed of, but instead as a material flows, the careful (re-)processing of which can fundamentally contribute to maintaining the cycle of life.

A SANITATION AND NUTRIENT REVOLUTION: SAVING WATER AND USING NUTRIENTS

What is called for is a socio-technical transformation from the linear wastewater system to a circular sanitation management. This change will be made possible through appropriate toilet systems and circular reuse technologies, which—while upholding high hygiene and quality standards—can reclaim nutrients from digested food to be used for local agriculture. A glance at the history of architecture shows that alternative sanitation systems such as dry toilets, urine-diverting toilets, or compost toilets are not new inventions by any means. In Germany, Austria, and Switzerland, social housing estates in the 1920s involved different typologies—from workers' housing estates with peat moss toilets and self-supporting vegetable gardens (e.g., the Rosenhügel estate in Vienna) to apartment buildings with their own vegetable gardens. Since the 1980s, composting toilets and plant-based sewage treatment facilities have been devised and included in many pilot projects for ecological housing estates. Today, they are likewise used around the world after natural disasters and in places without sanitation infrastructure.[22]

In recent years, researchers and practitioners have jointly developed new technologies and systemic approaches. One important concept is that of material flow separation, which involves the technical separation of urine, feces, graywater, and rainwater at their origin (i.e., in a neighborhood, in a building, in a bathroom, or even in a single toilet). By separating the collection of material flows, circular processing solutions tailored to the location and type of material flow can be flexibly applied. These tend to take the neighborhood or block as the starting point of wastewater treatment and not, as with conventional solutions, the rear end of the sewer. Moreover, by switching to alternative toilet systems (e.g., vacuum toilets, urine-diverting flush toilets, urine-diverting dry toilets, or composting toilets) large parts—if not all—of the normally used flushing water can be avoided. The major advantage of these toilets is that they do not need to be connected to the sewage system and can thus be placed more or less anywhere. By means of special bowl design, the natural separation of urine and feces can be upheld, and subsequent processing facilitated. Urine has a higher density of nutrients and also represents a majority of excretions in terms of volume. It usually exits the body in a sterile form, meaning free of germs. Drug residues are mostly excreted in the urine, making the elimination of toxins easier if the urine is separated. Feces, by contrast, contains fewer nutrients but a higher proportion of organic matter and intestinal bacteria, which can be eliminated and/or deactivated by targeted treatment of the sludge. While the main focus in processing urine is on nutrient recycling, volume reduction, and removal of drug residues, the treatment of feces concentrates on "sanitization," i.e., killing the germs, and the combined recycling of organic components and nutrients. The end products are high-grade forms of dry, liquid, and humus fertilizer.

Despite successful model projects aimed at implementing a circular sanitation infrastructure, a sanitary and nutrient revolution will require profound social change. The current, linear, unsustainable model is literally cemented at three different levels: physically in the infrastructure, legally in technical requirements, and mentally in our heads. In Germany, the existing legal situation puts a brake on the deployment of already developed and functional innovative wastewater treatment systems and the introduction of new, quality-controlled recycling fertilizers into the soil. The wastewater, waste, and fertilizer laws need to be amended to enable recycling to be practically implemented through circular economy legislation. Local authorities require support in authorization processes for plants designed to ensure circular utilization. And we all need more images and stories of a world with different toilets and circular nutrient hubs. Finally, architects, planners, and building cooperatives urgently require access to knowledge, plans, and detailed information.

NOW WHAT? THE FUTURE ROLE OF ARCHITECTS

The work of architects traditionally focuses on buildings as objects. The toilet and/or the bathroom is categorized as a utilitarian feature of any building, the design of which usually is predetermined by standardized floor plans, regulatory stipulations (e.g., accessibility), and the location of utilities shafts within the building. Planning and organizing what happens once the wastewater leaves the toilet proper is not typically considered to be within an architect's purview, but rather within that of technical building equipment specialists. Rooms for maintenance and operations (technical rooms, storage areas, locker rooms, etc.) are often given exceptionally tight dimensions in line with conventional briefs by specialist planners and developers. However, changing the perception of the bathroom from that of a purely functional room to a space which translates the aforementioned social, ecological, and technical standards into an architectural solution will be the task of architects.

For that to happen, the focus will need to be expanded beyond the actual building phase to include usage and maintenance, if we want to achieve a resource-oriented overall view. Planning and building, which make up a mere two percent of a building's total life cycle costs, have the potential to decisively influence its usage costs, which weigh in at almost 80 percent of the total figure. Significant leverage lies not only in saving energy but also in reducing the building's water footprint—in Germany, 45 percent of the latter is created during use.[23] Furthermore, alongside an extensive prolongation of the service life, other key parameters to consider in planning new buildings could include the regeneration of resources beyond their sparing use, along

FIG. 5
In the basement of Genevese housing cooperative Équilibre's six-story apartment building Soubeyran, wastewater is treated by means of worm composting. Urine and feces are passed through a plant-based, nutrient-binding filtration system made of straw, sawdust, and wood shavings, and gradually transformed into compost by earthworms. The percolated fluids are purified by a mineral filter and reused for flushing toilets and watering plants. The application of the humus fertilizer in the building's own garden closes the nutrient cycle locally.

FIG. 6
On the 3.4-hectare site of the former *Saint-Vincent-de-Paul* hospital in Paris, historical buildings are being renovated and converted to housing. As a pilot project for the implementation of circular sanitary systems on a neighborhood scale, the bathrooms are equipped with flushed urine-diverting toilets drained by separate piping. The urine is transported to a processing facility through a subterranean network. The recycled fertilizer produced here can be used in nurseries and Parisian parks. This keeps nutrients circulating in the city and avoids the need for additional fertilizers.

with an increase in the ease of maintenance (robust and easily cleaned materials, maintenance joints, large-enough rooms, etc.). The fundamental incorporation of these aspects into architectural practice will shift our notion of buildings as finished units, with the underlying object fixation this view entails, in favor of an idea of architecture as a metabolism that is embedded in ongoing/permanent metabolic processes and material cycles (water, nutrition, goods, electricity, heat, cooling, etc.), steadily (re)producing these by itself.

In contemporary Western academic discourse, increasing attention is being paid to the conversion of existing buildings. In Germany, modernization and conversion will soon replace newly built structures as the main task for planners. A sanitary revolution for existing—and new—buildings going beyond technically isolated solutions for single rooms with small collection tanks will require additional space that architects will have to factor into their plans. Here, technical and ecological issues must be structurally considered in combination with social questions of inclusion, accessibility, and widespread user-friendliness. In recent years, systems have consistently evolved, including new components devised for existing buildings in urban settings. Now, urine-diverting standing, sitting, and squatting toilets exist—either with or without flush systems. A separate transport of collected waste matter can be facilitated by a "pipe-within-a-pipe" system, whereby a second pipe is inserted into an existing pipe.[24] Pipes leading to a decentral urine treatment plant in the neighborhood—so-called "Urinodukte" [urinoducts]—could use existing sewage pipes as their service ducts. In some cases, no new pipes are required at all: New technological developments enable (partial) treatment with simultaneous reclaiming of nutrients right at the level of the individual bathroom (see for example the project inside the German Pavilion).[25] The range of options that planners have at their disposal to implement material flow-based solutions is expanding. However, planning solutions on their own will not suffice: We urgently require laws that allow exceptions to the mandatory connection to existing sewage systems and that enshrine innovation and experimentation clauses in building regulations to expand the possibilities for creative solutions. The sanitary revolution will need the reactivation of cultural techniques old and new regarding bathrooms, which architects need to support and mediate: How to discuss toilets with clients? What toilet systems function for which users? How is what cultural technique conveyed and nurtured? What role do daily cleaning and maintenance play in the design of these spaces?

Even if the ideas of inclusion and life-cycle analyses are gradually being incorporated into planning, we need a more systematic rethinking and appropriate action. Physical diversity is just as much a fact as is the threatened status of our planetary ecosystems. Today, we must ask ourselves how we can not only reduce (to achieve sufficiency) and repair, but also how we can reconstruct, nurture, and regenerate. With a sanitary revolution at the level of the individual building, the neighborhood, and the entire city, architecture can substantially contribute to greater social justice and the ecological regeneration of soils, the drinking water supply, and the production of food.

1 Beatriz Colomina and Mark Wigley, "Toilet Architecture: An Essay About the Most Psychosexually Charged Room in a Building," *PIN-UP*, no. 23 (2017–18): 231.
2 See klo:lektiv, eds., "Pissen* ist politisch: Feministische und kritisch-geographische Perspektiven auf Geographien der Notdurft," *Feministische Geo-Rundmail* 84 (Winter 2020), accessed February 16, 2023, ak-feministische-geographien.org/rundmail/.
3 See Lilith Kuhn et al., "Notdürftige Infrastrukturen: Öffentliche Toiletten zwischen Neoliberalisierung und Utopie," *Bürger & Staat: Öffentliche Infrastrukturen. Die politische Gestaltung der vernetzten Gesellschaft* 1/2 (Spring 2022), 69–75.
4 Leslie Kern, *Feminist City: Claiming Space in a Man-made World* (London: Verso Books, 2019), 106.
5 See Kuhn et al., "Notdürftige Infrastrukturen" (see note 3).
6 See United Nations, "Goal 6: Ensure availability and sustainable management of water and sanitation for all," *Sustainable Development Goals*, 2015, accessed January 30, 2023, sdgs.un.org/goals/goal6.
7 See Kathryn Anthony and Meghan Dufresne, "Potty Parity in Perspective: Gender and Family Issues in Planning and Designing Public Restrooms," *Journal of Planning Literature* 21, no. 3 (2007): 267–94.
8 See Lauren Berlant, "The Commons: Infrastructures for Troubling Times," *Environment and Planning D – Society and Space* 34, no. 3 (2016): 393–419.
9 See Katharina Ciax, "Flushing Down Hegemony: Public Toilet Infrastructure and the Politics of Accessibility," in *Jenaer Sozialgeographische Manuskripte*, vol. 20, ed. Simon Runkel (Jena: Friedrich-Schiller-Universität Jena, 2022).
10 See Yaffa Truelove and Hanna A. Ruszczyk, "Bodies as Urban Infrastructure: Gender, Intimate Infrastructures and Slow Infrastructural Violence," *Political Geography* 92 (January 2022), doi.org/10.1016/j.polgeo.2021.102492.
11 See Rob Kitchin and Robin Law, "The Socio-spatial Construction of (In)accessible Public Toilets," *Urban Studies* 38, no. 2 (2001): 287–98.
12 See Daniela Hayder and Wilfried Schnepp, "Umgang mit Harninkontinenz: Ergebnisse einer qualitativen Studie mit Betroffenen und pflegenden Angehörigen," *Pflege* 23, no. 3 (2012): 154–62.
13 See Alison Moore, "Colonial Visions of 'Third World' Toilets: A Nineteenth-Century Discourse That Haunts Contemporary Tourism," in *Ladies and Gents: Public Toilets and Gender*, eds. Olga Gershenson and Barbara Penner (Philadelphia: Temple University Press, 2009), 105–25.
14 See Alexander Kira, *Das Badezimmer* (Düsseldorf: Krammer, 1987).
15 Quote from an employee of the Berlin public water management agency BWB.
16 See "Welche Rolle spielt reaktiver Stickstoff für die Chemieindustrie?" *Umweltbundesamt,* accessed January 30, 2023, www.umweltbundesamt.de/umweltatlas/reaktiver-stickstoff/verursacher/energiewirtschaft-industrie/welche-rolle-spielt-reaktiver-stickstoff-fuer-die.
17 See Olaf Zinke, "Yara schließt Düngerwerke: Steht Europa bald ohne Dünger da?" *Agrarheute*, September 21, 2022, accessed January 30, 2023, www.agrarheute.com/management/betriebsfuehrung/yara-schliesst-duengerwerke-steht-europa-bald-ohne-duenger-598174.
18 See Dana Cordell et al., "The Story of Phosphorus: Global Food Security and Food for Thought," *Global Environmental Change* 19, no. 2 (May 2009): 292–305.
19 See Natasha White, "Toxic Shadow: Phosphate Miners in Morocco Fear They Pay a High Price," *The Guardian*, December 16, 2015, accessed February 1, 2023, www.theguardian.com/global-development/2015/dec/16/toxic-shadow-phosphate-miners-morocco-fear-they-pay-high-price.
20 See Cascade Tuholske et al., "Mapping Global Inputs and Impacts from of [*sic*] Human Sewage in Coastal Ecosystems," *PLOS ONE* 16, no. 11 (November 2021), doi.org/10.1371/journal.pone.0258898.
21 See Linn Persson et al., "Outside the Safe Operating Space of the Planetary Boundary for Novel Entities," *Environmental Science & Technology* 56, no. 22 (November 2022): 1510–21; see also Will Steffen et al., "Planetary boundaries: Guiding human development on a changing planet," *Science* 347, no. 6223 (February 2015): 736–47.
22 See for example the nonprofit SOIL in Haiti, which develops, tests, and deploys ecological sanitary systems worldwide, accessed February 14, 2023, www.oursoil.org.
23 See *Umweltfußabdruck von Gebäuden in Deutschland: Kurzstudie zu sektorenübergreifenden Wirkungen des Handlungsfelds "Errichtung und Nutzung von Hochbauten" auf Klima und Umwelt*, ed. Bundesinstitut für Bau-, Stadt- und Raumforschung (Bonn: Bundesamt für Bauwesen und Raumordnung, 2020), 15.
24 See Susanne Veser and Jörg Londong, *EVaSENS: Einsatz von Vakuum-Inlinern im Bestand; Integration von Unterdruck-Sanitärtechnik im bestehenden Gebäude zur Etablierung von NASS-Systemen* (Stuttgart: Fraunhofer IRB Verlag, 2017), 2, accessed January 30, 2023, www.irbnet.de/daten/rswb/17079006196.pdf.
25 See Michel E. Riechmann et al., "On-Site Urine Treatment Combining Ca(OH)2 Dissolution and Dehydration with Ambient Air," *Water research X* 13 (2021), doi.org/10.1016/j.wroa.2021.100124.

For the duration of the 2023 Architecture Biennale, the German Pavilion will see the installation of a prototype dry toilet developed for multistory apartment buildings combined with a downstream urine treatment reactor. The fully functional and usable infrastructure is the product of a collaboration between numerous scientists, planners, and practitioners, among which the Eawag aquatic research institute of the Swiss ETH Domain, Finizio GmbH, and the Leibniz Institute of Vegetable and Ornamental Crops (IGZ). The result is a sustainable alternative to conventional flush toilets.

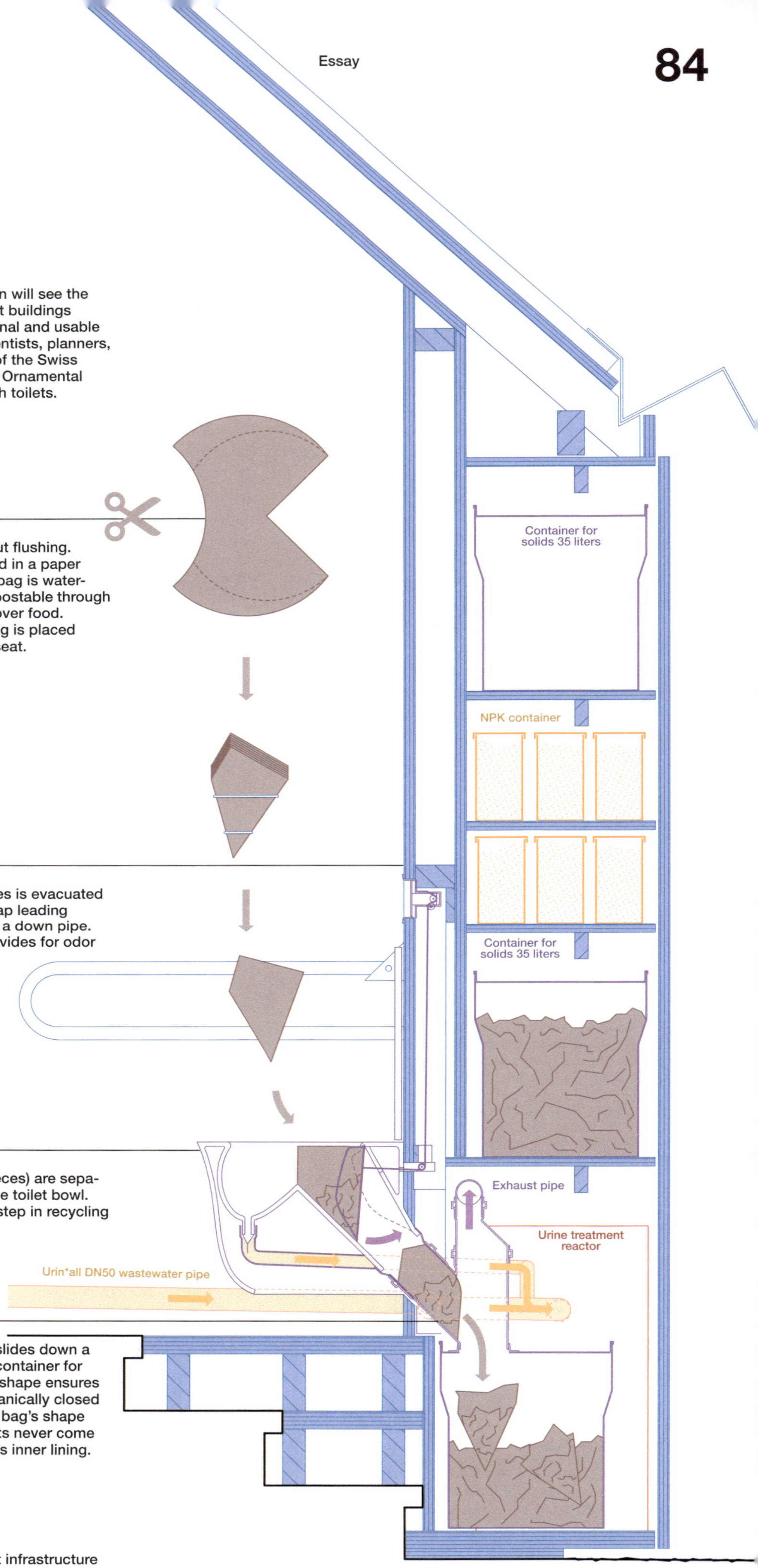

1. Paper bag
The dry toilet works without flushing. Instead, feces are collected in a paper bag during each use. The bag is waterproof yet completely compostable through its coating made from leftover food. Before each use, a new bag is placed manually below the toilet seat.

2. Hatch mechanism
Once used, the bag of feces is evacuated from the toilet through a flap leading to a sloped drain and then a down pipe. The flap, when closed, provides for odor impermeability.

3. Separation
Fluids (urine) and solids (feces) are separated from each other in the toilet bowl. The separation is the first step in recycling both raw materials.

4. Slide
Pulled by gravity, the bag slides down a 45-degree drain toward a container for solids. The drain's conical shape ensures the top of the bag is mechanically closed in the sliding process. The bag's shape guarantees that its contents never come into contact with the drain's inner lining.

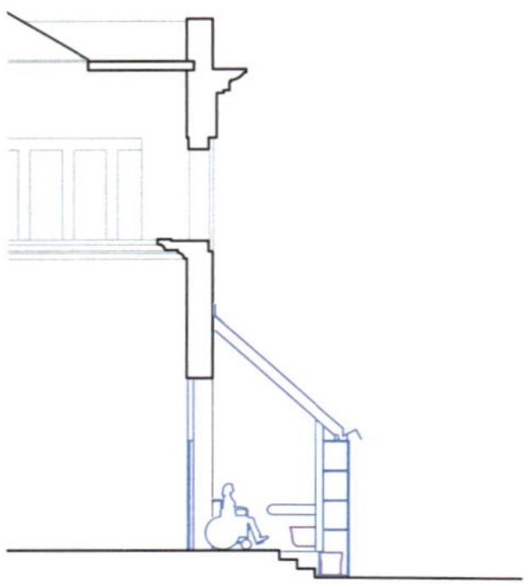

FIG. 7
Section of the toilet extension as part of the German Pavilion

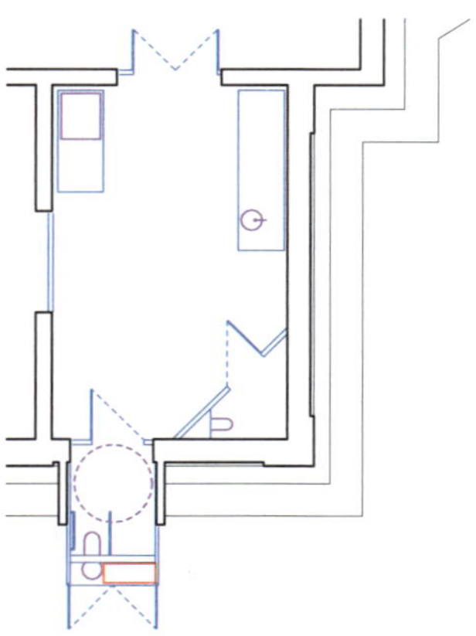

FIG. 8
Floor plan of the "bathroom" in the German Pavilion, including the toilet extension

FIG. 9
Cross section of the toilet infrastructure in the German Pavilion

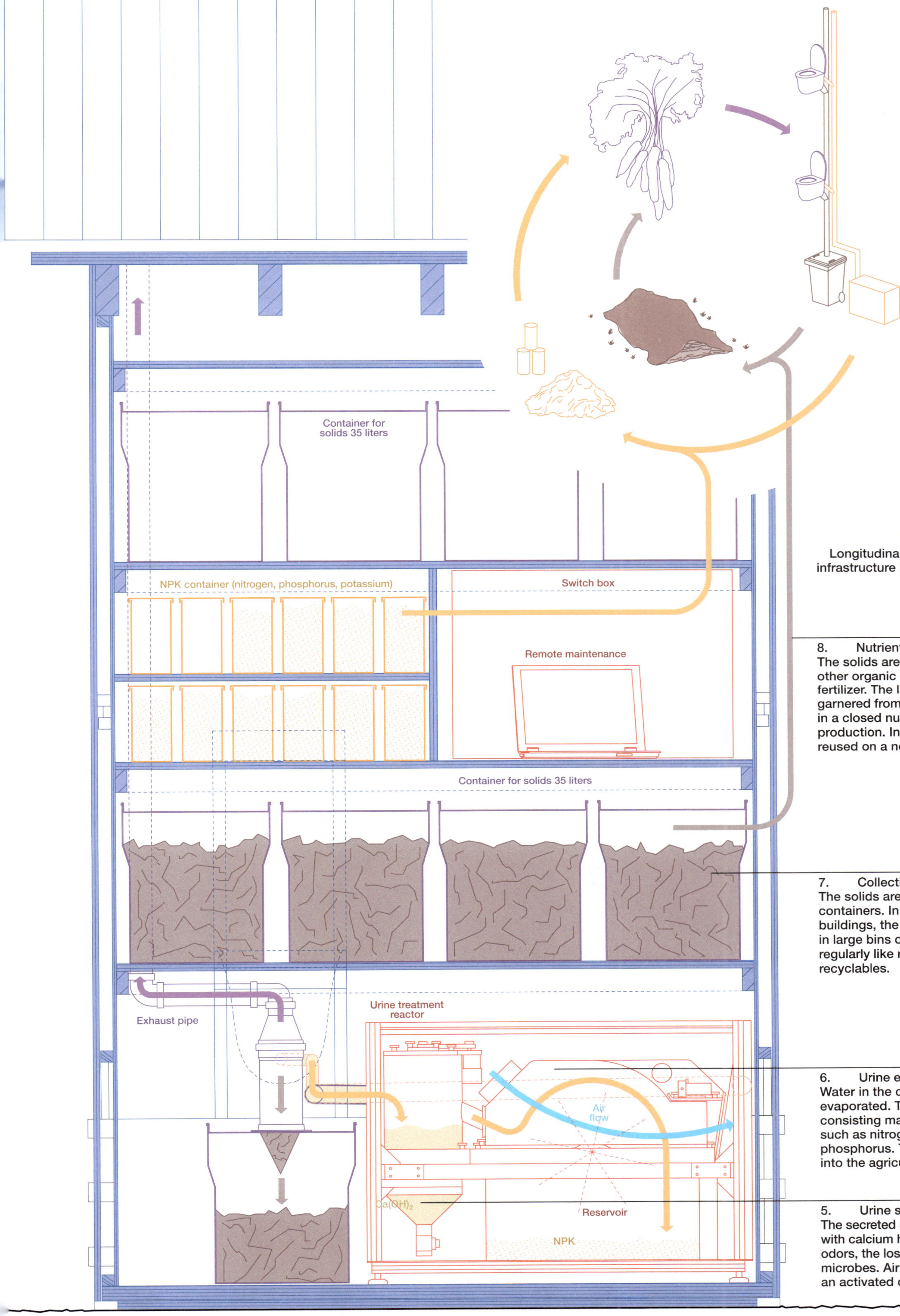

FIG. 10
Longitudinal section of the toilet infrastructure in the German Pavilion

8. Nutrient recuperation
The solids are composted after adding other organic residues, resulting in topsoil fertilizer. The latter, together with nutrients garnered from urine, is reused as fertilizer in a closed nutrient cycle in agricultural production. In Venice, the products are reused on a nearby farm.

7. Collection of solids
The solids are collected in 35-liter containers. In multistory apartment buildings, the collection happens in large bins or containers, emptied regularly like residual waste or recyclables.

6. Urine evaporation
Water in the collected urine is evaporated. The result is a concentrate consisting mainly of organic nutrients such as nitrogen, potassium and phosphorus. These are reintroduced into the agricultural cycle as fertilizer.

5. Urine stabilization
The secreted urine is immediately stabilized with calcium hydroxide, preventing at once odors, the loss of nutrients, and pathogenic microbes. Air leaves the reactor through an activated carbon filter.

THE POLITICS OF DISABILITY

Text:
Aimi Hamraie

One hundred stairs divide a gathering crowd from the US Capitol Building above. Numbering in the hundreds, they chant and hold signs. A group breaks off, leaving behind wheelchairs and crutches to lay flesh on stairs and crawl to the top. Framed against the building's steps, the bodies are clearly misfits: unanticipated, noncompliant, and taking up space.[1] Walking to their offices, irritated lawmakers step over and around misfit bodies; onlookers snap photographs; news anchors interview activists as they crawl to the top. Framed by the stairs in a striking image, these public bodies communicate what signs and chants alone cannot: this building, a symbol of governance and democratic citizenship for all—an embodiment of the nation itself—was not designed with disabled people in mind.[2]

The event was the "Capitol Crawl," a disability rights protest demanding that Congress pass the *Americans with Disabilities Act* (ADA) of 1990, landmark antidiscrimination legislation that identified a civil right to accessible buildings, public transportation, and workplaces for disabled citizens.[3] Widely credited as the final push that resolved congressional deadlock, the Capitol Crawl demonstrated the power of disabled people as resourceful agents whose novel tactics showed visible evidence of disability discrimination rather than patients in need of medical cure. In the Capitol Crawl, disabled people spoke back against the steps by deploying embodied speech and lived knowledge as architectural critique.

The built world is inseparable from social attitudes, discriminatory systems, and knowledge about which users designers must keep in mind. How we structure knowledge, interact with material things, and tell stories about the users of built environments matter for belonging and justice. When these stories embrace as common sense such values as freedom, access, and "a more inclusive world for everyone," it becomes all the more important to heed the critical lessons of the Capitol Crawl protestors, whose embodied architectural critique raised critical, material, and epistemological questions: Who counts as everyone and how can we know?

FIG. 1
On March 12, 1990, disability activists left their wheelchairs and crutches behind and crawled up the steps towards the seat of the United States Congress in what came to be known as the Capitol Crawl. The protest, widely publicized, is considered a milestone in the history of disability rights, impacting public opinion and urging Congress to finally pass the *American with Disabilities Act* (ADA), adopted on July 26, 1990.

USERS AS PRODUCTIVE CITIZENS

Since antiquity, architects imagined the inhabitant as an ideal or universal body reflecting cultural ideals of beauty and proportion. This "mythical average norm"[4] is not a neutral body but rather a particular white, European, nondisabled, youthful, and often masculine figure whose features remain unmarked. But to understand how the mythical average norm or normate became an unmarked template for good design, we have to engage more closely with histories of knowledge. Disability studies scholars and historians of science have argued that the concepts of "normal" and "average" are relatively recent phenomena, appearing in the nineteenth century with the birth of statistics to produce modern forms of power. Unlike the earlier, classical notion of the "ideal" body, which referenced mythic figures divine in form, the norm has a prescriptive function, which stems from its reference to real population data.[5] For disabilities studies scholar Lennard Davis, this is what makes the figure of the norm insidious: when norms purport to represent "real" populations, it becomes possible to attempt to align those populations with the average, consequently making normates appear as natural or neutral. In other words, norms do not simply reflect probabilities within populations. In shaping the "real" population, norms become prescriptions for normalcy.

In the nineteenth and twentieth century, the figure of the *user* began to signify a range of variation to subjects previously seen as universal. Statisticians, industrial scientists, and engineers identified this wide-ranging variation, termed the "human factor," as an unpredictable threat to industrial, military, and other technological systems. Studying this threat would enable its smooth assimilation into the machinery of production. As a scientific understanding of human diversity enabled the design of increasingly productive, efficient systems, flexible design for a range of users became the stuff of standardization and normalization. Concepts of human variation, disability, and injury configured the user as a site of human engineering and rehabilitation.

Before the twentieth century, the need for accessible design as a matter of public policy was unthinkable because disabled people were segregated from public space by eugenicist "ugly laws," as historian Susan Schweik has shown, confined in institutions, and hence illegible as public citizens.[6] In the post-World War II era, human factors research and ergonomics joined forces with postwar rehabilitation cultures, which brought particular disabled bodies—often white, male, physically disabled soldiers rather than people of color, women, or mentally disabled people—into public legibility as both users and citizens.

Proponents of barrier-free design argued that the world had been designed with an average user in mind, but the changing nature of human embodiment through war, industrial accidents, and medical advances demanded a new strategy. Barrier-free design challenged the idea that physical able-bodiedness is a prerequisite to occupying built space, but proponents did not challenge the imperatives of normalization. This was evident in the experts enlisted to create accessibility guidelines: architects and builders worked with rehabilitation scientists,

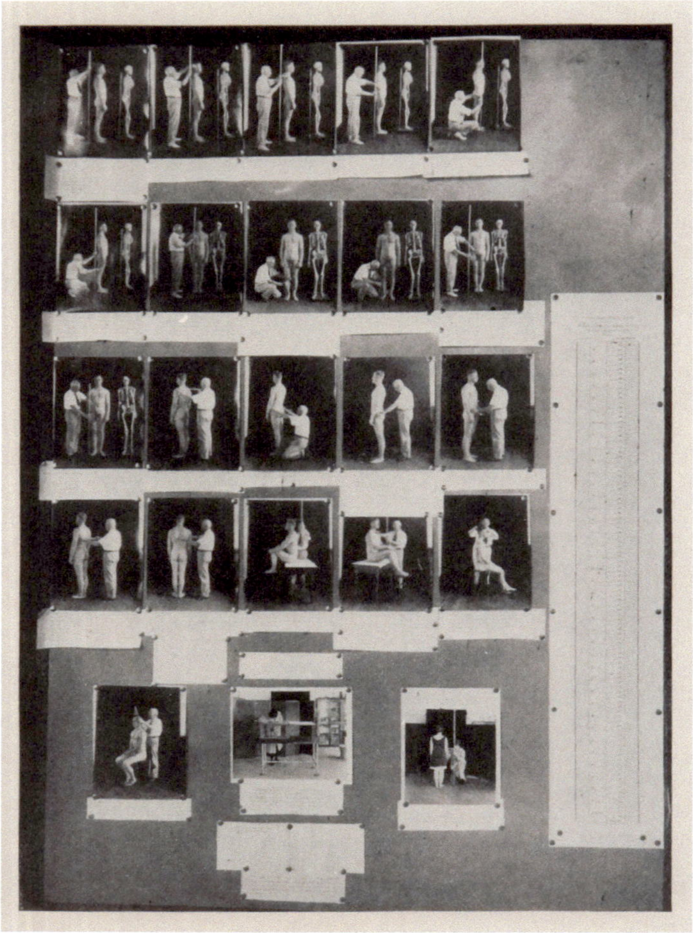

industrial designers, and scientific managers in tandem to produce barrier-free environments that would enhance productivity and human performance. As such, barrier-free design was firmly situated in twentieth-century notions of productive citizenship, which defined liberal belonging through the capacity for productive labor, as well as through the evident fruits of that labor: wealth accumulation, homeownership, and consumerism.

DISABILITY, GENDER, RACE, AND SEGREGATED CITIZENSHIP

Few spatial domains were closer to the epicenter of mid-twentieth-century constructions of whiteness as normal and Blackness as difference than the North American suburban home. In the late 1940s, laws which facilitated the ability of mostly white veterans to access property, as well as discriminatory lending practices by the Federal Housing Authority, enabled white US citizens to migrate from urban areas to middle-class suburbs.[7] This process consolidated spatial patterns of wealth distribution and entrenched the racial and economic segregation of African Americans through a disinvestment in cities and an accumulation of white suburban wealth.

FIG. 2
Anthropometric measurements illustrated in Harry H. Laughlin's catalog for *The Second International Exhibition of Eugenics*, held at the American Museum of Natural History, New York, in 1921

In the 1950s, architectural experiments in mass-producing standardized single-family houses to accommodate these migrations. Architects designed suburban homes as technologies for white, middle-class women whose labor they translated into "homemaking," a designation that both identified women's bodies as sites of efficient, extractable labor and reinforced the status of white women as model citizens.[8]

Concurrently, rehabilitation professionals turned to engineering disabled housewives, spatially bound bodies whose gender roles, perceived inherent weakness, and designated belonging in suburban homes made them appear as natural sites for scientific management. The visual and material rhetoric of rehabilitation interventions into the midcentury home recalled a longer history of depicting assistive technologies and built environments as enablers of white, middle-class women's comfort, agency, productivity, and quality of life. Consequently, white women's aging and gendered bodies became model organisms for the study of disability as a relationship between bodies and environments. Concerns with women as users began to surface in barrier-free design manuals for disabled and elderly people, with particular attention to wheelchair-accessible kitchens.[9]

For these users, rehabilitation through self-help entailed becoming autonomous consumers rather than productive factory workers or independent citizens. From the 1940s to the

FIG. 3

Anthropometric figures of wheelchair users. Charles Ramsey and Harold Sleeper, *Architectural Graphic Standards*, 7th ed. (New York: Wiley, 1981)

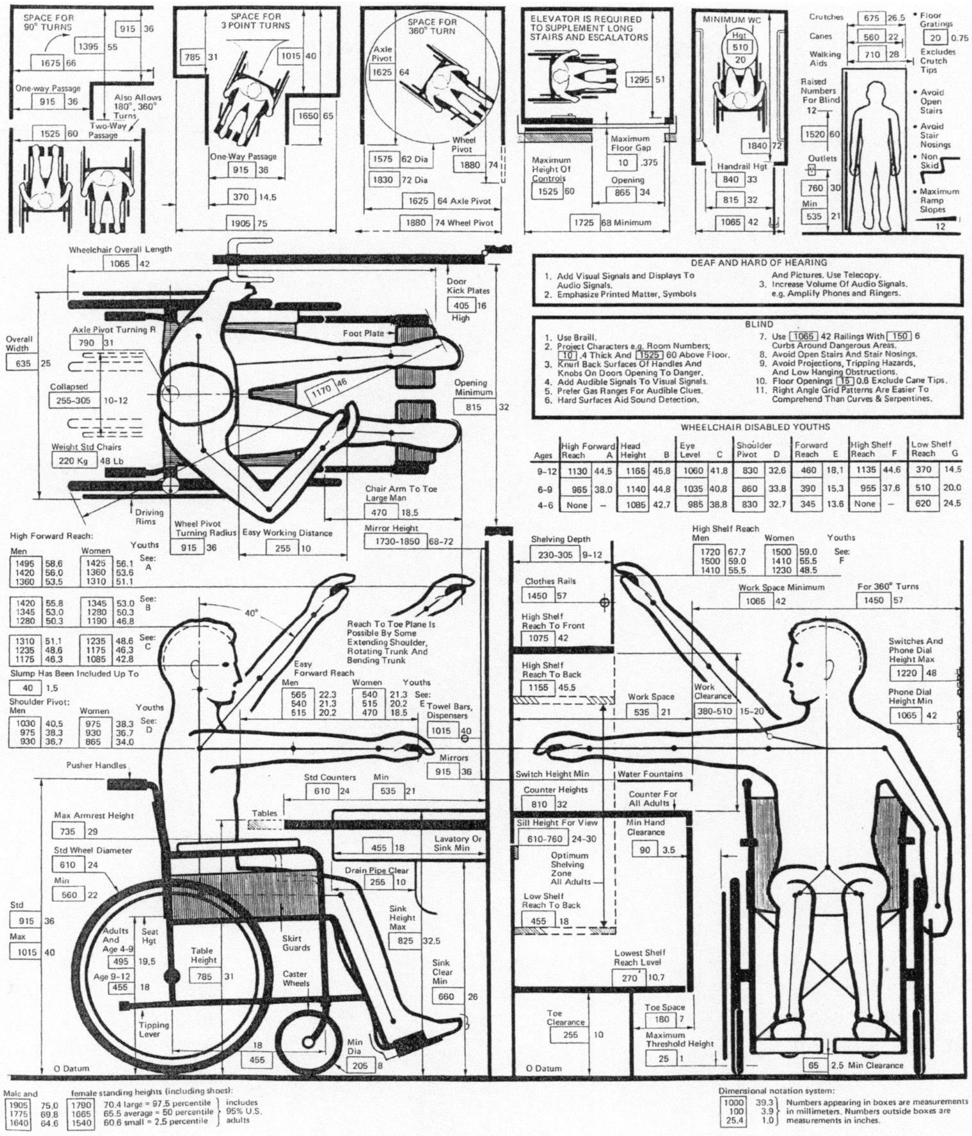

FIG. 4

In the postwar years, barrier-free design research was mainly focused on domestic settings, its main subject being the white, disabled housewife seen as a key target of both productive citizenship and consumerism. The photo shows a study conducted between 1961 and 1974 at the University of Illinois.

FIG. 5
An experimental ramp for accessibility research at the University of Illinois, ca. 1950s

1960s, barrier-free design attached itself to the tastes and preferences of white, middle-class consumers in the privileged, safe, and seemingly neutral spaces of the suburban home and the public university, where the design of new products and buildings would enable access to the material practices of normal life segregated from the stigmatized spaces of inner cities. Dominated by rehabilitation experts, ideologies of ability, and views of disability as tragedy or deficit in need of elimination, barrier-free design merely redesigned the language through which architectural and cultural norms of embodiment were enforced. There can be no doubt that these conditions came at a cost to those bodies that were deemed unproductive, incurable, or unamenable to rehabilitation. But in the following decade, a grassroots disabled peoples' movement emerged to challenge compulsory productivity, rehabilitation, and inaccessible environments.

CURB CUTS, RAMPS, AND CRIP TECHNOSCIENCE[10]

In the late 1960s, disability activists and their allies drove around Berkeley, California, under dark of night, smashing sidewalks with sledgehammers and pouring new curb cuts with bags of cement or asphalt—or so the rumor goes.[11] While those allegedly involved describe the circumstances surrounding activist curb cuts as far more mundane, heroic stories about sledgehammer-wielding activists have taken shape as the primal scenes of American disability activism, securing the movement's place within the broader memory of civil rights-era direct action and portraying disability as a social and cultural rather than medical category.

FIG. 6
In the early 1960s, federal US agencies pushed for standardized accessibility guidelines, which relied on research conducted on the bodies of young, white, wheelchair-using college students at the University of Illinois in Champaign—one of the first cities to adopt wide curb cuts as early as the late 1950s.

On the campus of the University of California in Berkeley, disabled students lived in the Cowell Hospital's third floor, which was established in 1962 as a "residence program for severely physically disabled students" with funding from the Department of Vocational Rehabilitation.[12] Isolated from Berkeley dormitories and student life, Cowell became a seedbed for crip community and activism through the independent living movement. Although the term "independent living" had originated within vocational rehabilitation to describe rehabilitation for those deemed unemployable, the movement appropriated this term to define a political position against compulsory productivity.[13] Espousing principles of self-determination, rather than rehabilitation-oriented self-help, the movement argued that everyone (regardless of their productivity) should have equal access to housing and care in the community rather than in nursing homes or institutions.

Despite its title, the movement invested in an ethics of interdependence. Similar to the feminist women's health movement centered on bodily autonomy, disabled people organized knowledge and expertise around their independence from medical authority and interdependence with one another.[14] Cowell was a site of crip culture-in-the-making, where disabled students shared space, formed mutual aid networks, transferred knowledge, and experimented with adaptive technologies of everyday life.

The independent living movement activists framed rehabilitation as a hegemonic system of medical expertise, in which biased "'professionals,' 'experts,' and 'specialists'" are "more likely to be knowledgeable about a person's limitations than about his capacities."[15] The problem with rehabilitation, they implied, was the exclusion of disability expertise and agency from the arenas of medical care and decision-making and the consequent exclusion of (what they deemed) more objective self-knowledge of disability grounded in life experiences. Instead, they insisted on disabled peoples' unique technoscientific literacies, with relevance for the politics of everyday life.

Curb cut and wheelchair ramp experiments materialized the independent living philosophy of gaining access to public life beyond the dictates of rehabilitation and productivity. Between 1969 and 1970, the Rolling Quads, a student-led activist group, lobbied the city of Berkeley to install curb cuts on sidewalks, requesting an annual budget for "wheelchair ramps in existing curbs" and for adding ramps "in all new construction as a matter of course."[16]

Disability activists produced a set of ideas that later influenced an academic theory of the "social model," which is often taken to argue that disability is a system of disadvantages that societies produce, and not solely embodied pathology.[17] Curb cuts (and their close cousins, wheelchair ramps) often signify the notion that disability is a social and environmental construction, produced in the relationship between bodies and built environments, and thus not something innate to the body.

UNIVERSAL DESIGN

In 1985, disabled architect Ronald Mace imagined "a way of designing a building or facility, at little or no extra cost, so that it is both attractive and functional for all people, disabled or not."[18] He called this idea "Universal Design" and offered it to architects as an aspiration for a more inclusive, functional built environment. The idea seemed straightforward, simple, common sense. It was easy to cite and quote. Nothing about Universal Design appeared radical, political, or confrontational. Mace had studied architecture in the 1960s, developing an analysis of architects' ignorance, which he described as a materially and historically conditioned arrangement resulting from the public invisibility of disabled people and from norms within the profession. Following his graduation, he began integrating barrier-free design principles into his own projects. Soon after, he turned towards architectural education as his field of action. In 1972, Mace was offered a job teaching architectural drafting at Fayetteville Technical Institute, where he found opportunities to infuse accessibility awareness into the technical dimensions of the design process.[62] Word of the disabled architect spread. Mace's professional networks in Fayetteville connected him to the North Carolina state government, which hired him to clarify and illustrate the state's new accessibility guidelines, the first state-level standards in the United States and a "national model."[19]

Mace came to be regarded as an accessibility expert, but he was also one of the compliance system's greatest critics. In the early 1980s, barrier-free design became synonymous with compliance and regulation. When accessibility practices became a matter of legal enforcement, barrier-free design came to signify a narrow, bureaucratic accessibility approach. Disability activists and accessibility experts contended with resistant architects, who insisted that accessible design was not "good design." He began establishing a relationship with a growing network of like-minded designers and scholars who desired creative accessibility solutions beyond code compliance.

Most importantly, Mace wanted to know how to promote accessible design to architects. He hypothesized that the best approach had to do with language and framing. Mace's 1985 article, "Universal Design: Barrier-Free Environments for Everyone," praised Universal Design as, "a concept whose time has arrived." It is also on the cutting edge of progressive design, and offers designers the chance to challenge conventional design thinking by designing products, buildings, and facilities which incorporate new ideas, and embody the essence of good design: that which is practical and can be used by all."[20]

Describing Universal Design as a "marketing concept," Mace clarified that the term was a strategy for overcoming architects' boredom and resistance to compliance by working within the market as a site of power with value and prestige for designers.[21] This strategy, he acknowledged, had not been successful because of what he identified as architects' "attitudes": so long as architects understood accessible products as only necessary on projects with disabled clients or explicitly for disabled users, the market for such products would not exist.[22] If accessible products and spaces appear in spaces of "mainstream commerce," such as corporate headquarters and government buildings, Mace proposed, "[t]hen we're winning."

Mace's comments suggest a shift in his thinking and in the broader Universal Design discourse. His earlier concerns had been with marginalized users. He experimented with foregrounding disabled users in their complexity and addressed intersectionality, particularly the disproportionate marginalization of disabled women, children, and the elderly who architects do not consider in design processes. But regardless of how nuanced and critical Universal Design's internal theory became, the public face of Universal Design marketing increasingly obscured these nuances.

Alongside terms like "green," "smart," "flexible," and "adaptive," "Universal" Design became a product description among other neoliberal forms, increasingly depoliticized and divorced from disability justice. Design magazines characterized Universal Design as simply a form of good design or quickly dismissed its potential for promoting justice for disabled people by remarking on its added value for nondisabled people—normate, mainstream consumers with a desire for freedom or more usable consumer products. Since the late 1990s, builders' magazines, newspapers, textbooks, and conference workshops began to tell a new story about Universal Design: that this approach was not about accessibility for disabled users at all but rather about a commonsense approach to "good design" for everyone.[13] The term has become a mainstay of popular discourse—not by centering disability as a category of marginalization but by disavowing it.

In 1997, the Center for Universal Design at North Carolina State University released "The Principles of Universal Design," a guide for inclusive and flexible design.[23] Since then, the "Principles" have become the most-often-cited reference to Universal Design, shaping public perceptions of its theory. Although the "Principles" uses terms such as "equitable" and "flexible," references to specific users, such as disabled people, do not appear in the text. The discourse of simplicity, common sense, and good design was not substantive or specific enough to encourage accessibility.

CONCLUSION

In the early 21st century, the term "Universal Design" gained popularity as an easy reference to the idea that inclusive design benefits everyone, regardless of disability or age. But what does "everyone" mean in a world that devalues particular bodies? Similar to the idea that we live in a post-racial society, wherein race is a fiction and civil rights laws have mandated equality, rendering oppression immaterial, terms such as "everyone" give the impression that legible belonging in a population is unmediated by historical, political, or social ways of knowing. Accordingly, it is often taken as common sense that because aging is a form of impairment, everyone is or will be disabled at some point. It follows that better design will benefit not only our present, youthful, able-bodied selves but also the bodies that we will be in the accessible future.

But aging is a marker of privilege in a dominant culture that does not anticipate or value all lives. For those of us whose bodies do not follow these smooth, predictable temporalities, whose ways of being and moving find friction with our social and built environments, and whose present and future belonging has been shaped by past conditions of inequality, the idea of universal disability is perplexing at best. Struggles for access, belonging, and citizenship are not contained in a linear march toward progress. The consumer-centric narrative that dominates much of Universal Design marketing tells us little about the sociopolitical economy of design or what purpose profitability serves, who benefits, and toward what ends. It ignores the intersecting imprints of racial injustice, poverty, ableism, and gender discrimination inscribed in the development patterns of our cities, suburbs, and landscapes.

Contrary to post-disability and post-racial narratives, physical structures and the stories that we tell about them matter for how we understand who gets to be in the world and under what conditions. As Universal Design extends into classrooms, education technologies, campus wayfinding projects, and academic publishing, our ways of reproducing claims about Universal Design matter. How we approach the intersections of disability with race, gender, class, and aging, how we study, teach, and claim knowledge about disability matters for the material arrangements we pursue.

This text is a slightly revised excerpt from Aimi Hamraie's Building Access: Universal Design and the Politics of Disability *(Minneapolis: University of Minnesota Press, 2017). Reprinted with the kind permission of Aimi Hamraie and University of Minnesota Press.*

1 See Rosemarie Garland-Thomson, "Misfits: A Feminist Materialist Disability Concept," *Hypatia* 26, no. 3 (2011): 591–609; Aimi Hamraie, "Designing Collective Access: A Feminist Disability Theory of Universal Design," *Disability Studies Quarterly* 33, no. 4 (Winter 2013), accessed February 14, 2023, www.dsq-sds.org/article/view/3871/3411.

2 "Disabled people" is the preferred usage for many disability activists, who argue that they are disabled by society and claim disability as an identity. "Person-first language," such as "people with disabilities," is often associated with medical and rehabilitative models, which identify personhood as separate from disabled embodiment and experience.

3 Americans with Disabilities Act (ADA), 42 U.S.C. § 12101, USA 1990.

4 Elaine Ostroff, "Universal Design: An Evolving Paradigm," in *Universal Design Handbook*, eds. Wolfgang F. E. Preiser and Korydon H. Smith, 2nd ed. (New York: McGraw-Hill, 2011), 1.9.

5 See Lennard J. Davis, "Constructing Normalcy: The Bell Curve, the Novel, and the Invention of the Disabled Body in the Nineteenth Century," in *Beyond Bioethics: Toward a New Biopolitics*, eds. Osagie K. Obasogie and Marcy Darnovsky (Berkeley: University of California Press, 2018), 63–72.

6 See Susan M. Schweik, *The Ugly Laws: Disability in Public* (New York: NYU Press, 2010).

7 See Martha R. Mahoney, "Residential Segregation and White Privilege," in *Critical White Studies: Looking behind the Mirror*, eds. Richard Delgado and Jean Stefancic (Philadelphia: Temple University Press, 1997), 273–75.

8 See Dolores Hayden, *The Grand Domestic Revolution: A History of Feminist Designs for American Homes, Neighborhoods, and Cities* (Cambridge: MIT Press, 1982), 285–6; see also Ruth Schwartz Cowan, *More Work for Mother: The Ironies of Household Technology from the Open Hearth to the Microwave* (New York: Basic Books, 1983), 28.

9 See Howard Rusk, *A Functional Home for Easier Living, Designed for the Physically Disabled, the Cardiac, and the Elderly* (New York: NYU Medical Center, Institute of Physical Medicine and Rehabilitation, 1959); Helen E. McCullough and Mary B. Farnham, *Space and Design Requirements for Wheelchair Kitchens*, Bulletin no. 661 (Urbana: College of Agriculture Extension Service, 1960); Helen E. McCullough and Mary B. Farnham, *Kitchens for Women in Wheelchairs*, Circular 841 (Urbana: College of Agriculture Extension Service, 1961).

10 See Aimi Hamraie, "Cripping Feminist Technoscience," *Hypatia* 30, no. 1 (2015): 307–13.

11 See Joseph P. Shapiro, *No Pity: People with Disabilities Forging a New Civil Rights Movement* (New York: Times Books, 1994), 126.

12 See John Hessler, "Grant Proposal for the Physically Disabled Students' Program, Proposed to Assistant Secretary/Commissioner of Education for Support Through the Special Services for Disabled Students in Institutions of Higher Education," 1970 manuscript in Michael Fuss, *Michael Fuss papers, ca. 1970–1972* (UC Berkeley Libraries).

13 See Gerben DeJong, "Independent Living: From Social Movement to Analytic Paradigm," *Archives of Physical Medicine and Rehabilitation* 60, no. 10 (1979): 435–46.

14 See Boston Women's Health Collective, *Our Bodies, Ourselves*, 2nd ed. (New York: Simon & Schuster, 1971).

15 Hessler, "Grant Proposal" (see note 12), 7.

16 See Bess Williamson, "The People's Sidewalks: Designing Berkeley's Wheelchair Route, 1970–1974," *Boom* vol. 2, no. 1 (2012): 49–52; see also Hale Zukas, "National Disability Activist: Architectural and Transit Accessibility, Personal Assistance Services," interview by Sharon Bonney (1997–98), in *Builders and Sustainers of the Independent Living Movement in Berkeley*, vol. 3, eds. Eric Dibner and Hale Zukas (Berkeley: Regional Oral History Office, The Bancroft Library, University of California 2000), 139, accessed February 14, 2023, oac.cdlib.org/view?docId=kt4c6003rh&brand=oac4&doc; see also Hessler, "Grant Proposal" (see note 12), 25.

17 See Union of Physically Impaired Against Segregation (UPIAS), "Policy Statement," 1972, accessed February 14, 2023, disability-studies.leeds.ac.uk/files/library/UPIAS-UPIAS.pdf; see also Tom Shakespeare and Nicholas Watson, "The Social Model of Disability: An Outdated Ideology?," *Research in Social Science and Disability* 2 (2002): 9–28.

18 Ronald Mace, "Universal Design: Barrier-Free Environments for Everyone," *Designer's West* 33, no. 1 (1985): 147.

19 See Ronald Mace, "Architectural Accessibility in North Carolina: The Quest for Barrier-Free Design," *N.C. Insight* vol. 6, nos. 2–3 (October 1983): 40–47.

20 Mace, "Universal Design" (see note 18), 152.

21 See Ronald Mace, quoted in *Designing the Future: Toward Universal Design*, symposium (Boston: World Trade Center, November 17, 1994), 61.

22 Ibid., 62–63.

23 Center for Universal Design, North Carolina State University, "The Principles of Universal Design," version 2.0, April 1, 1997, accessed February 14, 2023, design.ncsu.edu/wp-content/uploads/2022/11/principles-of-universal-design.pdf.

FIG.7

Visualization of an intervention showing a new ramp to access the front portico of the German Pavilion, as part of the contribution *Open for Maintenance – Wegen Umbau geöffnet* at the Venice Architecture Biennale

With a centrally positioned ramp welcoming everyone with the same level of respect, disabled people and maintenance workers with heavy equipment alike can use the same entrance as everyone else. At the same time, the ramp acts as a forum to renegotiate questions of access, citizenship, and spatial justice in architecture.

THE MATERIAL DIMENSION OF MAINTENANCE:

The annual cycle of Biennales in Venice is set out as a performative showcase and uses an incredible amount of resources. It is not exceptional for a single contribution to use more than 200 cubic meters of unrecyclable expanded polystyrene (EPS). The concept of the German contribution to the Architecture Biennale 2023 hinges on exclusively working with previously used materials. After the end of the Biennale Arte 2022, materials from over 40 pavilions and exhibitions—which would otherwise have been discarded—were gathered and exhibited in the German Pavilion as "spolia." However, this material repository is no immutable exhibition: Its contents will be made accessible for reuse in other projects across Venice over the entire duration of the Architecture Biennale. A fully operational workshop in the Pavilion will benefit this project and act as a platform to promote urban interventions in cooperation with local grassroots organizations. Fostering a building practice conscious of its material usage is in itself a form of maintenance work on the existing building stock.

REPAIRING

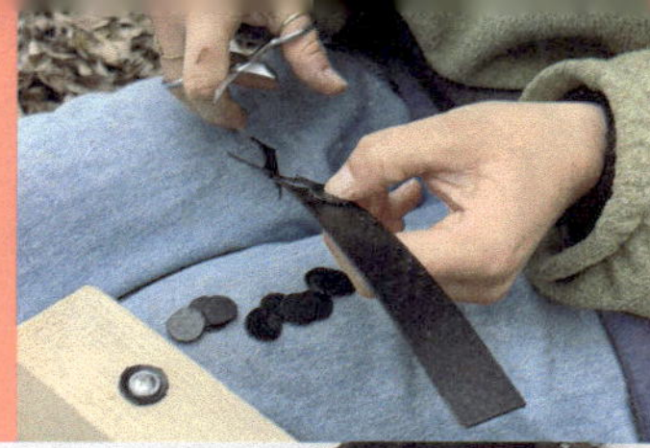

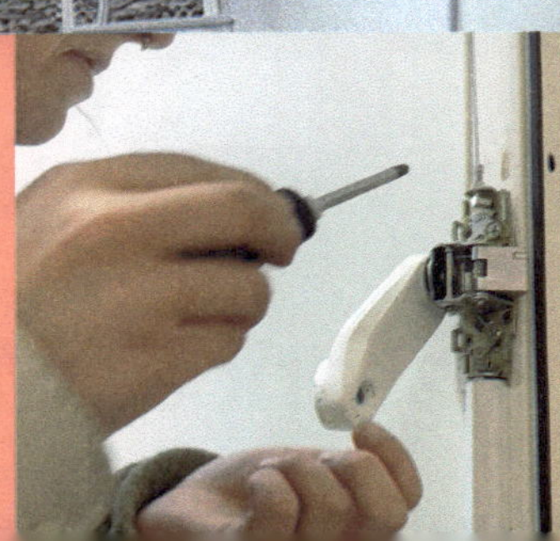

SPOLIA: IMAGE AND HISTORY

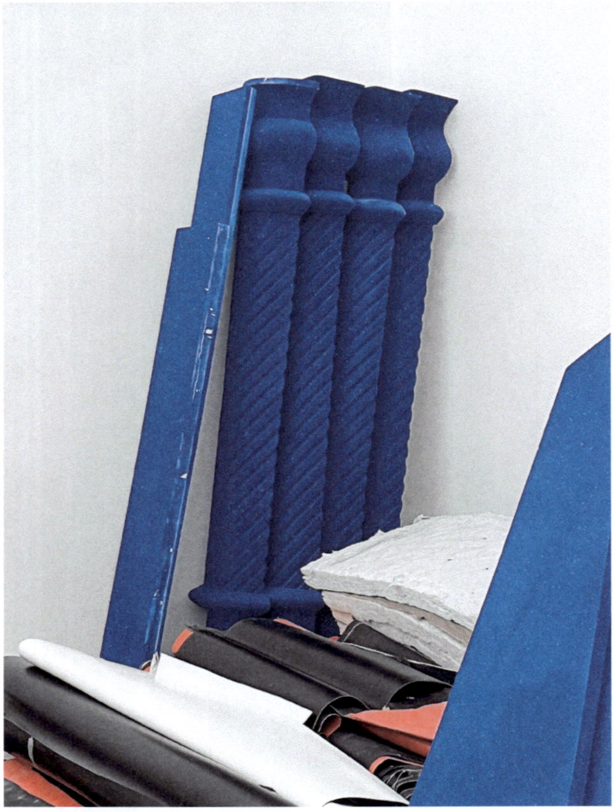

Text:
Johannes Odenthal

A Note on Historical Materialism

FIG. 1
Following the end of the Biennale Arte 2022, various materials and artifacts from the Arsenale and nearly 40 national pavilions have been collected and stored in the German Pavilion. They constitute the material basis for the concept *Open for Maintenance*. The integration of these "spolia" into new works multiplies their meaning.

The blue columns come from an installation in the Israeli Pavilion, the red and black sheeting from the Biennale Arte 2022's entrance tent, and the insulating panels from the exhibition spaces in the Complesso dell'Ospedaletto near the Fondamenta Nuove.

Spolia are elements of a structure—be it a building or work of art—that were not created for this purpose, meaning they were taken from a different context and put into a new one.

A building that makes use of spolia is, in this respect, heterogeneous. It displays a historical rupture. Spolia are enduring. Spolia are materials that persist into the present despite structural change. Metaphorically speaking, spolia are memories contained in material.

History is a material inherently present in spolia; indeed, it is doubly present: First, spolia represent material from a bygone time—a description that applies, of course, to all manufactured objects. Second, spolia embody a difference, because the use of spolia presupposes at least two separate periods of time.

Spolia form a structural unit with the newly created material. They are always part of a continuum, always *constructive*.

Spolia have therefore shed their original context and entered a new continuum. The material remains the same. It is the semantic structure, the frame of reference, that has changed.

Spolia can enter into a wide variety of connections. They always, however, represent a kind of natural inventory, a historical quarry. Still, spolia can *signify* and even *express*. The way spolia are used reveals a culture's conception of history. In a building that makes use of spolia, history vividly forms a continuum. The building is the present; the spolia are the past. The past cannot be fully reconstructed. The past is spolia. The past is always fragmentary, and, like spolia, it takes on a new function in the continually changing present. Herein lies the difference. Spolia function as a fragmented past in a building of the present.

The antonym of spolia is the monument. The monument strives for the illusion of reconstructing the past, of erasing difference. The preservation of historical monuments cultivates the past. The past is growing. One day the past catches up to us and we become our own history. The relationship between past and present has been inverted. The past's value rises while that of the present wanes.

Yet, if we set aside the illusion of historicist reconstruction, the monument is also spolia. Spolia are an image for the alterations to the semantic field despite the fixed identity of the historical material. What fluctuates is the cultural value of a structural element. And it is precisely this fluctuation that constitutes the dynamics of the historical sciences.

To summarize: Spolia represent history through material and in the continued use of material. Spolia represent history contained in the image. But spolia represent an *image of history* that corresponds to their material structure. Their meaning is an integral part of their materiality.

Spolia point to the possibility of constructively using historical material as a fragmentary piece in the present. Let us gather the debris of the past and use it consciously in a building of the present. Let us reintegrate the past into life, let us dare "the assault of the present on the rest of time." Let us allow difference to persist.

This text is an excerpt from Johannes Odenthal's dissertation published by Campus Verlag in 1986 under the title Imaginäre Architektur *(Imaginary Architecture), 11–13. Minor revisions from a later, unpublished version entitled* Spolie: Materialität und Differenz (Spolia: Materiality and Difference) *have been incorporated here. Reprinted with the author's permission.*

FIG. 2
Plywood panels previously used in a base structure for the exhibition *Re-enchanting the World* by artist Małgorzata Mirga-Tas at the Polish Pavilion in 2022

FIG. 3
Aluminum drywall studs of various sizes gathered from different exhibitions, namely from the Danish Pavilion and the Central Pavilion at the Giardini della Biennale, as well as from the Lithuanian Pavilion at Campo de le Gate

THE CONTEXTUAL RELOCATION OF MARIA EICHHORN'S RELOCATING A STRUCTURE

Text:
Vittoria Martini

FIG. 1
Maria Eichhorn, *Relocating a Structure*, German Pavilion at the 2022 Venice Art Biennale, concept study

When invited to represent Germany at the 59th Venice Art Biennale, Eichhorn began with the idea of physically removing the German Pavilion as a conceptual act, or an "exact imagination" (Theodor W. Adorno). This idea was later embedded as part of Eichhorn's multilayered contribution.

Architecture's function of symbolically representing the economic, political, and cultural power of a nation is exemplified at the Venice Biennale. Here, in the Giardini, the pavilions become devices for asserting national identity.[1] Countries owning a pavilion appoint a commissioner, "who will have to belong to the Governmental Authority or to the delegated Public Institution representing the Country."[2] The commissioner then selects a curator, who in turn invites an artist to represent the nation—normally, a citizen or at least a resident of that country, although this is not explicitly required.[3] In a sense, what is exhibited inside the pavilion is not all that important because the institutional machine is a medium that envelops and essentially neutralizes any critique. Fenced off and removed from public use, the Giardini become a fictitious realm, an exhibition space separate from the city.[4] Here, the container cannot be separated from its content, for any message launched from within such architecture will be ambiguous and ambivalent: the expression of institutions of power whose voices resonate within an architectural echo chamber. Moreover, a clause in the Biennale's Procedure for National Participations states that countries with pavilions in the Giardini "must carry out their artistic projects within the indoor space of their own pavilions" or in the area "immediately adjacent."[5] If the artist wants to emerge into "public outdoor spaces in Venice," they must apply to local authorities for a permit, showing that the project does not "interfere with the surrounding urban context."[6] The Biennale almost seems to fear that if the ideas produced within the fictitious space of the Giardini were to emerge into the real space of the city, they might elude neutralization and the institution would no longer be able to control or defend them. In this regard, Maria Eichhorn's work *Relocating a Structure*—the German contribution to the 2022 Art Biennale—stands as a rare exception.

The first time I met Maria Eichhorn was in those very Giardini. She told me she had been thinking about some photographs that showed leafy green trees in front of the old Bavarian Pavilion, which would later become the German Pavilion. These trees were cut down for the remodeling of the German Pavilion in 1938. Not long after that conversation, during a semi-legal site visit while the Giardini were closed to the public, I accidentally witnessed a real massacre of trees: this time on the grand avenue leading from the entrance to the Central Pavilion. The trunks, over fifty years old and still rooted, were left along the sides of the esplanade while new trees were being planted. The latter must have been at least fifteen years old and, as everyone knows, trees that size are quite expensive to replant. A chat with the workers confirmed that the felled trees had been perfectly healthy, and their replacement was a mere restyling operation—a facelift, as the artist Antoni Muntadas would say.[7] I was amazed by La Biennale's nonchalance in assuming the new trees would take root even in an environment that—as gardeners have known ever since the park was created in 1807 at Napoleon's behest—is hostile to plants, especially non-native ones.[8] Not to mention that some recent scientific research suggests trees might actually be in communication with one another, entangled in a collaborative network of roots and fungi known as mycorrhiza—a fusion of the Greek words *mýkēs* (fungus) and *rhiza* (root).[9] According to this theory, uprooting even one tree can constitute a shock for an entire symbiotic web. This episode sparked the idea in my mind that the German Pavilion, through Maria Eichhorn's work *Relocating a Structure*, had become part of such a symbiotic network.

Maria Eichhorn's work focuses on rigorously studying her operational framework. First and foremost, she builds personal relationships with the people who live or work there to study their "need, experience or desire."[10] In this case, they included Venetian curator and activist Marco Baravalle, who in 2020 launched the slogan "from exhibition to habitation,"[11] a call for reinterpreting the "Biennale as a commons,"[12] which means turning it from a place of national representation into a space of everyday production that serves its surrounding context. Further collaborators are Luisella Romeo and Giulio Bobbo of Iveser (Venice Institute for the Study of the History of the Resistance and Contemporary Society), with whom Eichhorn conceived an ongoing series of guided tours through places with historical ties to the struggles of the antifascist Resistance movement in Venice and the deportation and killing of its Jewish population; these will continue during the Architecture Biennale. Lastly, she forged ties with Chiara Buratti to learn more about her frontline work with Assemblea Sociale per la Casa, which advocates for the right to inhabit Venice—not just in terms of guaranteeing a right to affordable housing, but also in terms of preserving the network of social and material relationships buttressing Venice and threatened by mass tourism and tremendous pressure from the global industry of cultural events. With this deep grounding in the circumstances in which she operates, Eichhorn's work is quintessentially political—not for any ideological affiliation, but because it poses questions and reveals existing power mechanisms. Its material and immaterial elements lend themselves to a collective process of imagination with the power to spark effective long-term institutional change, as well as a shift in social and environmental relationships. The true complexity of her work can therefore only be fully grasped over the course of time, and if it finds welcoming terrain that will allow it to form a symbiotic web of social, material, and cultural interactions.

One year after the Art Biennale 2022, her sapling bears its first green leaves. As a matter of fact, the curators of the German Pavilion at this year's Architecture Biennale have unknowingly picked up in practical terms where Eichhorn left off conceptually by actively involving some of the same figures, as well as other local and international participants in their exhibition *Open for Maintenance*. But the curators have gone even further, working with them on tangible projects. In addition, they propose that the contextual relocation in Eichhorn's work—whose most visible manifestation she describes as the "exposure of the German Pavilion as two buildings"[13]—be integrated into their exhibition as found. To fully understand this decision, we have to take a step back and retrace Eichhorn's own path of reasoning.

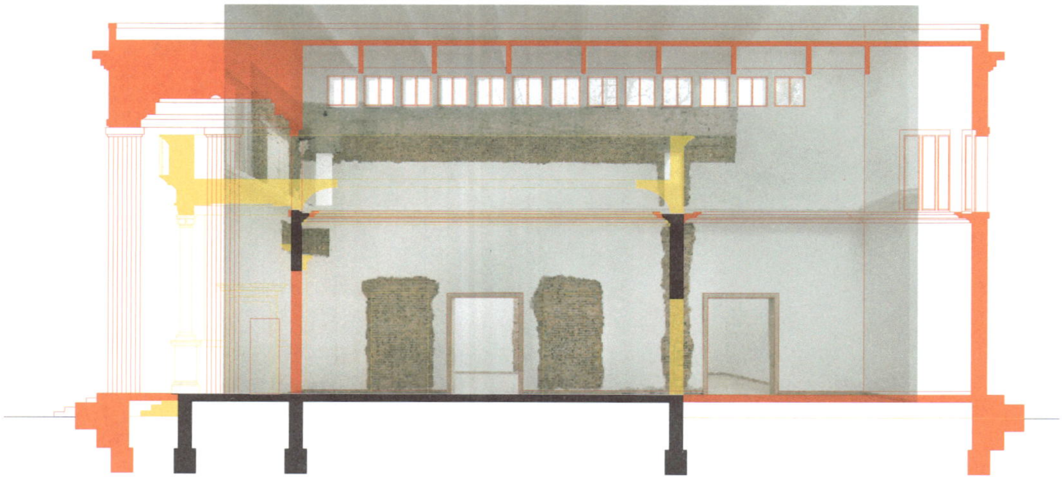

FIG. 2
Longitudinal section with an elevation of the left wall of the German Pavilion's main room. Remaining parts of the Bavarian Pavilion are shown in black, parts removed in 1938 in yellow, new components added in 1938 in red. The two exposed areas in the lower part of the elevation show doorways which were later walled up: the one on the right in 1928, the one on the left in 1938.

Although Germany's process of *Vergangenheitsbewältigung*—of confronting and coming to terms with its Nazi past—has been an important point of reference for postwar German society, the building, which still represents Germany at the world's oldest international art exhibition, is one designed to express the ideology of the Nazis. In 1998, the Italian Ministry of Cultural Heritage placed numerous national pavilions, including the German one, under the protection of the fine arts superintendency, essentially declaring them national monuments.[14] When Eichhorn was invited to represent her country at the 2022 Art Biennale and found herself working with this cumbersome piece of architecture, she began with the idea of "relocating" the Pavilion for the span of the exhibition.[15] The artist asked herself what such a radical act would mean, what consequences it would have, and what kind of further studies it would foster. To this end, she studied the history of structure relocation, communicating with the son of the famous civil engineer Eugeniu Iordăchescu and collaborating with specialists in the field, from whom she commissioned feasibility studies.[16] But as the curator Yilmaz Dziewior has pointed out, independent of its feasibility, "the temporary relocation of the German Pavilion is a work of art that exists without being realized in material terms."[17] The prospect of a temporary translocation is a conceptual element of her multipart project. The actual physical relocation is unnecessary, because once an image is in our heads, it has already changed how we see, think, and behave. Even if the radical act of removing the Pavilion's cumbersome presence from the landscape is not physically accomplished, the debate it creates about whether and how to exhibit within the framework of national pavilions is entirely real. With this work, Eichhorn does not escape the institutional mechanisms of the Biennale; yet, she confronts them. She takes responsibility for her participation by exposing the building's history and context. She examines them in depth and renders them fertile.

Eichhorn's extensive studies have revealed that the former Bavarian Pavilion still physically exists within the German Pavilion, that the current Pavilion is actually made up of two different structures: the Bavarian Pavilion from 1909, and its extension from 1938. This history can be retraced from the structural joints found in the walls and the old foundations discovered under the floor. The Bavarian Pavilion—which had already been renamed *Padiglione della Germania* in 1912—was only partly demolished before being rebuilt in monumental Nazi style by the architect Ernst Haiger. Haiger kept the walls and foundations of the preexisting building, but grafted onto them the arrogant, overblown architecture now familiar to us.

Based on this discovery, Eichhorn decided to make the process of architectural analysis visible to the public through an approach reminiscent of an archeological excavation. Visitors can see holes in the plaster revealing the locations where older bricks meet newer ones and a hole in the floor revealing the foundations of the previous Pavilion. Eichhorn added nothing, save for hand-painted wall texts in subtle white-on-white letters, such as "Join between sections of the building from 1909 and 1938," "Rear wall of the building from 1909, plastered as an interior wall in 1938," or "Foundations of the rear wall from 1909." A simple gesture, as silent as a pointed finger, makes the invisible visible and reveals the false nature of a historical document by unmasking it, stripping it bare. It deconsecrates the monument by

FIG. 3
Maria Eichhorn, *Relocating a Structure*, German Pavilion at the 2022 Venice Art Biennale

Maria Eichhorn's extensive studies have architecturally revealed that the current Pavilion is actually made up of two different buildings: the Bavarian Pavilion from 1909 and the German Pavilion from 1938.
Left, in the foreground, is the rear wall of the building from 1909, plastered as an interior wall in 1938. In the room behind it (left), two doorways from 1909 were walled up in 1912. Of these, the left doorway was reopened in 1928 only to be walled up again in 1938.

FIG. 4
Below the floor, near the German Pavilion's apse, the foundations of the rear wall from 1909 are visible (left), as well the remains of a preexisting building prior to 1909 (right). Under the wall plaster, the brick joint between the 1909 building and the 1938 building was exposed. The white-on-white wall text reads: "Fundament der Gebäuderückwand von 1909 / Foundations of the rear wall from 1909 / Fondamenta del muro posteriore del 1909."

FIGS. 5–6
As part of her contribution for the German Pavilion at the 59th Venice Art Biennale, Maria Eichhorn worked with Luisella Romeo and Giulio Bobbo of Iveser (Venice Institute for the Study of the History of the Resistance and Contemporary Society) to conceive a series of guided tours to monuments and places in Venice connected to the struggles of the antifascist Resistance and to the deportation of Venice's Jewish population. Among these are, for example, the commemorative plates at platform 8 of Santa Lucia station displaying the names of partisan railway workers who were deported to Dachau, and Augusto Murer's *Monument to the Partisan Woman* (1969), whose stone base was designed by Carlo Scarpa. The tours will continue on the occasion of the 18th Architecture Biennale in 2023.

consigning it to the sphere of memory, generating an awareness from which there is no return. Eichhorn's gesture shows the ambiguity of this architectural representation of national-socialist ideology, while also suggesting that it is unacceptable for a nation to continue representing itself through an architecture that does not reflect the needs, values, and wishes of a contemporary democratic society. She thus manages to make the container match its content. As Marc Augé would say, the architecture becomes "art because it assumes its own ambivalence and ambiguity,"[18] and through the artist's gaze, it becomes an integral support for the work. Eichhorn's undertaking is a counter-memorial, reflecting a new iconoclasm that is not aimed at erasing history, but at changing a point of view that can no longer be decided only by the institutions in power, whatever their claims—true or false—to universality. It is a call for a different kind of public commemoration, one that processes the past, deconsecrates it, and *relocates* it to what historian Enzo Traverso has called the "realm of memory in a non-oblivious democratic society."[19]

Fast forward to the 2023 Architecture Biennale. This year's curators have decided to perform another *relocation* of Eichhorn's work, shifting it in time rather than space. The exposure of the German Pavilion as two buildings will stay in place, but will be recontextualized, as part of the exhibition *Open for Maintenance*. Two different audiences will therefore experience the same artwork, in the same space, but at different times and in different settings that impart different meanings. Eichhorn's project will not be seen in all of the multilayered complexity encountered by visitors to the Art Biennale; but then again, this complexity may well have escaped most viewers because grasping the work as a whole required the sort of time and concentration that goes beyond the average biennial visit. Moreover, while some more intimate elements of the work may be harder to make out in this "relocation," many others will instead come across even more powerfully. To quote the curators, Eichhorn's work shows that "materials aren't neutral but cultural and political artifacts, whose connotations need to be reflected when dealing with the existing."[20]

The curatorial team emphasizes the importance of everyday reproductive care work for the maintenance of society, translating the notion of "maintenance" into the architectural sense of "repair," and in the political sense, into the practice of "squatting as a means of caring."[21] "Caring," because the building is used in real life. The very fact that the curators have chosen to "squat" the Pavilion as the central action in their project suggests that Eichhorn's work is indeed taking root. The building is taken care of by using it: It is "open for maintenance," as if in a transitional stage while awaiting a new function. Because now that it has been definitively unmasked and deconstructed by Eichhorn, it can no longer serve as a representation. Just as abandoned buildings often offer a space of autonomy where new artistic practices can be launched, metaphorically and physically "squatting" the German Pavilion provides a space for social organizations already active in the city of Venice, making them an operative part of the exhibition. Using the building in this way strengthens preexisting social and cultural networks and resources, while preserving and transforming them. The curators behind *Open for Maintenance* have taken Baravalle's phrase "from exhibition to habitation" quite literally. By "squatting" the Pavilion, they have made it a place for everyday life and work; a piece of the city's infrastructure. It becomes a building with a practical purpose, a place of dialogue, a workshop, a utility room, and a repository for valuable materials left over from the dismantlement of the previous edition of the Biennale. The latter are collected and stockpiled in the German Pavilion by the curators in collaboration with the local grassroots organization Rebiennale / R3B, which for years now has been repurposing leftover materials from the Biennale for the *autorecupero* [self-renovation] projects that Assemblea Sociale per la Casa carries out in abandoned public housing units. The curators behind *Open for Maintenance* have, in practical terms, matched the multilayered complexity of Maria Eichhorn's work by strengthening the same symbiotic network she created and helping it bear fruit. The Pavilion thus invites the reality of the city to cross over into the fictional realm of the Giardini and vice versa: Just as in Eichhorn's original work, the building moves out of the Giardini and into the reality of the city.

In Italian, the technical term used in agriculture for planting is *mettere una pianta a dimora*, literally "putting a plant in its home."[22] In other words, in its definitive location, in the ground where it will reside. As the recontextualization of Maria Eichhorn's work shows, the artist has already succeeded in fostering a fertile context for the *messa a dimora* of her ideas. The sapling has taken root, contributing to a mycorrhizal network that in part already existed and in part expands the German Pavilion's agency subterraneously, well beyond the confines of the Giardini.

1 Antoni Muntadas and Mark Wigley, "A Conversation between Antoni Muntadas and Mark Wigley, New York," in *Antoni Muntadas, On Translation: I Giardini*, ed. Bartomeu Marí (Barcelona: ACTAR, 2005), 277.
2 See La Biennale di Venezia, *58th International Art Exhibition: Procedure for National Participations*, accessed March 20, 2023, static.labiennale.org/files/arte/Documenti/58eia-nat-part-en.pdf, 2.
3 Ibid., 3.
4 See Vittoria Martini, "The Giardini: Status of the Property," in *Maria Eichhorn: Relocating a Structure*, ed. Yilmaz Dziewior (Cologne: Verlag der Buchhandlung Walther und Franz König, 2022), 294.
5 See *Procedure for National Participations* (see note 2), 4.
6 Ibid.
7 "The architectural changes on building facades and the remodeling of pavilions appear, over the years, as a cultural 'face-lift', echoing a political will to project a new image." See Antoni Muntadas, "Notes, November 2004," in *Antoni Muntadas* (see note 1), 143.
8 I am not claiming that the replanting operation used non-native trees, and since it involved the Venice Superintendence, a preliminary study was unquestionably carried out. Nonetheless, see Maria Marzi, *Giardini di Venezia* (Venice: Società Veneziana di Scienze Naturali, 1986), 14–5, 21–6; see also the comprehensive work by Tiziana Favaro and Francesco Trovò, *I Giardini napoleonici di Castello a Venezia: Evoluzione storica e indirizzi* (Venice: Cluva, 2011).
9 See Robert Macfarlane, "The Secrets of the Wood Wide Web," *The New Yorker*, August 7, 2011, accessed March 31, 2023, www.newyorker.com/tech/annals-of-technology/the-secrets-of-the-wood-wide-web.
10 See Carolyn Christov-Bakargiev, "Notes on Some Works by Maria Eichhorn," *Afterall* 1 (Autumn/Winter 2000), accessed March 31, 2023, www.afterall.org/article/notes.some.works.maria.eichhorn.
11 See Marco Baravalle, "On the Biennale's Ruins? Inhabiting the Void, Covering the Distance," *Institute of Radical Imagination*, May 2020, accessed April 5, 2023, instituteofradicalimagination.org/2020/05/02/on-the-biennales-ruins-inhabiting-the-void-covering-the-distance-by-marco-baravalle.
12 Marco Baravalle, "The Biennale as a Commons?" in *Maria Eichhorn* (see note 4), 317–21.
13 Maria Eichhorn, "Relocating a Structure: German Pavilion 2022, 59th International Art Exhibition, Venice Biennale," ibid., 118.
14 "È prescritta la conservazione dell'assetto architettonico e compositivo delle facciate … sono consentiti interventi di modifica del distributivo … purché siano compatibili con l'assetto architettonico esterno … è prescritta la conservazione delle caratteristiche formali delle coperture esistenti con possibilità di modifiche strutturali senza alterare la configurazione e la visione prospettica dell'edificio." See *Piano Particolareggiato "Giardini della Biennale," Fascicolo B: Progetto*, 19. ["The architectural and compositional layout of the facades must be preserved … alterations to the interior spatial organization are allowed … as long as they are compatible with the exterior architectural layout… the formal characteristics of the existing roofs must be preserved, although structural modifications may be made if they do not alter the configuration and perspective view of the building."]
15 Maria Eichhorn, "Relocating a Structure" (see note 13), 118.
16 Dana Andrei, "Interview with Adrian Iordăchescu," in *Maria Eichhorn* (see note 4), 219–23.
17 Yilmaz Dziewior, "Showing What's There: Maria Eichhorn and the German Pavilion in Venice, 2022," ibid., 8.
18 Marc Augé, "The Art of Separation," in *Antoni Muntadas* (see note 1), 27.
19 Enzo Traverso, "Tearing Down Statues Doesn't Erase History, It Makes Us See It More Clearly," *Jacobin*, June 24, 2020, accessed March 31, 2023, jacobin.com/2020/06/statues-removal-antiracism-columbus.
20 From an unpublished concept statement by the curatorial team of *Open for Maintenance*.
21 *Open for Maintenance*, curatorial statement, accessed March 31, 2023, archplus.net/en/open-for-maintenance/#article-37681.
22 *Dizionario Treccani*, s.v. "dimora."

FIGS. 7–10
Installation views during the construction process
at the German Pavilion, April 2023

REBIENNALE / R3B AND CONCULAR

FIG. 1
Cooperating with Rebiennale / R3B, the curators of *Open for Maintenance – Wegen Umbau geöffnet*, the German contribution to the 18th Venice Architecture Biennale, examined the exhibition materials left over from the Art Biennale 2022. In some cases, the collected residual materials have already received a second or third lease on life. For example, the pieces of wood painted in blue, gathered from the Chilean Pavilion, have already been used in multiple exhibitions.

Analogously to the model of the International Art Exhibition and its biennial rhythm dating back to 1895, an Architecture Biennale was held in Venice for the first time in 1980. The exhibition *La Presenza del Passato* (The Presence of the Past), curated by Paolo Portoghesi, laid the foundations for the 17 editions to date, which have alternated with the Art Biennale. The Biennale's format, as an international showcase of national competition and representation, consumes an immense amount of resources. Not only have many of the artifacts and tourists come a long way, a massive deployment of materials also occurs on site. Across the 200,000 square meters of exhibition spaces (Giardini and Arsenale combined), each year, thousands of tons of largely undamaged raw materials accumulate, which, owing to the high transportation costs, often simply get ferried to the nearest landfill after the end of the shows. Alongside the sheer waste of resources, the Biennale and its Collateral Events also impact the socioeconomic urban dynamics. Indeed, touristification as well as the real estate speculation that goes hand in hand with the commercialization of urban space displace both the established local population and everyday life.

Against the backdrop of a growing critical awareness of the "methods of production and … institutional structures and cultures" of the "Biennale machine,"[1] as the Venetian urban activist and theorist Marco Baravalle puts it, an initially informal alliance of Venetian citizens, students, architects, artists, and political activists formed: Rebiennale in 2008. By means of a performative occupation of the Italian Pavilion, which took as its programmatic title *L'Italia Cerca Casa / Housing Italy*, they criticized the Biennale, which, while taking the housing issue as its starting point, eschewed any institutional (self-)criticism of the Biennale as a driving force behind processes of gentrification and severe housing shortages faced by residents of Venice.

The activist group subsequently held a workshop together with the local architecture university, Università Iuav di Venezia, exploring practices of self-building as a tool to combat the housing shortage while reusing leftover materials from the Biennale. To this end, they cooperated with, among others, Assemblea Sociale per la Casa, a grassroots organization active in Venice since 1998, which squats publicly owned apartments that stand vacant and which, given their state, are considered unlettable. They then renovate the buildings and make them available to those in need of housing. The used materials the Biennale has disposed of find a new lease on life as part of the squatted apartments' interior fittings and furniture.

Over and above the formal context of the Biennale, Rebiennale has expanded its cooperation network to share methods, knowledge, and skills in the field of self-building. Their goal is to probe precisely what architecture is sometimes unable to reflect and what is hard to realize institutionally, namely "bottom-up" coexistence in the sense of a practice of commoning.

In 2017, Rebiennale rented a workshop and a small storage facility in Marghera, on Venice's mainland, where it provisionally stores many of the materials left over from the Biennale. It supports curatorial teams in the careful dismantling of their pavilions' installations and coordinates reclamation and reuse of the materials. In most cases, they are involved in the process at far too late a stage, making it difficult to offer all their experience, know-how, and methods. Materials are assembled in a way (glued, nailed) that renders reuse nearly impossible; product sheets that often contain relevant information on the materials' performance criteria, e.g., their fire resistance ratings, are thrown away or simply lost during the exhibition. This hinders getting renewed legal permission for their use. The deployment and (temporary) storage of some objects is frequently carried out in a way that is inappropriate for the material, for example, materials that are not water-resistant are used outdoors, thus sustaining long-term damage.

Within the activist group, a desire to be involved more systematically in the conception and implementation of the exhibitions' architectures was present from the very beginning.[2] In line with actively designing sustainable circular processes in the context of the Biennale, the group renamed itself "Rebiennale/R3B" (an acronym for Reuse, Recycle, Rebuild – Biennale) in 2017.

Reuse begins with the appropriate assembly and the accurate dismantling of the pavilions to reduce the scale and costs of waste disposal while also helping to safeguard the construction materials and use them longer. *Recycle* only comes into play when materials cannot be reused or given a second life cycle. To keep them from ending up as waste in landfills or incinerators, they are handed over to local companies in the business of building materials recycling. *Rebuild* aims to take care of the city's social infrastructure by allowing used materials to find a new lease on life in public, non-profit, or private spaces in the city. For example, Thomas Kilpper's *Pavilion for Revolutionary Free Speech* for the Danish Pavilion at the 54th Art Biennale in 2011 subsequently served to build a new gallery level in the occupied former salt warehouse and exhibition venue S.a.L.E. Docks; the materials from the German contribution *Bungalow Germania* at the 2014 Architecture Biennale were reused as furniture and fittings for the social cooperative Centro Sociale Rivolta, an autonomous cultural center in Marghera which, among other things, champions the cause of refugees. Moreover, Rebiennale/R3B also uses materials from past Biennales to make ordinary tables, cupboards, and kitchen cabinets, which are offered to private individuals for sale. With increasing demand, the activist group now faces a problem that confronts many circular enterprises: In cities and metropoles, where most of the construction activity takes place, space for storing and sorting large building components is both scarce and expensive—in the case of Venice, the problem is exacerbated by the confinement of the lagoon.

REBIENNALE/R3B
FOUNDED
2008 (as Rebiennale), since 2017 as Rebiennale/R3B
LOCATION
Venice

CONCULAR
FOUNDED
2012 (as restado), since 2020 Concular
LOCATION
Berlin

"OPEN FOR MAINTENANCE": THE GERMAN PAVILION AS A STORAGE SPACE FOR USED MATERIALS AND A SITE OF REPARATIVE WORK

It was out of this context that the curatorial idea for the Architecture Biennale 2023 arose: It focuses on using the German Pavilion year-round as a materials storage. To this end, the

space had to be taken over at an early date, as soon as the dismantling of the Art Biennale began in November 2022. In a large-scale "collection campaign," the curators, working together with Rebiennale / R3B, secured and stored several tons of material from more than 40 art exhibitions.

For a *circular* economy to be worthy of its name, it has to ensure that materials are reused after being saved. The curators brokered a cooperation between Rebiennale / R3B and Concular, an online platform for resource-efficient construction established in 2020. Concular digitizes architectural components and materials in existing buildings by means of life-cycle passports, published on its materials database. There, developers, architecture practices, and planning offices can match their needs with the supply in the database while the materials and components are still an integral part of the buildings. Once the buildings are demolished, the materials and resources become available for reuse. Concular also handles auditing for toxic materials, as well as transportation from the point of disassembly to the new construction site, which enables it to gather and integrate data on the reduction in CO_2-emissions and waste.

FIG. 2
Leftover materials sourced from the Arsenale exhibition grounds—such as the timber beams from the Chilean Pavilion pictured here—were gathered at the harbor and then shipped to the nearby Giardini by cargo boat. Due to the particular lagoonal topography of the city, most of the materials were transported by hand or with simple aids such as pallet trucks or handcarts.

The idea of documenting construction materials to potentially reuse them is, however, not new: Similar projects and companies have already existed for some time in other European countries where pre-demolition audits of construction materials is mandatory. Concular itself stems from the experience accumulated over almost ten years by its predecessor, restado. The latter launched in 2012 as an online marketplace where salvaged construction materials processed for reuse were offered in smaller volumes. By contrast, Concular's system, which is still being brought to full scale, offers a geographically wide-ranging and scalable infrastructure that can also be used in more complex dismantling projects and new constructions, and will in the future make it easier to calculate a building's life-cycle assessment.

There are, however, still many challenges, such as topical or geographical availability, various quality assurance audits and recertification processes, red tape, transportation, or processing. Responsibilities and costs, above all, often lack transparency. This makes the reuse of building components hard to plan, which in turn deters planners. Concular aims to counter this by acting as an ecosystem for

FIG.3
After the Art Biennale closed in November 2022, materials were sourced from more than 40 national participants and exhibitions and transported to the German Pavilion, where they were stored. In addition to construction materials such as beams, wooden boards, and metal girders, the team also salvaged fragments of artworks, almost as "spolia"—for instance, these bipartite columns originated from the exhibition *Queendom* for the Israeli Pavilion at the Art Biennale 2022.

FIG.4
Rebiennale / R3B, a local grassroots organization, provided tools and machines, including a forklift, to transport the materials. Pictured here is a heterogeneous collection—ranging from wood and metal profiles to insulating materials and rolled-up pieces of carpeting—representing a cross section of materials typically used at the Biennale.

FIG. 5
All materials were collected and stored in the German Pavilion in the weeks following the end of the 2022 Art Biennale. Taking over the German Pavilion ahead of schedule, along with Maria Eichhorn's existing work, allowed for several tons of construction materials to be saved from the landfill, making them available for further processing.

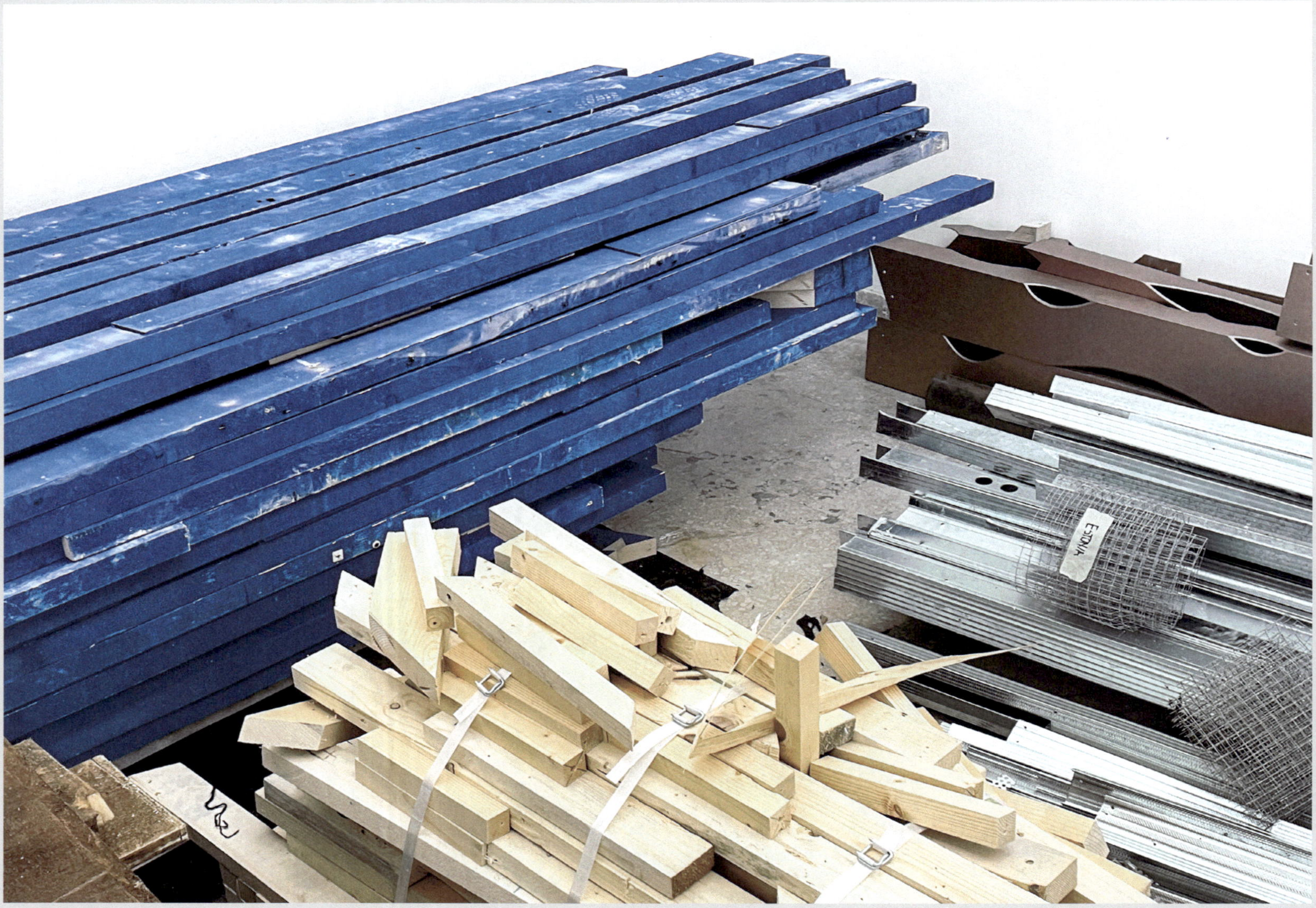

circular construction in which different players from the building of origin and the destination building are connected with one another, and factors such as availability, quality, costs, processes, and responsibilities are presented transparently. Using the online platform provided by Concular, the materials collected from the 2022 Art Biennale and presented in the German Pavilion at the 18th Architecture Biennale will be examined and cataloged before being made available to local projects for reuse. Each individual collected item will be carefully measured, cleaned, and documented. In the process, not all objects will be completely disassembled into individual components; some will be left as objects—or even as individual pieces of art—making it possible to understand their history. The digital twin of the objects on Concular's online platform therefore not only provides information on the technical measurements and physical properties, such as the state of the materials or viability for dismantling and reuse, but also on their origin and the cultural context (i.e., which pavilion or exhibition they once belonged to). With its extensive collection and cataloging of the Biennale's leftover materials, *Open for Maintenance* aims to culturally valorize what was formerly treated as waste. They now become "spolia" and make a practical contribution toward testing and fostering more systematic methods of reusing and "preserving the value" of the tons of materials that accumulate each year in connection with either the Art or the Architecture Biennales. *FG*

1 Marco Baravalle, "The Biennale as a Commons?" in *Maria Eichhorn: Relocating a Structure*, catalogue of the German Pavilion 2022, 59th International Art Exhibition – La Biennale di Venezia, ed. Yilmaz Dziewior (Cologne: Verlag der Buchhandlung Walther und Franz König, 2022), 318.

2 See Rebiennale, *Call for Second Life: a sustainable challenge!*, accessed March 31, 2023, rebiennale.org/en/call-for-second-life-a-sustainable-challenge

Bipartite EPS columns
ca. 240 × 50 cm
Israeli Pavilion
4 in stock

Jute fabric on wooden frame
ca. 180 × 60 cm
Chilean Pavilion
16 in stock

Maritime pine plywood 16 mm, colored
max. 160 × 90 cm, various shapes
Chilean Pavilion
26 in stock

Solid structural timber, red/black
various lengths and cross sections
Chilean Pavilion
ca. 150 in stock

Wooden frames, structural timber
ca. 160 × 110 cm, triangular
Albanian Pavilion
11 in stock

Sheet steel door with frame
ca. 210 × 85 cm
Italian Pavilion
1 in stock

Structural timber, untreated
ca. 120 × 18 × 2 cm
ECC – Giardini della Marinaressa
ca. 170 in stock

PVC banner film, red/black
ca. 120 cm, various lengths
Biennale entrance tent
18 in stock

Geotextile, black
ca. 140 × 500 cm
Swiss Pavilion
21 in stock

Spiral ducts, white
various lengths and cross sections
Austrian Pavilion
18 in stock

Multiplex sheets 18 mm, red
ca. 115 × 75 cm
Chilean Pavilion
12 in stock

2-wire copper cables, ca. 0.5 mm^2
various lengths
Italian Pavilion
52 in stock

FIG.6
All construction materials collected were measured, photographed, and inventoried. An online platform developed by Concular hosts a "digital twin" of the physical stock and a visual archive of the materials. The platform is also a tool for the materials' reuse. During the Biennale's six-month run, these materials will find new applications in repair and maintenance works in the City of Venice, within the framework of the workshop program *Maintenance 1:1*.

THINK MORE,

FIG. 1
In the early 1970s, the British architect Martin Pawley initiated the research project *Garbage Housing*, working together with students from various British and US universities. Pawley's 1975 eponymous book is both a pragmatic guide for building resource-efficiently with recycled materials and a manifesto against the neoliberal politics of privatizing and commodifying housing.

BUILD LESS

Architecture in the Anthropocene

Text:
Eva Stricker

For half a century, the Club of Rome has patiently warned us about the impending "limits to growth."[1] We can no longer ignore it: The world stands at a crossroads, and we are the ones who forced it there. Indeed, the conviction has taken root that, somewhere between the dawn of plantation slavery, the industrial revolution, and the end of the Second World War, we entered a new geological epoch, the so-called "anthropocene." Humans and their terrestrial activities have become a formative geological force, one that will significantly determine planetary living conditions over the coming millennia.[2] Usually, the geosciences monitor processes underlying the earth's history—whose effects are measured in millions of years—from a temporal and emotional distance. That it would be the geosciences of all disciplines discussing a new name for our present epoch at the outset of the 21st century—one that, from the perspective of geological time, has barely begun—is revolutionary. It lays bare the scope of what is happening: We humans are responsible for the factors that define the anthropocene, and only we can take responsibility for and counteract them. The task at hand is nothing less than negotiating a restructuring of the relationship between humanity and nature, as a prerequisite for preserving future living conditions on Earth. In this sense, the anthropocene is much more than a geological term; it should be understood above all as a social and political call to action, one that puts special responsibility on the emissions-heavy, resource- and waste-intensive construction sector.

WE THE CHILDREN OF THE GREAT ACCELERATION

Architecture has always been the medium that situates us within our environment. It is as elemental for the protection and continuity of our existence as food and clothing—two other basic needs, it should be noted, whose industrial satisfaction accounts for a significant share of global greenhouse gas emissions. That we invest the majority of our primary energy consumption (around three-quarters) in satisfying these basic needs is understandable. The total consumption of energy and materials, however, is increasingly erasing the boundary between what we protect ourselves *with* and what we protect ourselves *from*. Since the mid-20th century, human activity on Earth has grown at an unprecedented pace, as has the construction industry. The result is that the economic activity of Western industrial nations, geared toward growth and prosperity, have profoundly impacted the Earth's systems.

West Germany's meteoric economic growth in the postwar years hailed as *Wirtschaftswunder*, or "economic miracle," did not fail to impact architectural production. In 1959, architect Konrad Wachsmann euphorically proclaimed a "turning point of building," referring to the breakthrough of rationalized construction.[3] As predicted much earlier by classical modernism's pioneers, this turning point heralded the boom years of late modernism. The "Great Acceleration" of prefabricated concrete construction defines European suburbs into the present—with varying degrees of triumph and debacle. With a little hindsight, however, this development now looks like an absurd acceleration in the history of human energy and resource consumption, a spike neither the oil crisis nor ecological catastrophe have managed to halt. Nearly everyone holding a position of responsibility today—as educator, planner, builder, or commissioner of architecture—is a child of this Great Acceleration, and it is only right that we critically interrogate our values and valuation criteria accordingly.

FROM AN INDUSTRIAL TO AN ECOLOGICAL TURNING POINT OF BUILDING

It has long been clear that the role of fossil fuels in operating buildings needs to be minimized, if not eliminated entirely. It has also become clear, albeit more recently, that greenhouse gas emissions effected by the construction of buildings need to be curbed. This puts a focus on materials: The construction materials we choose, their provenance, how and to what degree they are processed, how long they survive in a building, and how we reuse and recycle them is fundamental for both resource consumption and our building stock's climate footprint. Across centuries of architectural history, a conscious, far-sighted, economical use of materials was taken for granted—until the increasing rationalization of construction under modernism reduced the costs of processed building materials to a point where their use became untethered from their actual life cycles. The development of industrially processed materials, composites, and coatings contributed to the uncoupling of architectural expression from the aesthetic qualities of raw materials and their handcrafted processing and joining. In this respect, postwar modernism is a perceptible break with a long tradition of building that sought to preserve resources and was conscious of material cycles. All the same, the postwar era saw plenty of counterproposals to the construction industry's boom-era fixation on linear consumption and routinized attrition. In the mid-1960s, Bernard Rudofsky's famous exhibition at New York's Museum of Modern Art, *Architecture without Architects*, celebrated the genuine beauty of vernacular architecture. In 1972, using the term "adhocism," Charles Jencks and Nathan Silver advocated for a playful aesthetic that emerged from the improvisational richness of bricolage. The following year, influenced no doubt by the oil crisis, Martin Pawley's *Garbage Housing* discussed quite pragmatically how the residues of consumer society could be employed as a resource for affordable housing construction. And even beyond the burgeoning protest and environmental movements, the work of many of the period's architects eludes the clear dialectic between abstract/serial slash-and-burn modernism and the joyful discovery and reappropriation of local peculiarities, building traditions, and materials. Alison and Peter Smithson, for example, placed confrontation with that which has developed over time, a strategy they dubbed "as found," at the center of their architectural practice from the very beginning: "Setting ourselves the task of rethinking architecture in the early 1950s, we meant by the 'as found' not only adjacent buildings but all those marks that constitute remembrancers in a place and that are to be read through finding out how the existing built fabric of the place had come to be as it was. … Thus the 'as found' was a new seeing of the ordinary, an openness as to how prosaic 'things' could re-energise our inventive activity."[4]

As we have seen, the course of architectural creation has been anything but linear since the declaration of a "turning point of building" over 60 years ago. Various detours and U-turns have anticipated the issues facing us today in a transformed political and ecological environment. The climate and resource crises of our times demand a collective course correction once again, the widely demanded *Bauwende*, or (resource-friendly) turning point of building, for which not only environmental groups and critical professional associations but also key political actors appeal. And there is no shortage of forward thinkers and visionaries to invoke. In honor of its 100th anniversary, modernism's think tank par excellence may even serve as a namesake once again: Bauhaus Earth is the name of a nonprofit organization, initiated by prominent climate researcher Hans Joachim Schellnhuber, whose director Philipp Misselwitz believes construction can undergo a metamorphosis "from climate killer to climate healer";[5] meanwhile, the New European Bauhaus is an EU initiative with the express goal of linking the European Green Deal policy package to the design of our built environment. Professional associations are equally unsparing with visionary manifestoes, among which the 2019 white paper issued by the Association of German Architects (Bund Deutscher Architektinnen und Architekten, BDA), entitled *Das Haus der Erde* (Planet Home).

BACK TO NATURE?

In the face of ongoing ecological crises, what could be more obvious than a return to simple building methods, to natural and regenerative materials such as stone and clay, or wood, hemp, straw, and wool, which can be garnered from the biotic cycle and returned to it? In recent years, wonderful buildings have sprung up in Switzerland and across Europe that borrow their material unobtrusively from the earth and understand themselves as part of the cultural landscape from which they derive. These include Atelier Schmidt's load-bearing straw bale buildings (Haus B–D) in Disentis, Gilles Perraudin's mortar-free natural stone buildings, the rammed-earth home (Haus Rauch) built by Roger Boltshauser for and alongside Martin Rauch in Schlins, and the adhesive-free wooden building with a rammed-earth core (Haus K) built by Seiler Linhart Architekten and Küng Holzbau in Alpnach. Each of these makes a respectful and subtle contribution to the preservation of local materials and artisan traditions, radiating far beyond their relatively modest scale. However, they are not able to answer the pressing question facing architecture and urban planning in the 21st century: How do we achieve enough affordable, dignified, and well-tempered homes for an ever-growing population without exceeding the maximum load our feverish planet can bear?

Great hopes are pinned on wood in particular—a natural, regenerative, high-performing construction material that has proven to be reliable in various building cultures over centuries. In Switzerland, since the revision of fire-safety regulations in 2003 and 2015, wood has been allowed to be used again for multistory residential and office buildings, which has given an enormous boost to research and development into using structural timber as a replacement for reinforced concrete, which hitherto has faced little competition. Nevertheless, timber construction is straining to bring the construction industry appreciably closer to its target of net-zero emissions. One example: Upon completion in 2010, the residential and commercial building on Zurich's Badenerstrasse by pool Architekten, a six-story timber structure designed to fit the criteria of Switzerland's "2000-watt society" [an environmental per-capita target for primary energy usage by Global North countries introduced by scientists at ETH Zurich in 1998; editor's note], undoubtedly set standards in energy- and climate-conscious construction. However, subsequent comparisons of its thermal transmittance (U-value) to similar buildings made with conventional solid construction materials like reinforced concrete and masonry showed that the timber construction method chosen by the architects only reduced gray greenhouse gas emissions by around 12 percent.[6] This, of course, is better than nothing, but it is far—*very* far—from net zero. The demonstrable advantages of wood as a natural construction material seem to get lost somewhere in the production line and supply chain.[7] If this is the case even for solid timber construction, we better not look at wood that needs to be glued to form glued-laminated timber (glulam) or laminated veneer lumber (LVL) to fulfill structural requirements. Hardwood timber in particular, the most prevalent European variety given our expectations for the continent's future climate, needs to be subjected to intensive processing to be used in timber construction. Current figures for these sorts of materials according to ecological assessment data are sobering, and raise doubts about the value of wood as a universal "climate healer," not to mention the raw material's wavering availability in recent times.[8] If it becomes possible to incorporate wood into buildings in a permanent way, it could store biogenic carbon dioxide and function as a temporary carbon sink—a promising ecological potential that would unfold over a very long-term perspective.[9] But what use is this for the reduction of greenhouse gas emissions in the shorter term, something so desperately needed in the face of impending climate tipping points?[10] Practice shows: If we want to "build our way out of the climate crisis with wood,"[11] we need more than a good narrative, as the urgency of the situation demands more than simply achieving social acceptance of an undoubtedly seductive idea. Ultimately, a dispassionate comparison of vision and reality is important if we ever hope to bring the two into actual alignment.

FIG. 2
This seven-story building located in Zurich's Badenerstrasse was planned by pool Architekten with prefabricated wood elements, the only exception being the ground floor built with site-mixed concrete. Finished in 2010, it was the first building in Switzerland to comply with the guidelines of the 2000-watt society.

ARCHITECTURE AS A RAW MATERIAL REPOSITORY?

Perhaps this would be the most logical way of processing the implications of the anthropocene architecturally: by not only acknowledging our role as a geological force but by actively appropriating that role, building not just our own carbon sinks, but also creating the construction material we need from anthropogenic sources. A full 41 percent of today's housing stock in Germany was built between 1949 and 1978, and has therefore already exceeded its life cycle according to the logic of the economic investment cycle—or will do so shortly.[12] Why not address the problems arising from the Great Acceleration by using the (real) estate it has bequeathed us as a substrate? Might this not give rise to a new, contemporary form of vernacular construction that no longer feeds on a site's natural circumstances but instead on its anthropogenic sediments? It is a fascinating thought experiment, but sometimes

FIG. 3
This three-story residential house in the Swiss village of Alpnach was realized in 2019 by Seiler Linhart Architekten together with (and for) the family-owned Küng Holzbau carpentry firm using their own solid-timber construction system. Built around a rammed-earth core, the timber house, which does not require any insulation materials, combines elements of traditional and contemporary timber architecture. The structure is built on a concrete foundation reinforced with bamboo.

FIG. 4
The Emmenbrücke Recycling Center by Huber Waser Mühlebach was designed with its disassembly in mind. In 2040, with the completion of an adjacent highway tunnel, the plot is expected to make way for other uses. So as to be easily reassembled at another location afterwards, the facility is made of dismountable steel supports, solid timber elements, and reusable materials.

FIG. 5
Over a period of two and a half years, the architectural office baubüro in situ collected various building components from more than 20 demolition sites. Many of the building components of the K.118 building in Winterthur are reused, resulting in a 60 percent decrease of emissions during the construction phase when compared to a conventional new building.

also a tautological argument: Urban mining presupposes obsolescence, after all. It is both a means of damage control and a systematic component of a construction industry inherently structured around growth and innovation. Precisely those inner-city developments that are desirable for various reasons—less urban sprawl, less individual motorized traffic, more synergetic use of infrastructure—trigger the same pattern of redevelopment processes within cities. Without doubt, recovering building components and secondary raw materials will always be better than producing new waste. But before we start giddily turning existing built environments into quarries, the obligatory question of preservation arises even in the case of cumbersome building stock. This is not least because the built fabric is often only reusable to a limited extent due to the variable construction quality of the postwar years and the construction practices typical of the era (composite materials, glued joints, prodigal use of contaminants). But we can learn our lessons from this. When we design new buildings today, as natural resources are dwindling, we need structural and administrative frameworks that project far into the future; buildings will be "designed for disassembly" from the very start, so that they can be dismantled and sorted with as little waste as possible. Each component, each material will be outfitted with a digital identity, stored in the BIM model. To simplify anthropogenic mining for future descendants, digital ecosystems will be necessary to bundle all this knowledge. These are exciting approaches, which only emerge when architecture is no longer conceived as a momentary snapshot taken immediately after its completion and handover, but rather as a process that encompasses its entire life cycle. But where do we obtain the necessary foresight? Will our descendants in 60 to 100 years really remember what and how to disassemble, what and how to reuse and reprocess? Will they still be able to actually use the components we have designed for them, to read the digital instructions? Who will ensure the maintenance of this data over the span of generations? Architectural history is full of examples of architectures designed for the future that never lived up to their carefully and enthusiastically developed potential. Take, for example, Jean Prouvé's elegant Maison Tropicale, whose clever joints ultimately proved to be less reversible than originally planned after heavy-duty exposure to the unfamiliar climates of French colonies in Western Africa; or various European construction systems of late modernism, whose vision of infinite flexibility and expandability, at least in German-speaking countries, became obsolete around 1980 with the introduction of the first thermal insulation regulations. Penetration of the buildings' envelopes by their load-bearing structure, immanent to those systems, and which made future expandability possible in the first place, were suddenly unmasked as thermal bridges. Who can know today which standards and expectations will be topical in a few decades? Hermann Czech's reply to a 1967 competition invitation springs to mind: Solicited to design "a piece of furniture for the year 2000," he politely declined, requesting to be contacted about the matter in 30 years.[13]

CIRCULATION AND PERMANENCE

From time to time, the discomfort surrounding the assumptions—sensible and important as they may be—of building in a circular and reversible manner become almost palpable. Indeed, there is a certain tragedy in suddenly measuring the quality of architecture according to its potential to be disposed of with as little trace as possible. We have only recently begun to realize the inordinate extent to which our construction industry has been herded forward by the diktat of linear economic growth. Do we really want to subordinate everything once again to the rules of an economic system and its commercial models, only this time with a commitment to circularity? Might this not encourage a certain arbitrariness and impermanence in building, in which randomly found objects and standardized products are cobbled together on a short-term basis into unspecific constructions, only to be reused in another context at the next opportunity? If building components are no longer developed for specific sites and buildings, but only leased or rented out for temporary, site-independent use, then suddenly the constellation of ideas behind circular building veers disconcertingly close to the Bauhaus ideology of standardized construction systems from the early decades of the Great Acceleration. The reservations against tendencies of this sort are quite understandable, since they are associated with qualities that many people see as essential for architecture: *specificity* and *durability*. At the same time, however, such reservations fail to recognize that the point of circular construction is not primarily to boost economic circulation through constant and clever moves of material components; rather, the goal is to maintain material cycles over the long term by avoiding waste and preserving material and immaterial value, ideally through maintenance and repair—with their deconstruction, reuse, and reprocessing as a last resort. When planning tomorrow's built environment today, it helps a great deal if we agree on a few rules and basic principles that leave room for individual developments and designs. Simple, self-explanatory, "revealing" connections and constructions capable of being comprehended intuitively offer the best prospects for remaining repairable and deconstructible in the future, and materials that can be separated and sorted by type will retain their value.

Demanding a readiness for future disassembly and reuse can also enrich architectural design processes, as demonstrated by the building program developed by Huber Waser Mühlebach for the Emmenbrücke Recycling Center of the municipal association REAL (Recycling, Waste Management, and Sewerage services of Lucerne), completed in 2020. The building's presumably modest lifespan in a rapidly developing environment is effectively incorporated into the design through structurally staged separation of systems and reversible joints between materials and components.

RESEARCH MORE, BUILD LESS

These days, any potentials for circular use we imagine when planning new buildings are nothing more than theoretical possibilities, until these buildings are actually dismantled in a hopefully distant and post-fossil future. No one knows whether and how these potentials will ever be exploited and, in any case, they do nothing to reduce the environmental impact of new construction. The same applies to the goal of building as permanently as possible; when it comes to this, unfortunately, there are also no guarantees. Charles Berg and Edward Clark presumably never dreamt that their proud Gillender Building, completed in 1897 in New York City, would be dismantled for a replacement skyscraper only 13 years later. The architects of postmodern corporate palaces currently being phased out in the overheated Zurich real estate market, complete with their flawless natural stone facades, might feel the same way today.

The only way to guarantee our built fabric a long service life is to use already existing buildings and components longer. In recent decades, our Western industrial society has gone overboard when it comes to overall resource and energy consumption. Might we not then be obliged to help our building stock, created at the expense of others, to reach a better ecological balance? At least retrospectively, this would be possible by offsetting the ecological costs already incurred through ensuring the longest possible service life, achieved via preservation or at least by reusing building components. That the latter approach can make a serious contribution to reducing greenhouse gas emissions in "new" buildings was demonstrated by the K.118 Case Study in Winterthur, where the architectural firm baubüro in situ realized a three-story extension of a historical industrial production hall using, as much as possible, reused building parts—ranging from steel structural components, to elements

FIG.6
The former telephone exchange in Bad Hindelang, a town in southern Germany, stood vacant for 40 years before the Munich-based architecture office Kofink Schels converted the building from 1923 into a residential house in 2017. The architects, who had already sourced used components from online resale platforms for previous projects, opted for an ecological conversion by using minimal resources and doing as much work as possible themselves.

of the building's facade, to interior fittings.[14] Taking into account dismantling, transport, processing, and reinstallation, the savings in greenhouse gas emissions per component during the construction phase ranged from 85 to 99 percent when compared to new ones.

Every year by which we delay the necessary turnaround in greenhouse gas emissions makes it more difficult to achieve the reduction target of 1.5 degrees Celsius acknowledged in the Paris Agreement. Crossing the first irreversible climatological tipping points is already all but inevitable. Halting new construction and focusing instead on repurposing and reusing is currently the only viable strategy available to initiate a course correction in the building sector. Beyond lofty visions of an architecture for a post-fossil, post-linear, post-growth future, we need, quite desperately, an architecture of the present, one that concentrates on creating high-quality habitats for as many people as possible with the built fabric already at hand.

More space to live. Less building. How can these be reconciled? On the one hand, we can preserve existing structures and spaces, using them as cleverly and economically as possible. Vacancies produced by structural change—churches, movie theaters, department stores, and so on—need to be invested with new meaning. Spaces designed for different living and working conditions need to be adapted to contemporary needs. Spaces that are only used at specific times—offices, schools, opera houses—could open up anticyclically and be used for new purposes. Where the available space does not offer sufficient options, additional density can be achieved through annexes, renovations, or added floors. This would prevent further soil sealing and allow costly investments such as infrastructure, circulation areas, and foundations to be used synergistically. Further, we will not be able to avoid interrogating entrenched approaches and standards: What quality of life do they generate, at what ecological and social cost? Above how many square meters of living space per person does abundance fail to make our lives happier and more livable, instead making it more wasteful and lonely?

In parallel, the task is to continue developing architecture as a discipline over the long term, in a collaboration between research and practice—and through critical feedback via standards, norms, and laws. From materials research into structural and typological questions to studies of new processes of building and planning, there is a broad field open to experimentation.

AND THE PROFESSION?

Suddenly, much that was taken for granted—even only a few years ago—is being put to the test. What does it actually mean to be or to become an architect today? In this era of uncertainty and disorientation, there is an opportunity, on the one hand, to move toward a more economical, sustainable building culture. On the other hand, the oppressive ubiquity of the climate crisis should not lead us to the misapprehension that architectural expertise can simply be replaced by life-cycle analysis and an Urban Mining Index. We cannot simply calculate the difference between good and bad architecture—although the impression is not uncommon in contemporary discourse. Recyclability and a favorable ecological balance alone can make a building, at best, less damaging to the environment. When it comes to designing valuable, livable spaces, architects are still necessary. The crisis, however, does open up space for new structural diversity; only a few years ago, experimental constructions with straw bales or reused components would not have generated the enthusiastic and extensive discussion within professional circles they foster today.

In recent years, it has become common to hear the complaint that the loss of importance and the increasing fragmentation of the architectural field into various individual disciplines has degraded us from proud generalists to mere design specialists. At the same time, the urgent need to deal with climate issues, material cycles, and fundamental physical and biological phenomena when designing and planning a structure brings us back, in a surprising way, to the supposedly lost ideals of the generalist-humanist practitioner. Nevertheless, we cannot dismiss the fact that a change in orientation toward the existing building stock represents a serious paradigm shift for our professional self-image. Suddenly, the primary focus in designing a building is not the singular creation of an individual author. To the contrary: If conversion becomes the rule, we will have to grow accustomed to devoting ourselves with undivided attention to the work of others, even when we find said work to be not particularly accomplished. Looking closely and understanding, comprehending structures and strengthening them in minimally invasive ways, making sense of spaces, reinterpreting and complementing them … these approaches demand a great deal of empathy and thinking, without due recognition. As architecture critic Tibor Joanelly wrote in the Swiss journal *werk, bauen + wohnen*: "How, for heaven's sake, are architects going to make money with acupuncture?"[15]

This may reflect a particularly Swiss view of things, but it speaks to important truths. First: Architects' fees are still generally tied to construction costs, i.e., to the consumption of material and energy. The more you consume, the more you earn—a perverse anachronism! Second: If we are to take the climate crisis seriously and to commit ourselves to caring for the existing built environment, we must prepare for the fact that our practice's status and systemic importance may sometimes diverge, as they do for countless others who provide indispensable care work.

1 See Dennis Meadows et al., *The Limits to Growth: A Report for the Club of Rome's Project on the Predicament of Mankind* (New York: Universe Books, 1972).
2 See Paul J. Crutzen, "Geology of Mankind," *Nature* 415, no. 23 (2002), doi.org/10.1038/415023a.
3 See Konrad Wachsmann, *The Turning Point of Building: Structure and Design*, trans. Thomas E. Burton (New York: Reinhold Publishing Co., 1961).
4 Alison Smithson and Peter Smithson, "The 'As Found' and the 'Found,'" in *The Independent Group: Postwar Britain and the Aesthetics of Plenty*, ed. David Robbins (Cambridge: MIT Press, 1991), 20.
5 Alexander Stumm, "Roadmap für das Bauhaus Erde," *Bauwelt* 13 (2022): 64–67.
6 See Matthias Klingler and Ueli Kasser, "Graue Energie: Holz- versus Massivbau," in *Espazium*, January 15, 2012, accessed March 6, 2023, www.espazium.ch/de/aktuelles/graue-energie-holz-versus-massivbau.
7 For more on this topic, see Daniel Savi and Matthias Klingler, *Kohlenstoffspeicherung im Holzbau: Potenzial des Gebäudeparks in der Schweiz* (Zurich: Stadt Zürich, Amt für Hochbauten—Fachstelle nachhaltiges Bauen, 2022).
8 See for example *Ökobilanzdaten im Baubereich* (Schweizerische Koordinationskonferenz der Bau- und Liegenschaftsorgane der öffentlichen Bauherren, 2022), accessed March 6, 2023, www.kbob.admin.ch/kbob/de/home/themen-leistungen/nachhaltiges-bauen/oekobilanzdaten_baubereich.html; see also eid., *Ökobaudat: Informationsportal Nachhaltiges Bauen* (2021), accessed March 6, 2023, www.oekobaudat.de/no_cache/datenbank/suche.html.
9 See Savi and Klingler, *Holzbau* (see note 7).
10 See Timothy M. Lenton et al., "Tipping Elements in the Earth's Climate System," *PNAS* 105, no. 6 (February 2008): 1786–93.
11 Hans Joachim Schellnhuber, "Können wir uns mit Holz aus der Klimakrise herausbauen?" (lecture, 42. Fachtagung Holzbau Baden-Württemberg, Stuttgart, October 1, 2020).
12 See *Wohnungen nach Baujahr und Bundesländern 2018* (Statistisches Bundesamt), accessed March 6, 2023, www.destatis.de/DE/Themen/Gesellschaft-Umwelt/Wohnen/Tabellen/wohneinheiten-nach-baujahr.html.
13 See Hermann Czech, "Eine Wettbewerbseinsendung," in *Zur Abwechslung: Ausgewählte Schriften zur Architektur* (Vienna: Löcker Verlag, 1996), 62.
14 See *Bauteile wiederverwenden: Ein Kompendium zum zirkulären Bauen,* ed. ZHAW Institut Konstruktives Entwerfen (Zurich: Park Books, 2021), 256–63.
15 Tibor Joanelly, "Das wertvolle Obsolete," *werk, bauen + wohnen*, November 23, 2021, accessed March 6, 2023, www.wbw.ch/de/online/werk-notiz/das-wertvolle-obsolete.html.

CRCLR HOUSE

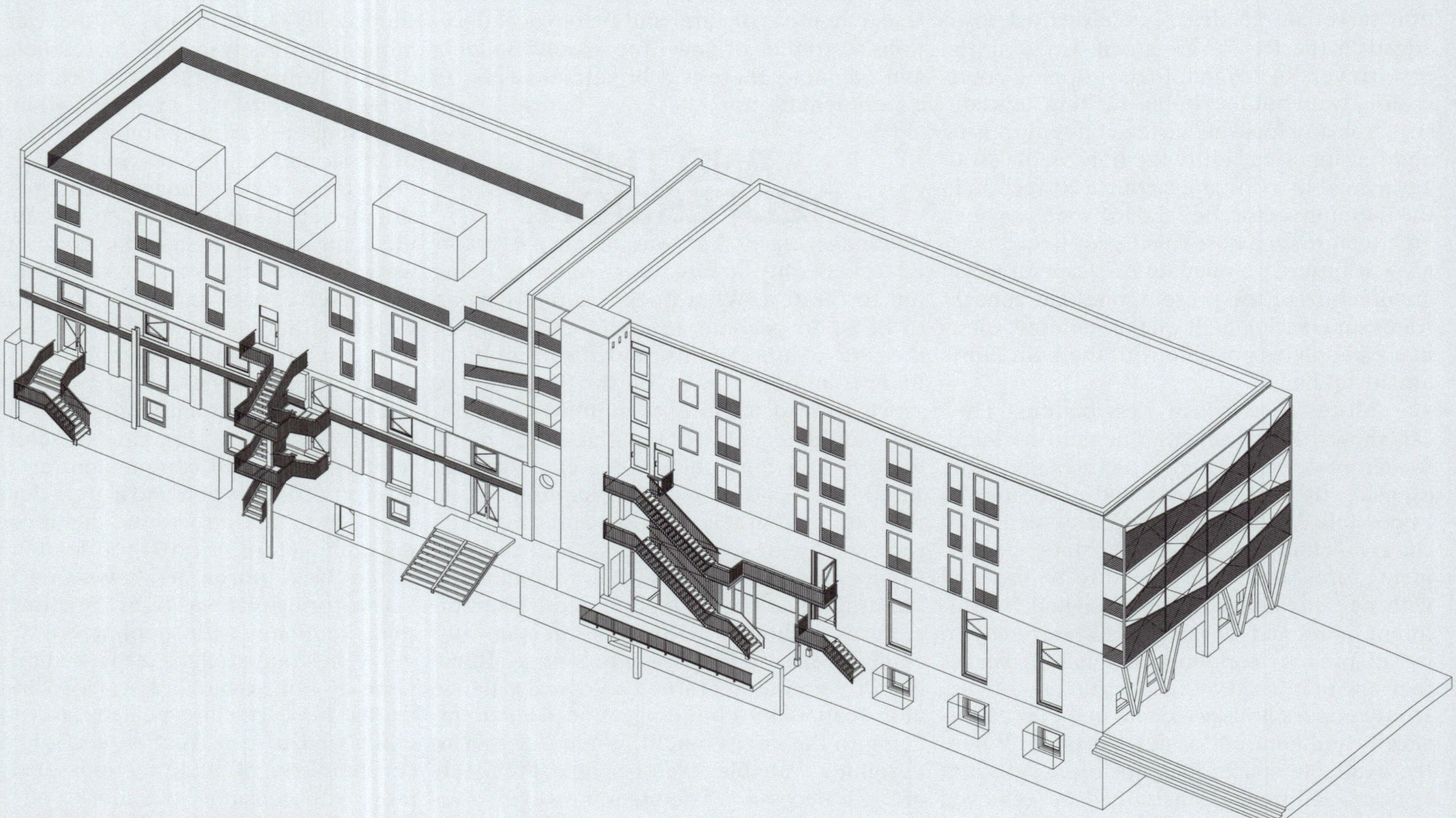

USES
Housing, work, laboratory and workshop spaces, repair café, cafeteria, event venue, greenhouse with a communal roof terrace, common rooms, playground
SIZE
6,100 m²
USERS
CRCLR Living eG and Impact Hub Berlin
DEVELOPER
TRNSFRM eG
LEASEHOLD LANDLORD
Terra Libra Immobilien GmbH, a subsidiary of the Edith Maryon Foundation
DESIGN
Die Zusammenarbeiter – Gesellschaft von Architekten mbH (Berlin) with baubüro in situ AG (Basel)
INTERIOR ARCHITECTURE
LXSY Architekten
MATERIAL PASSPORTS AND INVENTORY
Concular
STRUCTURAL ENGINEERING
ZRS Ingenieure GmbH
STRAW-BALE WALLS AND INTERIOR CONSTRUCTION
Kollektive Baustelle / Heap59 GmbH
BEGINNING OF CONSTRUCTION
2019 (planning started in 2015)
LOCATION
Berlin

FIG. 1
Axonometric drawing of the CRCLR House as seen from the northwest, with the commercial House East on the left and the residential House West on the right

The construction industry is the economy's most resource-depleting sector, accounting for roughly half of all raw materials used. It needs to be reevaluated in a circular way.[1] Contrary to the logic of a linear construction economy (extraction of raw materials—production—consumption/use—disposal/accumulation of trash), building according to the principles of a circular economy (cradle-to-cradle) considers the life cycle of resources and raw materials differently. Materials, instead of ending as waste, are preserved with the least loss of quality possible and reused as part of a closed technical cycle, or completely degraded and reintroduced into the biological cycle. To preserve gray energy and prevent construction and demolition waste—which amount to over half of today's total waste accumulation in Germany—maintaining the existing building stock must be prioritized over demolition and new construction.

The CRCLR House, which has been under development since 2015 on the grounds of the former Kindl brewery in the Rollberg neighborhood of Berlin's Neukölln district, is a model of circular construction based on three central principles: maintaining and converting existing buildings, reusing entire building sections and pre-used materials, and making (new) construction ecological and disassemblable. For the cooperative TRNSFRM eG as developer, the architecture studio Die Zusammenarbeiter planned a new hub combining work, housing, and community-oriented life in close consultation with the Basel-based baubüro in situ and interior architecture studio LXSY Architekten. Construction on the 6,100 square meter site is carried out by Kollektive Baustelle / Heap59.

The plot on which the CRCLR House is being built lay vacant for several years until it was acquired in 2015 as part of the 20,000 square meter Vollgut site by Terra Libra Immobilien GmbH, the German subsidiary of the Edith Maryon Foundation. Established in 1990, the Swiss non-profit aims to save land and property from real estate speculation in order to enable permanent ecologically and

FIG. 2
View of the CRCLR House's southern facade in the Rollbergkiez neighborhood, which is part of Berlin's Neukölln district

FIG. 3

New residential spaces in the House West were created by adding stories to the existing structure. The stories' height was determined by the size of the reused wood and aluminum windows. All other materials are biobased.

FIG. 4

View of Impact Hub Berlin's reception area on the first floor of the former keg loading hall with the newly constructed gallery. The structural and fastening elements are left visible to facilitate their retrofitting and disassembly in the future.

FIG. 5

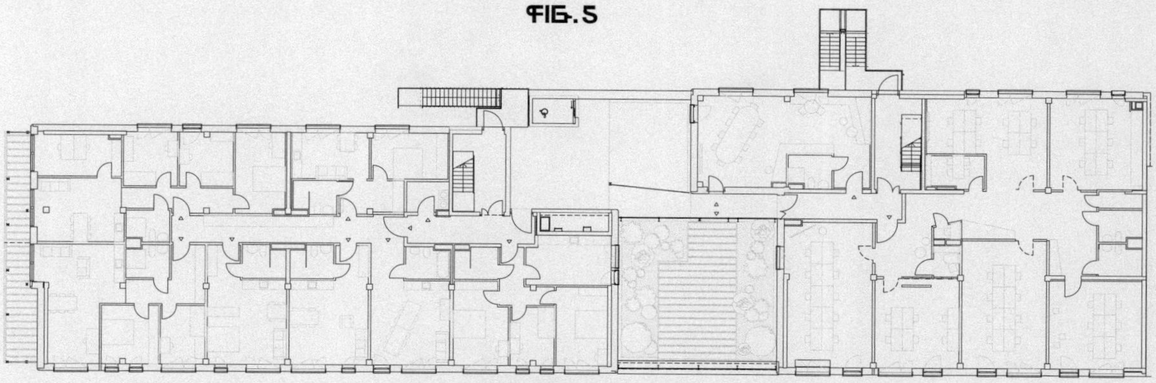

FIRST FLOOR

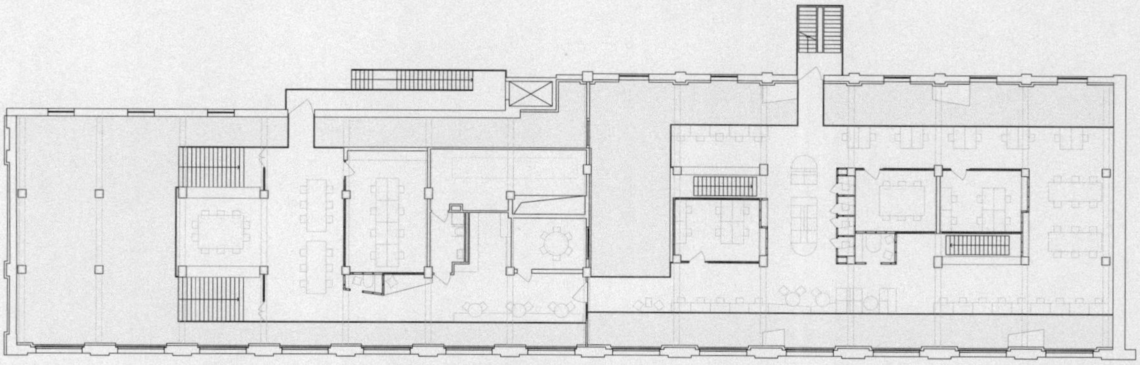

GALLERY

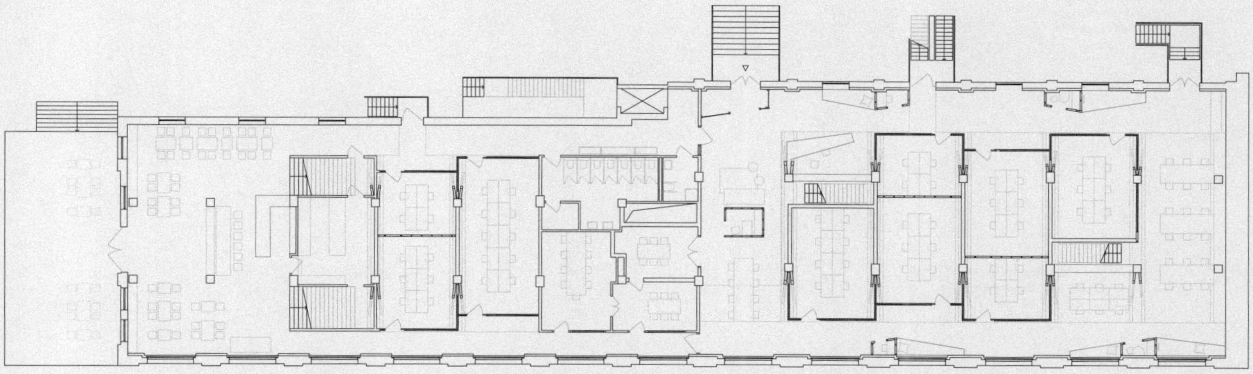

GROUND FLOOR

LONGITUDINAL SECTION

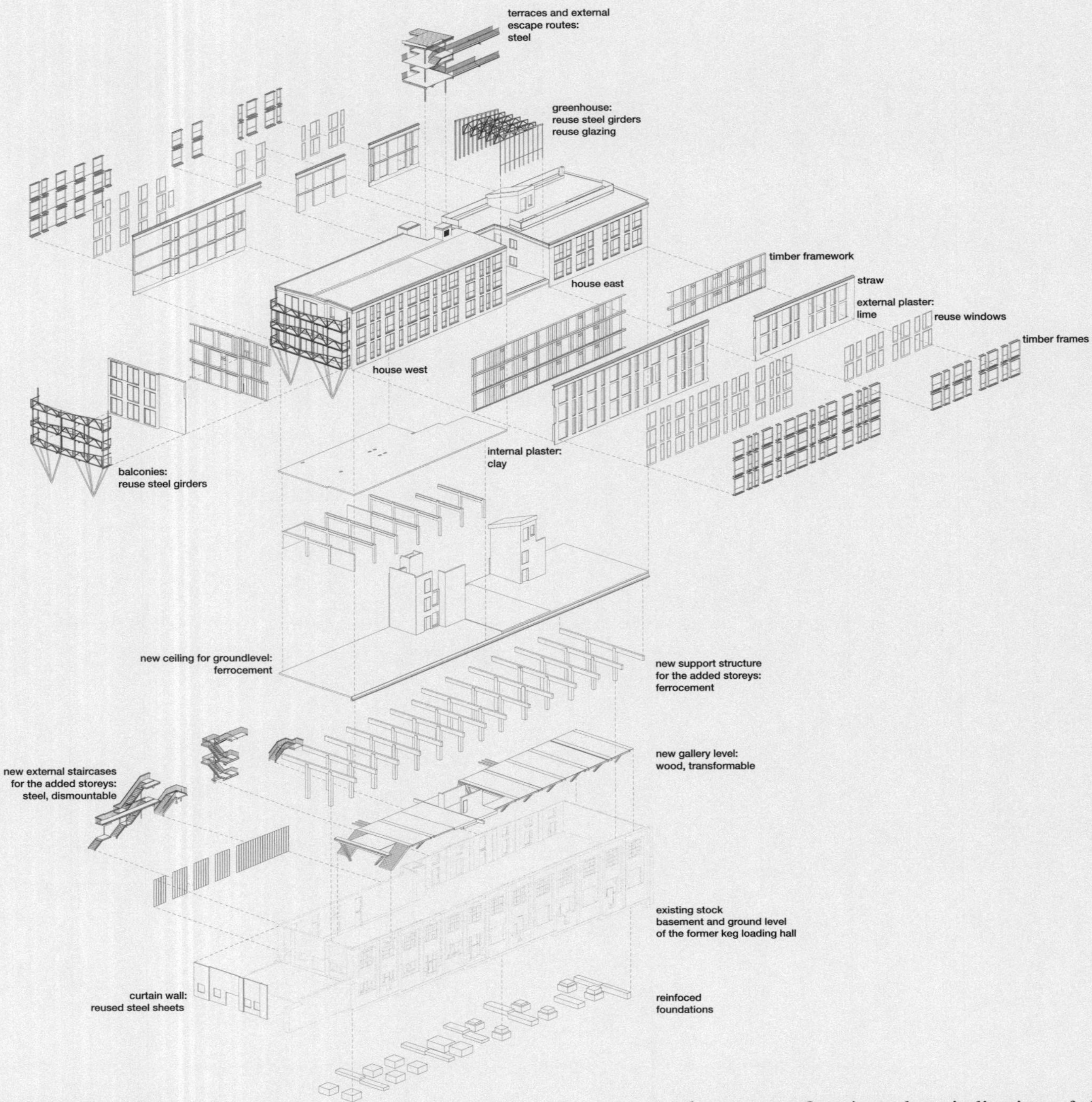

FIG.6
Exploded axonometric drawing of the load-bearing structure and the structural elements reused in the conversion of the existing building, as well as the newly added upper floors

socially responsible projects. To this end, it assigns land to developers and users under leasehold agreements. This method was already implemented in 2008 in cooperation with Mietshäuser Syndikat [apartment buildings syndicate] to secure the continued use of Rigaer Strasse 78, one of the first buildings to be squatted after the fall of the Berlin Wall; likewise, the tenants of Schokoladen, an alternative residential and cultural building squatted in the early 1990s in Berlin's Brunnenviertel neighborhood, were saved from eviction by the transfer of property from private ownership to that of the foundation in 2012. In 2017, the Edith Maryon Foundation assigned the Kindl brewery's land and existing buildings to the construction cooperative TRNSFRM eG through a leasehold agreement with a maximum duration of 99 years. The agreement stated that any profit-oriented capitalization of the land must be prevented by ensuring that user fees and rental income are not pegged to possible increases in the value of the land. Moreover, the programmatic terms set out in the agreement mandate the establishment of structurally, ecologically, and socially circular processes between users, residents, and the neighborhood, ensuring the creation of spaces for new forms of work and affordable yet varied housing for people with special needs or in situations of particular hardship.

The CRCLR House's starting point was the preservation and conversion of the former 19th century brewery's existing keg loading hall. Modernizing the basement and ground floors and adding new stories was predominantly accomplished with used building components and materials sourced through urban mining on building demolition sites in Berlin and by the partial dismantlement of the existing building, as well as from exhibitions, trade fairs, museums, warehouse inventory stock, and off-cuts from carpentry workshops around the city. The practice of urban mining views the built environment as an anthropogenic material repository enabling the "lossless and value-preserving repeated use and recovery of materials, building components, and substances."[2] The recuperated materials were stockpiled first in the hall on the ground floor, and subsequently in a neighboring building, before being repurposed in the newly established workshop in the basement: Lacerated drywall panels were lacquered with natural paints and secondhand windows upgraded from double- to triple-glazing to bring them up to highest insulation standards. The stored materials—ranging from commonplace components like tiles, limestone blocks, multiwall sheets, profiled sheeting, perforated sheet metal, metal panels, drywall paneling, and wooden materials to technical elements like acoustic insulation panels, cable ducts, ventilation tubes, step grids, to architectural elements like doors, windows, parapets, dividing walls, steel girders and supports, and roof beams—were cataloged with so-called material passports by TRNSFRM, LXSY Architekten, and Concular. The documentation recorded evaluation criteria such as proper functioning, material properties, source, and storage, as well as data on avoiding waste and on the item's integration into new use cycles to improve the overall process of installation and future reintegration into further cycles of usage. The goal of circular construction creates new challenges to the conventional workflow and routines, as planning and construction have to be geared to the principle of "form follows availability," as regards the existing stock of materials. In contrast with the traditional construction and planning phases, where design defines the choice of materials, a circular approach oscillates between (prototype) design and the sourcing of appropriate materials. A broad implementation (i.e., scaling) of digital inventory systems, secondhand materials exchange platforms, and material passports, as well as the related warranty and certification structures would make the arduous process of reusing materials easier in the future. In the case of the CRCLR House, flexibility and improvisation were prioritized both in planning and on the construction site itself. Under the given circumstances, the search for specialist firms proved difficult, which led to the founding of the construction collective named "Kollektive Baustelle" [collective construction site], which in turn gave birth to the construction company Heap59, specialized in circular construction. In close consultation between the construction workers and the architects, specific structural schemes were developed to respond efficiently to inconsistencies and irregularities in the design and implementation. Here, the close interaction with baubüro in situ, which concentrates on circular construction, played a crucial role. To enable the reuse of 600 square meters of large-format wood and aluminum windows salvaged during the planning phase, a special permit was issued to raise the maximum cornice height set in the zoning plan to adapt to the existing windows' size of 2.80 meters.

For the building's interior, LXSY Architekten approached planning by defining desired spatial qualities and allocating different degrees of transparency, translucence, and opacity for the walls, without identifying specific materials in advance. Choosing a smaller standard size of 62.5 centimeters for the wood-frame grid enabled the easy repurposing of usually small-sized offcuts from carpentry workshops. Panes of tempered glass from a dismantled curtain facade of the headquarters of Berlin's public transport agency BVG were reused as interior wall cladding for the existing floors, and old metal grating steps were recycled to function as guardrails. Such potential for reuse is, however, constrained by the legal framework set by building regulations: Stipulations for reuse are not uniform in structure, building components lose their certification if dismantled, and, depending on the case, time-consuming and costly special permits need to be sought.

Where recycled materials were unavailable for construction, the team behind CRCLR House resorted to using sustainable,

FIG.7
View of the new gallery level with the collectively used kitchenette and open seating, lounging, and working areas. Following the principle of "use as is," high-quality old and new materials are incorporated without prior treatment, whereas damaged or rough materials are upcycled to meet the design concept.

FIG.8
In addition to the open-plan office, secluded booths and meeting rooms enable a variety of work settings.

FIG. 9

One of LXSY Architekten's strategies for circular construction was to approach interior design by defining desired spatial qualities without designating specific materials. To easily integrate salvaged materials and their respective qualities into the spatial concept later on, three types of walls were defined: partition walls (blue), transparent/translucent elements (red), and flexible bookcase units (green).

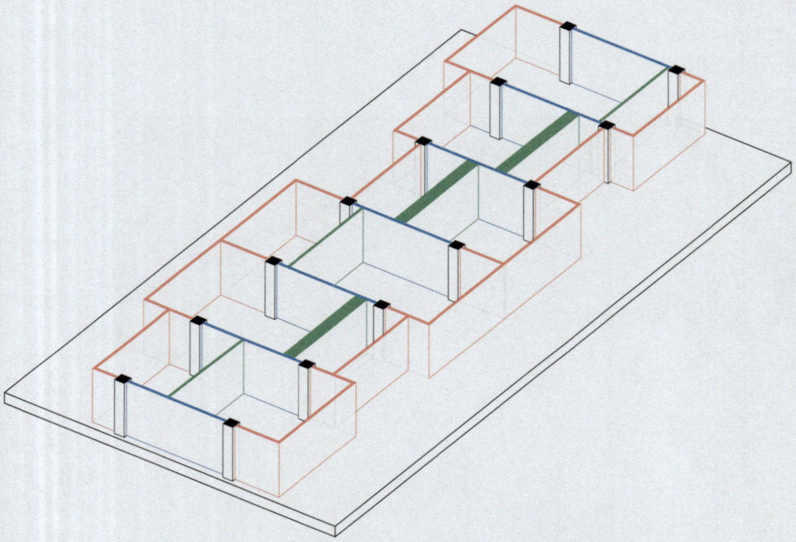

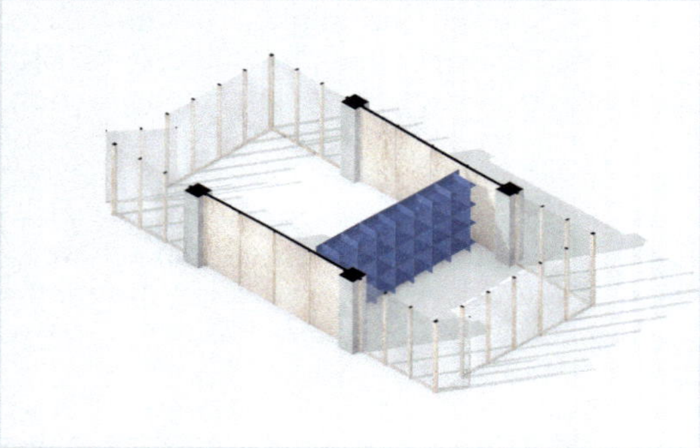

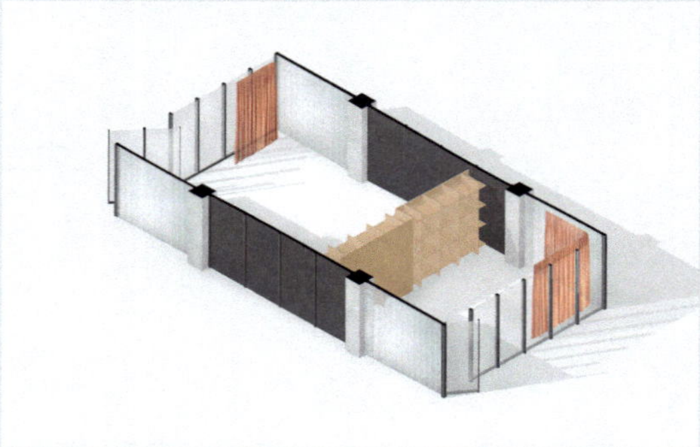

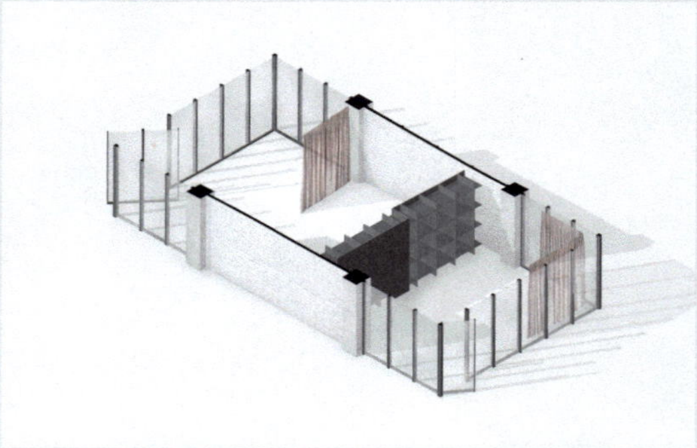

regenerative raw materials and components that can each be disposed of separately and reintroduced into the biotic cycle after use: wood as the main load-bearing material, straw-bale outer walls, hemp-based walls with high noise insulation properties for individual work spaces, limestone or clay plaster and straw panels instead of plasterboard. The new roof was realized as a back-ventilated wood-beam ceiling using wood-fiber insulation and a reusable, mechanically fastened (i.e., detachable) plastic film instead of heat-sealed bitumen for waterproofing.

To ensure future circularity, the CRCLR House is built for disassembly, meaning it has been devised with further usage and production cycles in mind for the materials and building components, should the building be torn down at some point in the future. The components' properties are recorded in the material passports. The building itself thus becomes a "material reservoir" that "temporarily stores" the building components until they are used again in the possible later context of a new construction. Structurally, this "design for disassembly" prioritizes simple bonds between disparate elements, straightforward requirements for building components, and a decoupling of the functional elements of the load-bearing structure, which means that less plaster was used and thermal bridges were geometrically avoided. The utmost importance is placed on the connections between construction elements, which were rated on repairability, as well as ease of disassembly and separation, which is why screwing, interlocking, or wedging elements together was chosen over gluing or nailing them, preferably with wood being connected to wood. The key principle here was adjusting the complexity of the connections for the duration of each element's use cycle, thus avoiding irreversible bonds between elements that are part of different use cycles, and enabling repair and dismantling without special expertise. All such connections were left unclad and the floor free of electric installations and piping. This facilitates repair and disassembly, conveys the simplicity and sufficiency the design seeks to achieve, and enables users to more easily adapt the built structures in the future.

Alongside the circular construction method, the CRCLR House's expressed goal is to link housing and workplaces in a socially sustainable manner, taking cues from circular processes by closely interlocking the technical, organic, and social material cycles of various

FIG. 10
A partition wall on the gallery level, consisting of a wooden post and beam structure, reused glass, and cross-laminated timber.

parties across the different stories of the building. Divided into two structures, one for working, the other for housing, two and three stories were respectively added to the existing building, increasing its floor space by 2,800 square meters. A rooftop terrace offering a communal zone for tenants and users connects the two volumes. The three-story residential building, House West, is predominantly organized in so-called apartment clusters, where one to three rooms can be interconnected to form housing units together with shared spaces such as laundry rooms and restrooms, communal kitchens, a bicycle shed, guest rooms, or shared bathrooms that can be assigned respectively to a single cluster or to the entire community.

FIG. 11
Locally produced hemp walls allow for the separation of individual working zones withing the existing building's commercial use area. As a natural product with acoustic, thermal, and moisture insulating qualities, and acting as a natural carbon sink, hemp represents an environmentally sustainable alternative to conventional walls.

The increased proportion of shared usages and shared spaces in the residential section is aimed not only at nurturing the social aspect, but also at reducing the surface used by each person. After all, improvements in ecological efficiency of construction methods will not reduce humanity's overall ecological footprint over time if the average person continues to use up more and more space each year. The specially established CRCLR Living eG is the organization underpinning the communally oriented housing model in the CRCLR House: It is a tenants' cooperative that seeks to provide affordable housing for groups often disadvantaged on the housing market, such as members of the LGBTQ+ community, Black people, and

FIG. 12
Double-glazed windows are reused as partitions between the hallway and individual meeting rooms.

FIG. 13
Impact Hub Berlin's publicly accessible restaurant in the CRCLR House is open to the surrounding neighborhood. Differently colored joint sealants made with discarded paints were used between the tiles, mirroring the experimental and resource-mindful approach down to the most detailed level.

FIG.14
Scraps of wood in various shapes and colors were reused as wall paneling in the Rollwerk workshop's kitchen.

People of Color. The two-story commercial extension, House East, consists of flexible spaces for different office layouts, with smaller phone booths for privacy and one adjacent optional space per floor available to both residents and commercial users for larger events.

The ground floor of the existing building is enhanced by a gallery level which offers both a cafeteria and office spaces for various companies that join forces in the Impact Hub, a network of young companies and non-profit NGOs working around the topics of circular economy, sustainable nutrition, social innovation, and green technologies. The collective working spaces, which can be appropriated in a variety of ways, have different sizes, shapes, and degrees of privacy, ranging from small booths to a large open-plan office, to an event area that can host up to 190 people. Prototypes and ideas can be tested in specialized workshops and laboratories for crafts manufacturing, research, and educational activities relating to resource-preserving applications located in the basement. Here, Made of Air take agricultural waste to produce carbon-negative components that capture CO_2 from the environment and will find application, among other things, as new building material. Mujō produces biodegradable packaging films for food, cosmetics, and goods, while Proteme manufactures coatings that prolong the shelf life of produce and protects it against pathogens. Moreover, a repair café is on site, integrated into the material and social circuits of the immediate neighborhood as well as charitable organizations such as Reviving Home, a crowdfunding platform for the repair of destroyed cities in crisis-stricken regions, or Hudara, a non-profit NGO focusing on issues of mental health, life under the impact of climate change, and social development through

FIG.15
In their basement laboratory, Made of Air transform agricultural waste into carbon-negative components that capture carbon dioxide from the environment and could be used, among other things, as new building materials.

FIG. 16
Prototypes of products and ideas developed in the CRCLR House can be implemented and tested in the basement's Rollwerk workshop. The workshop community dedicated to various aspects of sustainable and circular economics offers an openly accessible repair café as well as tools and services for 3D printing and upcycling metal, wood, and glass.

access to renewable energies. To ensure adequate energy provisions for the various usages of the CRCLR House, the building relies on geothermal and heat pumps, solar thermal systems, photovoltaic panels, heat recovery systems, and a seasonal heat accumulator. Excess power is fed into the local heating network.

Across different scales, the CRCLR House offers an example of a circular construction methodology that goes beyond the implementation of durable material cycles and envisions a sustainable and decidedly holistic approach to all resources—from the plot of land to the extreme reduction of primary resources, to the social inclusion of users. The oftentimes very specific decisions made in planning and construction as well as the measures developed on a transdisciplinary basis are not universally reproducible but do reflect trends on how a circular approach changes the assessment of materials, construction methods, structures, and spatial programs in their totality. Learning from and widely disseminating these is a necessary precondition for new construction to be an ecologically viable option to solve the pressing spatial problems we are faced with today. *DK*

FIG. 17
The office of Skyseed, a company using drones and pelleted seeds for reforestation and climate change-resilient forest transformation, was refurbished only to the extent necessary for the long-term preservation of the existing building.

1 According to the European Union, the construction sector is responsible for 40% of CO_2 and other greenhouse gas emissions, 50% of primary energy consumption, as well as 50% of primary raw materials consumption and at least 37% of solid waste volume in Europe. See European Commission, "LEVEL(S): Taking action on the TOTAL impact of the construction sector" (Luxembourg, 2019), 5; see also Eurostat, "Waste statistics," 2023, accessed January 16, 2023, ec.europa.eu/eurostat/statistics-explained/SEPDF/cache/1183.pdf.

2 Dirk Hebel and Felix Heisel, "Introduction," in *Urban Mining und kreislaufgerechtes Bauen: Die Stadt als Rohstofflager*, eds. eid. (Stuttgart: Fraunhofer IRB, 2021), 13.

HAUS DER MATERIALISIERUNG

Center for Climate-Friendly Resource Usage

FIG. 1
Haus der Materialisierung's graphic identity is conceived as a toolbox encompassing a range of fonts, format templates, symbols, color codes, etc., giving the participating organizations an easily accessible means to independently design their external communications.

A transformation of the current economic, social, and cultural model is inescapable given the dramatically changing environmental conditions and their direct consequences on our life and survival on the planet. Therefore, the question is not *whether* a fundamental change will take place, but rather *how*, "by design or by disaster."[1] A proactive design approach is presented by Haus der Materialisierung [House of Materialization] in Berlin, a transdisciplinary coalition founded in 2019, currently consisting of 23 activist groups and organizations who research and practice climate-friendly resource usage and sustainable economics. To counter the unbroken growth imperative currently structuring our linear economics, provoking resource wastage, and fanning the flames of the climate crisis, an array of activist groups have found sanctuary at Haus der Materialisierung, including rental and repair organizations; craftspeople working with wood, textile, metal, and gold; upcycling and bicycle workshops; markets for leftover and secondhand materials; as well as agencies for crafts and trades, and social and educational work. Here, people reuse, reprocess, and repair; they get guidance and learn how to do things differently. Used items that are usually considered trash serve as the source material for further cycles of use and production.

Haus der Materialisierung is part of the larger model project Haus der Statistik in the

USES
Studios for wood, textile, and metal works and goldsmithing, as well as upcycling and repair, especially of bicycles; markets for scrap, leftover, and secondhand materials; rental agencies, workshop spaces, crafts and trade agencies, social and educational work

SIZE
780 m²

ORGANIZATION
Koop5, as part of the Haus der Statistik (House of Statistics) pilot project

PIONEER USERS SINCE 2019 (*FORMER USERS OF HDM)
Baufachfrau Berlin e. V., Berlin Repair*, Berliner Stadtmission, Circular Berlin*, Circular City – Zirkuläre Stadt e. V.*, Cosum, Essbar, Extinction Rebellion Bau AG, FahrArt (Bruce Brenner, Chainless-D, Larsito), Freifunk, Habibiship*, Kostümkollektiv e. V., Kunst-Stoffe e. V., Material Mafia, Meltmeister*, Merijaan, Mitkunstzentrale, MRTZ, MURKS? NEIN DANKE! E. V.*, NIE Druckerei, Ort-schafft-Material, Plastikberg, Raumlabor Berlin, S27 – Kunst und Bildung*, Searchwing, Selbstgebaute Musik, Stefan Is Doing Things, Streetware Saved Item, Upcycling Mobi*, Zebraap, ZK/U – Zentrum für Kunst und Urbanistik

SCIENTIFIC PROJECT MONITORING
Reallabor Zirkuläres Wirtschaften im urbanen Raum (living laboratory for a circular economy in urban space) at Technische Universität Berlin, funded by DBU German Federal Environmental Foundation

FOUNDED
2019

LOCATION
Berlin

FIG. 2
The Werkhof [builders' yard] next to Haus der Materialisierung's two-story low-rise building offers communal spaces for workshops, building activities, parties, meetings, and raised-bed planting, as well as for cultivating crops and breeding aquatic animals in eco-circular aquaponics systems.

FIG. 3
"Discursive-subjective drawing" by Erik Göngrich showing Haus der Materialisierung and the pioneer users' locations

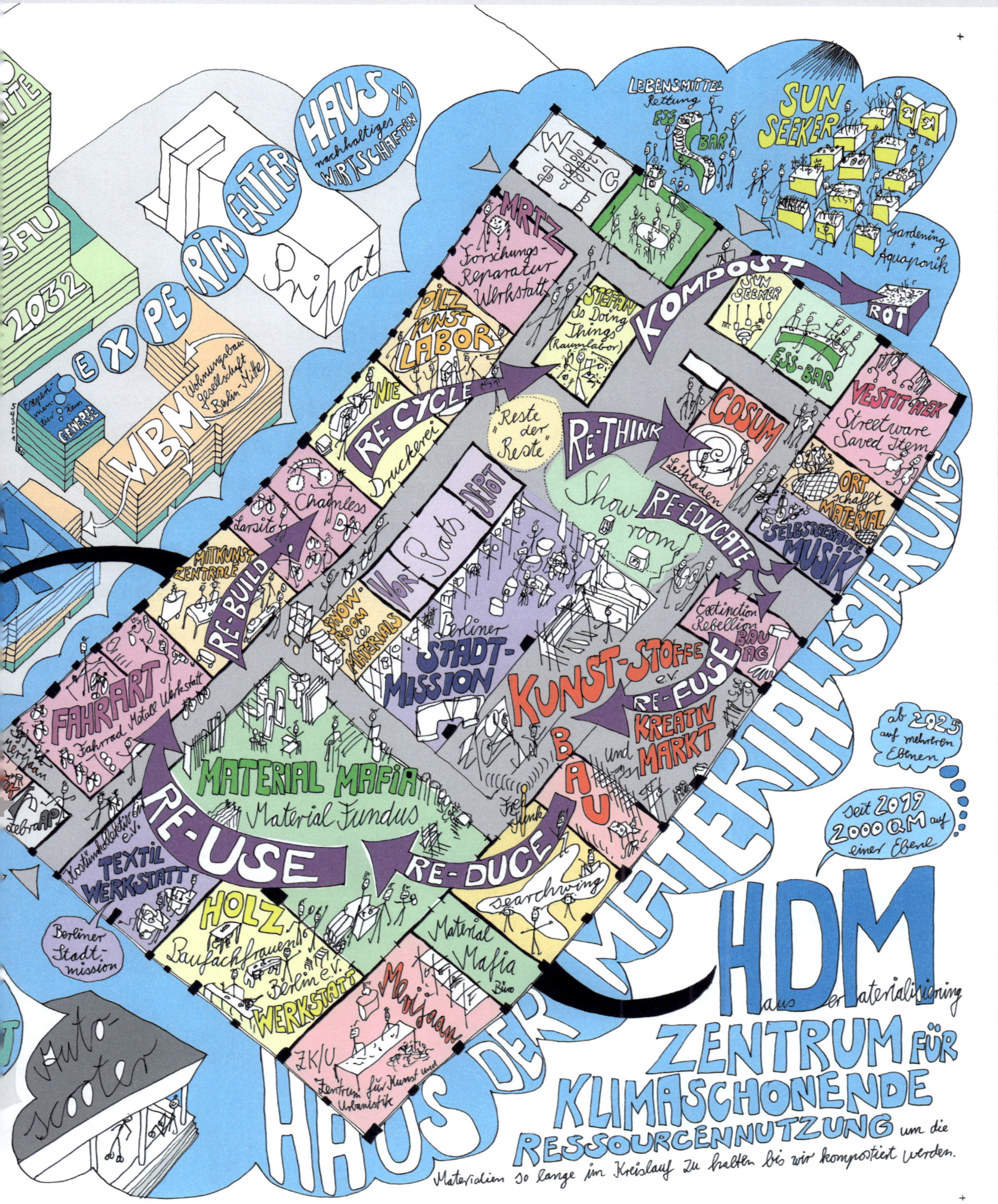
HAUS X1
nachhaltiges Wirtschaften
EXPERIMENTER
Privat
WBM
Wohnungsbaugesellschaft Berlin-Mitte
BAU 2032
LEBENSMITTEL Rettung
ESS BAR
SUN SEEKER
Gardening + Aquaponik
KOMPOST
ROT
MRTZ
Forschungs-Reparatur Werkstatt
PILZ KUNST LABOR
STEFAN Is Doing Things Raumlabor
NIE Druckerei
RE-CYCLE
Reste der Reste
RE-THINK
COSUM
Leihladen
VESTITHEK
Streetware Saved Item
ORT schafft MATERIAL
SELBSTGEBAUTE MUSIK
Show-room
RE-EDUCATE
Chainless
Larsito
MITKUNSTZENTRALE
RE-BUILD
Vorrats DEPOT
SHOW-ROOM des MATERIALS
Berliner STADT-MISSION
Extinction Rebellion
BAU AG
KUNST-STOFFE e.V.
RE-FUSE
KREATIV MARKT
FAHRRAD
Fahrrad Metall Werkstatt
MATERIAL MAFIA
Material Fundus
RE-USE
RE-DUCE
BAU
Searchwing
Kostümkollektiv e.V.
TEXTIL WERKSTATT
HOLZ Baufachfrauen Berlin e.V. WERKSTATT
Berliner Stadtmission
Material Mafia Büro
ZK/U Zentrum für Kunst und Urbanistik
Autoscooter
ab 2025 auf mehreren Ebenen
seit 2019 2000 QM auf einer Ebene
HAUS DER MATERIALISIERUNG
HDM
Haus der Materialisierung
ZENTRUM FÜR KLIMASCHONENDE RESSOURCENNUTZUNG um die Materialien so lange im Kreislauf zu halten bis wir kompostiert werden.

Mercure HOTEL
ALLESANDERSPLATZ

FIG. 4
Haus der Statistik,
view of south facade as seen from Alexanderplatz

former headquarters of the GDR's Central State Administration for Statistics, which is spread across a complex of some 46,500 square meters near Berlin's Alexanderplatz. The architectural ensemble dating back to the 1960s was due to be torn down ahead of the site's redevelopment by a private investor, sparking a protest campaign by artists of the activist group Allianz bedrohter Berliner Atelierhäuser [Alliance for Threatened Studio Buildings in Berlin] in 2015. The activists prevented the buildings from being demolished and the land from being sold by the federal government and the State of Berlin, co-owners of the complex at the time. The artists hung a banner from the facade which read, "Here, spaces for art, culture, and social welfare for Berlin are under development." This led to the founding of Haus der Statistik, an alliance of actors from civil society, artists, and architects, as well as social and cultural institutions, associations, and foundations. The alliance launched a debate on urban policy with demands and ideas for the subsequent use of the site, which eventually prompted the State of Berlin to enter into negotiations with the Federal Government to hand over its shares in the property to the municipality. Since 2018, the site has been managed by Koop5, an alliance consisting of Berlin's Senate Department for Urban Development, Building and Housing, Berlin's Mitte District Office, the municipal housing company WBM, the city's real estate management provider BIM, and the cooperative ZUsammenKUNFT Berlin eG – Genossenschaft für Stadtentwicklung (ZKB), a newly-founded subsidy of Haus der Statistik. The joint cooperation agreement aims to collectively develop Haus der Statistik as a neighborhood for the common good and to secure long-term affordable space for housing, working, and culture. Early in the modernization process, as the upper stories were being gutted, so-called "pioneer users" moved into the ground floor. They appropriated and repaired the space themselves after the cooperative ZKB negotiated temporary usage rights with Berlin's real estate management firm BIM. The call for applications to activate the building at the beginning of the pioneering phase addressed organizations coalescing around the topics of social learning, healthy future, local democracy, urban cultural venues, diversity, and sustainable economics. Haus der Materialisierung as an association spawned from these common goals in 2019.

FIG. 5
At Haus der Materialisierung, the welfare organization Berliner Stadtmission offers a textile workshop and courses around repairing, upcycling, and sewing textiles, as well as a second-hand market for furniture and other household items.

THE WORKSHOP PRINCIPLE

Haus der Materialisierung is an answer to the realization that capitalist growth has material and social limits. The throwaway mentality behind the consumption, squander, and exhaustion of resources is countered by the activists' and organizations' strategies of reuse and reprocessing. The workshops promote new forms of experimentation with different materials and encourage people to "start doing things together": Following an inclusive DIY principle, participants—users as well as producers—learn new craft techniques and skills. In Haus der Materialisierung's open workshops, the implementation of sustainable and transformative practices is internalized through participatory processes. This applied transfer of knowledge creates moments of self-empowerment and fosters an awareness of what alternatives to a linear form of life and economy could look like. The social practice of participation therefore communicates not only *how*, but also *that* an ecological transformation is possible if enough people participate. Haus der Materialisierung repairs bicycles and relations of production—by means of *sharing*, *procuring*, *repairing*, and *reusing*.

FIG.6
Baufachfrau Berlin e.V.'s ReUse wood workshop offers free services and city-wide classes for learning about the reuse and reprocessing of different materials from Haus der Materialisierung's large stock.

SHARING

One of the most effective measures to restrict resource consumption and consumerism, while also breaking with the capitalist logic of ownership based on exclusive property relations, is to *share*: tools and workshops, objects and knowledge. This commoning of goods represents an intensification of each individual object's use and contributes to reducing the consumption of resources. At the same time, collective usage reduces financial barriers, lowering the threshold to broader participation. This connects the dimension of sustainability with that of justice, an essential step for a comprehensive socio-ecological transformation. Cosum makes this possible through rentals, either digitally via its online rental platform of the same name, or physically at its rental store at Haus der Materialisierung, both of which enable access to the types of goods that are not a matter of everyday use such as sporting equipment or construction tools. The printing workshop NIE Druckerei offers a job press for the production of leaflets or posters. Freifunk provides free-of-charge and independent communication structures by means of a mesh network of Wi-Fi routers on the roofs of Berlin. Kostümkollektiv sources costumes that would otherwise be thrown away, making them available for the independent theater scene while offering courses in textile repair. Performatively acting as modern rag collectors, Streetware Saved Item moves through the urban space with mobile clothes drying racks and collects clothing items that have been thrown away, cleans and patches them up, and then lends them out. Searchwing builds drones to locate people in danger at sea and offers them to NGOs such as SARAH-Seenotrettung or Mission Lifeline, thereby appreciably expanding the search radius of their rescue boats. Raumlabor understands itself as an experimental architectural practice that aims to use temporary urban interventions to share locally produced knowledge and built structures that can be repurposed in other places.

FIG.7
As an artistic contribution to the art and culture festival *48 Stunden Neukölln*, Streetware Saved Item presented an interactive installation in Berlin's Körnerpark, consisting of 48 mobile laundry racks with saved clothing items, which could be exchanged and restocked by residents and visitors during the two-day runtime.

PROCURING

A circular economy requires the physical procurement of what was formerly understood as waste, steering it to places where it becomes a resource for further production and usage cycles—a practice also called "urban mining," analogous to extractive mining. All kinds of raw materials and goods mined from anthropogenic material depositories such as buildings earmarked for demolition, cultural venues, abandoned apartments, urban spaces, etc. are placed on offer at Haus der Materialisierung for reuse or are processed and refurbished in the workshops on site. The Essbar food-sharing café saves produce from going to landfills, which it prepares and offers at weekly meetings, which also serve as informational events and networking and exchange platforms around sustainable food sourcing. Berliner Stadtmission sells donated furniture and textiles, which can be refurbished in their textile workshop. Kunst-Stoffe e.V. acts as a collecting point and interface for materials that have been declared waste, offering them for re-use at their zero-waste builders' and creatives' market. The Material Mafia functions as a climate-friendly hardware store, offering the full range of building supplies from wooden planks to paint, which have been donated by traditional hardware stores, craftspeople, businesses, trade fairs, or private individuals. Zentrum für Kunst und Urbanistik hosts the GüterMARX market, which not only sells reprocessed goods and arts and crafts items, but also provides space for workshops on collective design processes. Ort-schafft-Material also hosts workshops to explore the use of experimental ecological processes and materials science, such as dying fabrics using plants cultivated in the urban space or processing food waste to create biologically degradable tableware. Mitkunstzentrale is a space for collective knowledge production and co-creation, whose artistic practices and interventions interact with public space in order to develop "visions for climate-neutral sculptures, cities, and architecture born from the spirit of solidarity" and test them locally using art.

FIG.8
In addition to the Material Mafia's hardware store at Haus der Materialisierung, all materials and found objects are also listed on a digital open-source platform that records the storage, handling, resale, and sustainability of materials and products. Material Mafia not only offers hands-on workshops on the reuse and repurposing of materials, but also provides comprehensive educational programs on material cycles—including the origin of raw materials, commodity chains, reusability, and recycling.

REPAIRING AND REPROCESSING

Repairing and reprocessing that which has been thrown away plays a crucial role in overcoming the often artificial discrepancy between economic service life (built-in obsolescence) and material life cycle. In other words, things that are commonly considered waste under the capitalist throwaway mindset have to be made productive (again) to serve as the starting point for additional continuities of usage and production. This approach is doubly sustainable, as it prevents not only new waste, but also the squandering of resources in new production output. At the same time, this practice of "maintaining value" allows for independence from capitalist surplus production and profit-driven valorization (e.g., by artificially induced scarcity). In the same vein, anyone using the Baufachfrau Berlin e. V. woodworking shop to build furniture from secondhand materials does not need to buy new items. In its workshop, Extinction Rebellion Bau AG manufactures signs and other materials for their climate protests. FahrArt is an open bicycle and metalworking shop for repairing bicycles and building bike trailers, as well as manufacturing lamps and doing goldsmithing work. Recently founded Merijaan manufactures surfing equipment from reprocessed and recyclable plastic. MRTZ is a research workshop for lighting technology, material reuse, and recycling, dedicated to collecting, reprocessing, and renting out old and new projectors of all kinds as well as hosting workshops for young people to transmit knowledge in handling (and repairing) technical appliances. The Plastikberg initiative develops and manufactures furniture from local reprocessed plastic. Selbstgebaute Musik experiments with the construction of musical instruments and their individual parts from secondhand everyday objects, such as mouthpieces for wind instruments made from champagne corks or guitars made from laminated paperboard food packaging. Zebraap repurposes secondhand furniture to give it another usage cycle, which results in experimental design objects, such as a chair that doubles as a planter. Pursuing the principle of "form follows material," Stefan Is Doing Things uses reprocessed components to build furniture and tools, as well as temporary working and performance spaces in front of Haus der Statistik, in which the pioneer users stay during the construction phase.

By rooting the material dimension of maintenance and care in a multiplicity of social practices, Haus der Materialisierung uproots the understanding of "'production,' 'consumption,' and 'the market' as the fixed focal points of the capitalist economy"[2] in order to internalize the necessary fundamental social change through practice on a smaller scale and in everyday life. The scalability of this approach is being studied by the TU Berlin's state-funded research project "Reallabor Zirkuläres Wirtschaften im urbanen Raum"[3] [living laboatory for a circular economy in urban space], which is integrated into the building complex as a space for the overarching advancement and transmission of knowledge, to test the efficacy of the pilot project, and ultimately transfer it to other locations nationwide. At the same time, Haus der Materialisierung—alongside B-Wa(h)renhaus in Neukölln and NochMall, which is run by the Berlin's municipal waste management company BSR in the district of Reinickendorf—is one of three "centers for climate-friendly resource usage" promoted in the context of the city's zero-waste initiative "Re-Use Berlin." Alongside the modernization of the existing buildings around Haus der Materialisierung in the new Haus der Statistik neighborhood, an additional 65,000 square meters is planned for cultural and social uses, education, administration, and affordable housing, as well as for the "Rathaus der Zukunft"—the city hall of the future for Berlin's Mitte district. In the long run, one of the new buildings will be dedicated to sustainable economics to grant a continued lease to the pioneer users on site, whose activating presence on—and maintenance of—the site around Haus der Statistik has had a significant influence on society well beyond the neighborhood itself. *DK*

1 Davide Brocchi, *By Disaster or by Design? Transformative Kulturpolitik: Von der multiplen Krise zur systemischen Nachhaltigkeit* (Wiesbaden: Springer VS, 2023).

2 Hans-Joachim Bürkner and Bastian Lange, "Situierte Raumkonzepte zur Erklärung von Arbeitsprozessen im Kontext von Postwachstumsökonomien," in *Postwachstumsgeographien: Raumbezüge diverser und alternativer Ökonomien,* eds. Bastian Lange et al. (Bielefeld: transcript, 2020), 36.

3 "Reallabor Zirkuläres Wirtschaften im urbanen Raum: Kompetenzaufbau und Umweltkommunikation im 'Haus der Materialisierung' in Berlin," Technische Universität Berlin, accessed December 15, 2023, www.tu.berlin/circulareconomy/forschung/hdm.

FIG. 9
The MRTZ experimentation workshop specializes in the repair and reprocessing of lighting equipment and second-hand electronic goods.

FIG. 10
The Sun Seeker e.V. association experiments with various forms of urban gardening and sustainable food production, such as pearl oyster mushroom farming in the basement of Haus der Materialisierung.

THE URBAN DIMENSION OF MAINTENANCE:

The Venice Biennales and their growing number of so-called Collateral Events accelerate the unfettered commodification of space by the profit-oriented culture industry, which in turn leads to an increase in mass tourism. As a consequence, everyday life—and its networks of social and material acts of care not geared toward turning a profit—are progressively being driven out of the city. While the commercialization of space leads to the city's depopulation, more than 2,000 publicly owned apartments across the city stand empty and are left to decay. Organizations from civil society are trying to reverse these trends. They understand the care for urban and community structures as a means to ensure the right to housing and the right to the city: a form of urban maintenance. Their work, reminiscent of historically rooted practices of squatting and maintaining, is more than mere self-help. It addresses social inequalities and translates them into political demands for society as a whole. Reappropriating and defending public spaces constitutes the backbone of these organizations' activism.

MAINTAINING

(THROUGH SQUATTING)

HOMES IN ITALY — A POLITICAL TALE

FIG. 1
Luigi Ghirri, *Modena*, 1971–72, 13 × 8 cm
From the series *Fotografie del periodo iniziale*

Text:
Sarah Gainsforth

I grew up in a tiny apartment in Rome that my father adapted over the years to accommodate the growing family. He built the furniture himself, each piece fitting the others to make use of all the space available, not unlike a sailboat. One day, when I was ten, he sat the family down at the kitchen table and asked, "Where would you like to live? We could stay here or move into a bigger house in the suburbs." We had no doubt: Moving out was not an option. Rent was low and our small terrace overlooked the Palatine and Aventine hills to the left, the Tiber straight ahead, and the Capitoline hill to the right; why would we ever want to leave this place? I used to walk through the Roman Forum every day. I would follow the quiet paths through the ancient ruins and exit at the opposite side into the bustling city.

In summertime, we would picnic between the ruins and play under the pine trees or inside the fountains. Of course, even back then, this was not allowed; my mother would be told off by police officers. Nevertheless, the Forum was an integral part of the city. Today, it is fenced off and one must buy a ticket to pass the turnstiles. Once inside, you can only look. Picnics and playing are not allowed. Over the years, our rent increased, but never too much. The landlord, a Catholic institution, gradually raised rents for new tenants, but old-time residents like my father paid rent based on their income. We stayed, but around us, the neighborhood changed. It started to feel empty. Old neighbors died, others left, new ones moved in. Judging by the closed shutters, they were never in. Many homes became second homes and, more recently, Airbnb rentals.

When my father first came to Rome in 1963, the majority of Italians was still renting: In 1961, only 45.9 percent of households were homeowners. Today, that number has risen to 70.8 percent; another 20.5 percent rent, and an astonishing 8.7 percent live in usufruct, meaning they neither own nor pay rent for the home they live in.[1] The high percentage of homeowners in Italy is often portrayed as a natural and historical fact. Official reports are invariably convinced that Italians display a marked "preference"[2] for ownership, presenting it as some kind of anthropological evidence. But something is missing from this narrative: Over the decades, homeownership has been actively promoted by national policies and funded with public investments and tax incentives, quite suddenly turning everyone into a mortgage holder. As a result, and more than ever, housing is at the center of a fundamental conflict between the idea of the home as the physical space where life, care, and social reproduction take place, and that of the home as a financial asset. These two dimensions are not compatible, as it is precisely the value of housing as a financial asset that erodes its social value as an inhabited place. The effects of this process of erosion have become more apparent as unaffordable housing markets worldwide continue to push low-income tenants out of cities. At the same time, the invaluable public housing stocks accumulated by states in the postwar years are either being sold off or left to decay. Italy is no exception; on the contrary, due to a combination of demographic trends, economic policies, and the extraordinary appeal the country holds as a global tourism destination, Italy presents us with a textbook case study that is worth looking at in depth.

HOUSING POSTWAR ITALY

The first legislation in Italy providing for public housing to be built for those in need dates back to 1903 and the introduction of the so-called Luzzatti Law.[3] Prior to this, poverty and housing exclusion had been dealt with exclusively by charity institutions. The law called for the establishment of local, decentralized *Istituti Autonomi Case Popolari* [Autonomous Institutes for Public Housing, or IACP] to provide housing to the less affluent. But in Rome, at a time when unauthorized, informal settlements were the main solution to the housing crisis, the local IACP was unable to catch up with the immense task of housing their inhabitants. Under the fascist regime, poor people were pushed out of the city center by high rents and evictions aimed at crafting Mussolini's vision for a capital city of monumental grandeur and emptiness. Moreover, a steady influx of migrants from rural areas was pouring into growing industrial cities in search of work. Between 1955 and 1970, 17 million Italians migrated to cities.[4] They found no housing, so they built shacks. The 1951 census revealed that within the city, around 100,000 people lived in 30,000 shacks, caves, basements, warehouses, and attics.[5] For decades, the lack of official data on this silent housing emergency was also a convenient way to ignore it. In Rome, entire neighborhoods were built with no planning authorization. It is estimated that one third of the city originated from the sprawl of informal or quasi-formal settlements. Over time, this praxis consolidated into an established cultural phenomenon known in Italy as *Abusivismo*—a word commonly used to describe the illegal development of entire stretches of land by individual plot owners. This urban Wild West remained unchallenged until at least the 1950s, when clearing the slums at the edges of the city and providing affordable housing for newly arriving workers would be transferred to a national program, drafted by the Christian Democrat Minister of Labor and Social Security Amintore Fanfani, who would later go on to become prime minister. The much glorified program, called INA-Casa [*Istituto Nazionale delle Assicurazioni-Casa*, or National Insurance Institute-Housing], was approved in 1949 with the dual intent of fostering employment and solving the housing emergency. By the time the so-called "Fanfani Plan" was discontinued in 1963, almost 355,000 housing units had been built across the country, and over 40,000 construction workers had found steady employment in each year of its run. The program was funded by a mix of international postwar grants, deductions from the salaries of workers and employers, and state contributions.[6] INA-Casa was an unprecedented experiment in which the government firmly took the lead deploying centralized housing policies on a vast scale. Nine housing projects were built in Rome, with space for more than 55,000 people.[7] The plan was scheduled to run out, but its success led to it being replaced by another program, dubbed Gescal [*Gestione Case per i Lavoratori,* or Workers' Housing Management], a fund with the same purpose and financing model.[8]

Even before the conception of the INA-Casa program, cities were mandated to draft urban master plans regulating land use by a national urban planning law passed by the fascist government in 1942.[9] However, it took two decades before master planning started to be effectively adopted by municipalities nationwide. Rome, for example, only adopted such a plan in 1962 after Fiorentino Sullo—the Christian Democratic Minister of Public Works who had overseen its drafting—set an ultimatum for the plan's adoption and suspended all building permits until then; an unprecedented and courageous act against land speculation. The same year, Sullo introduced an affordable housing law requiring municipalities to select areas to be allocated for the construction of public housing covering between 40 and 70 percent of the total housing demand for the next decade.[10]

Sullo's proposal went even further. He understood rent as the extraction of value from land, which is increased by planning regimes of urbanization and public investments for infrastructure and services. These were, and still are, a key factor in determining market prices and housing affordability. It is for this reason that Sullo also proposed to reform the 1942 national urban planning law and campaigned for the executive branch to have the right to purchase undeveloped real estate at a price usually reserved for agricultural land, then sell it after development at a value increased by the servicing cost they had borne, or sell only the right to surface as a concession. Traditionally, as in most countries, Italian law assimilates land ownership with the right to build. Sullo's proposal would have separated the two by nationalizing building rights. This way, developers would profit if they actually built housing on their property, but not from speculating on their real estate's surplus value. Sullo's visionary proposal was designed to structurally tackle the single most important issue at the root of the housing crisis: the private appropriation of inflated land values through speculative real estate transactions. Needless to say, his reform proposal did not sit well with the construction lobby and Sullo became the subject of a defamatory media campaign accusing him of wanting to abolish private property in Italy. His political party isolated him and the most radical elements of his proposal never reached Parliament.

In an attempt to address widespread social uprisings—crystallized in the historical general strike of November 19, 1969—a second attempt was made a few years later to achieve public control of urban rent through the housing law of 1971, followed in 1977 by the Bucalossi Law, named after one of Sullos successors, Pietro Bucalossi, which reintroduced the possibility of land expropriation based on agricultural value.[11] The law remains ambiguous on the concept of expropriation, but many considered it a success because it stated ownership rights and surface rights to be two different things. Private ownership of the land therefore no longer automatically implied the right to build. This right is now allocated by local governments with building permits termed *concessioni*. A pioneering form of rent control was also introduced in 1978 with the *Equo canone* [Fair Rent] law, which capped the rent of any unit through a complex matrix based on factors such as location, size, and state of maintenance.[12] These, however, were often too difficult to assess and calculate for the authorities, leading to frustration towards a heavily bureaucratic system and, more generally, towards any form of state intervention in the private housing market. Results fell short of expectations, partly due to administrative delays and planning mistakes, and partly due to a global cultural shift already underway: From the late 1970s onward, as homeownership increased steadily, housing was less and less perceived as a public resource; instead, it increasingly became a commodity.

INVENTING A RIGHT TO BUY

With the elections of Margaret Thatcher and then Ronald Reagan, the period between 1978 and 1980 is a turning point in global social and economic history. The advent of neoliberalism, facilitated by national legal systems, was marked in Italy by a 1980 Constitutional Court ruling which declared that compensations for compulsory acquisitions based on agricultural value were unlawful expropriations and mandated the reimbursement of incurred losses.[13] The ruling left national and local authorities reeling from the compensation payments for previously acquired land and suddenly facing huge costs when trying to acquire new real estate. As free market ideologies gained traction, Italy began to sell off its public housing stock in 1993. Until 2011, according to estimates by the Italian social housing federation Federcasa, 190,000 publicly owned units worth 9 billion euros had been sold well below market value for only 2.5 billion euros.[14] In 1998, state funding for public rented housing ended altogether when the Gescal fund—which, on average, had subsidized 1 billion euros' worth of public housing construction per year—was abolished altogether. A law from the same year, which still regulates the rental sector today, abolished rent control and left rent prices to be determined by the market; rents below the market rate are now ensured through tax incentives for landlords and housing subsidies for tenants.[15]

With a twenty-year delay, Italy thus followed in the path opened by the United States with the 1974 Housing and Community Act. Its passage ended funding for the construction of public housing and subsidized the private market through housing allowances, known as the Section 8 program, to cover rental costs exceeding 30 percent of a tenant's income.[16] This paved the way for a systematic shift of public resources to the private sector. Two main arguments were employed to justify this shift: first, the need for social mixing by *dispersing* poor tenants, otherwise concentrated in public housing areas. This argument holds some truth in that concentrating poverty in ghettos is never a good idea, but it does not deal with the root causes of poverty, nor with the prohibitive private housing market that allowances end up supporting. The second argument employed to justify the shift lies in the very name of the program: Housing Choice Voucher Program. In true neoliberal speak, so the argument goes, even poor tenants should have a right to *choose* where to live, again ignoring the economic conditions of tenants and the simple evidence that under the voluntary voucher program, many landlords *choose not to* rent homes to tenants on welfare. For too many people, high rents mean that there is simply no choice about where to live. This way, the decimation of public housing continued, now seen as the last resort for the poorest segments of society rather than as a valuable resource for all.

A look back across the past four decades confirms that neoliberalism never had much to do with economic efficiency and much more with pure and simple ideology: While the divestment of public housing stock was justified with the need to reduce government spending, in the long run, the shift to subsidizing the private rental market has seen an increase in spending, not a decrease. For example, under Margaret Thatcher's notorious "right to buy" program, which allowed tenants of public housing to acquire their unit from their local council at a steep discount, the British government has sold property totaling 47 billion British pounds to this day; meanwhile, it spends around 16.5 billion British pounds each year on housing benefits.[17] In Italy, inefficiency within the public administration—itself also a consequence of disinvestment—motivated further cuts to public spending, fueling a vicious circle that turned out to be quite functional for presenting the free market as a solution to the shortcomings of state welfare.

A NATION OF HOMEOWNERS

As the myth of homeownership spread around the world, the cost of housing increased. Beginning in the mid 1990s, as Mario Draghi, then Director General of the Italian Treasury, was enacting radical reforms and privatization programs that were aimed at ensuring Italy's membership in the eurozone starting in 1999, the annual number of housing units sold rose sharply in Italy, almost doubling until 2008.[18] As a result of the restructuring of the Italian financial system homes truly began to be understood as financial assets: Whereas in industrial capitalism, companies used their fixed assets, such as real estate, as collateral for loans for purposes of production, now companies began to create special purpose vehicles to which they conferred their real estate assets, obtaining capital not as means of production but for incrementing profitability for shareholders. This mechanism relies on a steady increase of real estate values boosted by state programs subsidizing homeownership, as well as by bank loans at low interest rates. It is no coincidence, then, that in 1998, the Italian government abolished rent control, triggering a sharp increase in rents and property values; between 2000 and 2007, home prices in Italy increased by almost 40 percent.[19]

Over a period of 30 years, between 1971 and 2001, the proportion of housing occupied by renter households in Italy as a percentage of total available housing declined dramatically, from about 40 percent to 16 percent.[20] Since 2008, thanks to digital platforms such as Airbnb, a further share of the already scarce private residential stock has been converted into more profitable short-term holiday homes. Today, close to half a million rentals are available in Italy via the platform.[21] This has hollowed out entire urban districts, especially in the city centers, where homes are increasingly bought as assets and often left empty, or only temporarily inhabited by tourists. Those Italians who do own property have a trump card: Unlimited rent-seeking from real estate is now socially accepted and viewed as a legitimate substitute for declining salaries.

FIG.2
Completed in 1984, the 986 meter-long block on the southwestern outskirts of Rome known as Corviale houses about 4,500 people. It was commissioned by the local chapter of the public housing authority *Istituto Autonomo Case Popolari* (IACP) and planned under the supervision of Mario Fiorentino. After decades of abandonment and neglect, Corviale is currently undergoing extensive renovation.

With short-term rentals like Airbnb, landlords' profits yield more, at the expense of long-term tenants. As of today, renting up to four homes as vacation homes yearlong is considered by the Italian law as a noncommercial activity and the income generated is taxed at only 21 percent—2 percent less than for the lowest income bracket. On the flip side, the mismatch between housing prices, rents, and income levels means that both the rental sector and the property ladder are no longer accessible to an increasing number of people who will not inherit property. The share of people aged 20 to 29 still living with their parents in Italy is therefore disproportionally higher than in most OECD countries, trailed only by Greece and South Korea.[22] Furthermore, according to INPS [Italian National Institute for Social Security], half of full-time workers in Italy have a monthly gross income of less than 2,058 euros.[23] Stagnating salaries and soaring rents constitute insurmountable obstacles to class mobility and to the emancipation of younger generations. Confronted with this scenario, it becomes painfully clear that the promotion of private *home* ownership was pivotal to the ongoing conservative revolution that has been eroding postwar welfare since at least forty years. Homeownership was promoted as a means of generating the cultural consensus needed to present the project of the richest members of society as being in the general interest, justifying the return and rise of sharp class inequalities. The latter are often exacerbated by other civil inequalities, as for example migrants—and their descendants—are much less likely to inherit wealth or property.

FIG.3
Saverio Muratori and Mario De Renzi's INA-Casa blocks in the Tuscolano quarter of Rome, 1953

From 1949 until the scheduled end of the national public housing program INA-Casa in 1963, almost 355,000 public units had been built across the country.

CONCLUSION

As of today, in Italy, there are no national policies for public housing in place, nor any coherent form of rent control for short-term leases. Renters and those in need of housing are exposed to the whims and structural limitations of local governments and authorities on a shoestring budget when it comes to housing security. The alternative to *public* housing is commonly referred to as *social* housing, i.e., housing built by private developers with

FIGS. 4–5
Alessandro Guida's 2017 photographic series *The Waiting City* presents a collection of unfinished properties in the shrinking village of Cagnano Varano, Apulia. The development of small plots of land into multigenerational properties is typically understood by households as a long-term investment intended to ensure that younger family members inherit property.

the aim of providing dwellings at an intermediate cost, usually with the aid of tax breaks and public funding. Social housing units are often let-to-buy, meaning that ultimately they are targeted at middle class buyers who can afford to get a mortgage and eventually disappear from the rental market. With virtually no public debate on the issue, a new housing emergency is on the rise. According to a 2017 estimate, 650,000 people were on the waiting list competing for the 850,000 public housing units remaining across Italy, of which, astonishingly, 55,000 stand empty because the local public housing companies in charge are structurally underfunded and unable—or unwilling—to undertake essential works of maintenance.[24] Conversely, since 2020, in an attempt to boost the economy, more than 60 billion euros have been generously distributed to landlords choosing to retrofit their properties in order to meet higher energy standards, de facto financing the renovation of private homes with public money, possibly leading to an increase in private rents in some cities.[25]

In October 2022, in Venice—a city whose exceptional struggles to resist the pressure of the touristic industry are well known—the independent research collective Ocio counted at least 2,208 empty dwellings among those owned by the two public housing agencies active in the city, ATER and Insula.[26] Many of these are in a state of permanent or semipermanent decay. As one of the most desirable global touristic destinations, Venice is often in the spotlight due to its exceptional geographical and economic circumstances. But in a country like Italy, whose economy is increasingly reliant on tourism, which systematically expels poor people from city centers, the case of Venice is no longer an exception; it is the norm. Italy badly needs a new public investment program in public—not social—housing. Accordingly, the maintenance of and care for the invaluable existing public housing stock should be at the top of any political force's agenda if it wishes to save Italy from its tragic destiny of becoming the empty representation of its past splendors and present failures.

1 See Istituto Nazionale di Statistica, *Audizione dell'Istituto Nazionale di Statistica, Dott.ssa Cristina Freguja, Direttrice della Direzione centrale per le statistiche sociali e il welfare, Ministero del Lavoro e delle Politiche Sociali, 6 settembre 2022*, 6, accessed March 1, 2023, www.istat.it/it/files//2022/09/Istat-Audizione-Politiche-per-la-Casa_06_09_22.pdf.

2 Ibid.

3 See *Legge sulle case popolari* [Public Housing Law], L. n. 254, Italy 1903.

4 See Vezio De Lucia, *Se questa è una città: La condizione urbana nell'Italia contemporanea* (Rome: Donzelli, 2006), 75.

5 See Giovanni Berlinguer and Piero Della Seta, *Borgate di Roma* (Rome: Editori Riuniti, 1960), 23.

6 See Paola Di Biagi, "La 'città pubblica' e l'Ina-Casa," in *La Grande Ricostruzione: Il piano Ina-Casa e l'Italia degli anni cinquanta*, ed. Paola Di Biagi, 2nd. ed (Rome: Donzelli, 2010), 11.

7 See Italo Insolera, *Roma moderna: Da Napoleone I al XXI secolo* (Turin: Giulio Einaudi, 2011), 202.

8 See *Disposizioni per favorire l'acquisizione di aree fabbricabili per l'edilizia economica e popolare* [Provisions to Facilitate the Acquisition of Areas for the Creation of Affordable and Social Housing], L. n. 162, Italy 1962.

9 See *Legge urbanistica* [Urban Planning Law], L. n. 1150, Italy 1942.

10 See *Piani Edilizia Economica Popolare* [Affordable Public Housing Plans], L. n. 167, Italy 1962.

11 See *Programmi e coordinamento per l'edilizia residenziale pubblica* [Programs and Coordination for Public Residential Construction], L. n. 865, Italy 1971; *Norme in materia di edificabilità dei suoli* [Rules on Land Suitability for Building], L. n. 10, Italy 1977.

12 *Equo Canone: Disciplina delle locazioni di immobili urbani* [Fair Rent: Ordering of Urban Property Rentals], L. n. 392, Italy 1978.

13 See Corte Costituzionale, *Sentenza 5/1980*, January 5, 1980.

14 See Federcasa, "Abitazioni sociali: Motore di sviluppo, Fattore di coesione," April 2014, 12–13, accessed March 1, 2023, www.senato.it/application/xmanager/projects/leg17/attachments/documento_evento_procedura_commissione/files/000/001/276/federcasa.pdf; for the law authorizing the sale of public housing units, see *Norme in materia di alienazione degli alloggi di edilizia residenziale pubblica* [Rules on Repurposing Public Housing Units], L. n. 560, Italy 1993.

15 See *Disciplina delle locazioni e del rilascio degli immobili adibiti ad uso abitativo* [Ordering the Lease and Cession of Property Used for Residential Purposes], L. n. 431, Italy 1998.

16 See *Housing and Community Development Act*, 12 U.S.C. 1706e, USA 1974.

17 See "Government expenditure on housing benefit in nominal terms in the United Kingdom from 2000/01 to 2021/22," *Statista*, November 4, 2022, accessed March 1, 2023, www.statista.com/statistics/283949/housing-benefit-united-kingdom-uk-government-spending; John Perry, "The Treasury has made £47bn from Right to Buy but we have paid a price in lost social housing," *Inside Housing*, March 23, 2021, accessed March 1, 2023, www.insidehousing.co.uk/comment/comment/the-treasury-has-made-47bn-from-right-to-buy-but-we-have-paid-a-price-in-lost-social-housing-70199.

18 See Giorgio Gobbi and Francesco Zollino, "Tendenze recenti del mercato immobiliare e del credito," in *Le tendenze del mercato immobiliare: l'Italia e il confronto internazionale* (Rome: Banca d'Italia, 2012), 17, accessed March 1, 2023, www.bancaditalia.it/pubblicazioni/collana-seminari-convegni/2013-0015/Atti_convegno_immobiliare_lug13.pdf.

19 See ibid.

20 See Salvatore Chiri, et al., "Tassazione delle abitazioni e mercato degli affitti," in *Le tendenze* (see note 18), 208.

21 See Francesco Luigi Milone, et al., "Airbnb e gli affitti brevi in Italia: le prospettive di un mercato in forte ascesa," *Agenda Digitale,* December 21, 2022, accessed March 1, 2023, www.agendadigitale.eu/mercati-digitali/airbnb-e-gli-affitti-brevi-in-italia-le-prospettive-di-un-mercato-in-forte-ascesa.

22 See Boris Cournède and Marissa Plouin, *No Home for The Young? Stylised Facts and Policy Challenges*, ed. OECD Directorate for Employment, Labour and Social Affairs, 2022, 4.

23 See *Relazione annuale del presidente: XXI rapporto annuale*, ed. INPS (Rome: July 2022), 8.

24 See "La pratica della Mediazione Sociale nell'attività di gestione del patrimonio ERP: Risultati dell'indagine rivolta alle Aziende Casa associate a Federcasa," ed. Federcasa, 2018, accessed March 1, 2023, cms.federcasa.it/download.aspx?id=ae2f36f4-905f-4ab5-8716-d0d1e16e7bea.

25 "Enea, non si arresta la corsa del Superbonus 110%: a fine ottobre detrazioni per oltre 60 mld," *Il Sole 24 Ore*, November 7, 2022, accessed March 1, 2023, www.ilsole24ore.com/art/superbonus-enea-a-fine-ottobre-detrazioni-oltre-60-mld-AEMJ6rEC.

26 See "Lo Stato Degli Alloggi Pubblici non Assegnati a Venezia," *Osservatorio ClvicO sulla Casa e la Residenza*, October 22, 2022, accessed March 1, 2023, ocio-venezia.medium.com/lo-stato-degli-alloggi-pubblici-non-assegnati-a-venezia-aggiornamento-2022-bee156b8db99.

INHABITING VENICE

The Squatting and Maintenance of the Casette Neighborhood in Giudecca

Chiara Buratti and Laura Fregolent
in conversation with Mirko Gatti
Photos: Giovanna Silva

FIG. 1
In this photographic series, Giovanna Silva captures the everyday reality of the working-class neighborhood Casette, on the island Giudecca. The Casette (lit.: little houses) were built in the early 1940s by the now-defunct local Istituto Autonomo Case Popolari. Today, the majority of dwellings are owned and managed by the local public company ATER.

Chiara Buratti is an activist with Assemblea Sociale per la Casa (ASC, or Social Assembly for Housing), a grassroots organization that has been fighting for the right to housing in Venice for years. ASC works with residents to restore and maintain abandoned public housing units, offering an alternative to fleeing the city's soaring rents. We met her at Laboratorio Occupato Morion, a self-governing, occupied community center, where we were joined by Laura Fregolent, professor of urban planning at Università IUAV di Venezia, to discuss the maintenance of public housing, the rental market, tourism, and the right to inhabit Venice.

MIRKO GATTI:

In the 1960s and 1970s, developers in West Berlin tore down one turn-of-the-century residential block after another in the name of urban renewal. As the urban fabric of the city center was gradually being replaced, evicted residents were typically offered apartments in newly built large-scale housing projects on the city's outskirts. The resulting social tensions gave rise to a dedicated squatters' movement, especially in the district of Kreuzberg. Different models of political activism formed within the movement, often very distinct from one another. One notably successful practice that emerged in the late 1970s was the so-called *Instandbesetzung*—a play on the German words *Instandsetzung* [maintenance] and *Besetzung* [squatting]. These groups not only squatted abandoned buildings that were left to decay, they also fixed them up and maintained them; as a result, what had started as illegal occupations often came to be tolerated by the administration. Many of these squats even came to be legally recognized. The turnabout in the city's urban policy strategy engendered by the movement is best reflected by the landmark 1984–87 International Building Exhibition (IBA Berlin). The IBA formalized the concept of Instandbesetzung by funding the restoration of several historic Kreuzberg housing blocks, which would otherwise have been demolished and which went on to become symbols of participatory urbanism. [For more details on the Instandbesetzung movement, see the essay by Andrej Holm in this issue.] Assemblea Sociale per la Casa has adopted a similar strategy in Venice, an approach you call "autorecupero." Chiara, tell us about ASC. How did it come about? And what exactly does autorecupero mean?

CHIARA BURATTI:

Assemblea Sociale per la Casa started operating in Venice in the late 1990s, inspired by the experiences and struggles of Venetian and non-Venetian activists in the city. The idea originated here, in the Laboratorio Occupato Morion, a squat run as a social, cultural, and political hub since 1990. We're a very mixed group. Many of us had moved to Venice to study and have since built lives here, which we don't want to give up. Rising prices are forcing more and more people to move to the mainland. Of course, people have been talking about the depopulation of Venice forever. But in recent years, partly because of big structural changes in the tourism industry caused by the digital platform economy, rent has become impossibly high for many Venetians. But there's another side to it that doesn't get as much attention: Venice has a large—massive, even—public housing stock, which has been mostly abandoned and left to decay. In light of this, ASC's mission is twofold. We want to take action against the rent crisis and also to denounce the abandonment of public housing, pushing for that housing to be renovated, maintained, and assigned to residents who want to stay in Venice but have difficulty accessing the housing market. This was the motivation for the first occupations. The squatters then began a process of autorecupero, or "self-recovery," meaning that they do all the internal renovation work themselves, at their own expense, with support from ASC. ASC runs on a collaborative model, allowing for the sharing of knowledge, skills, and resources. These range from everyday life experiences to useful information on the legal and bureaucratic aspects of eviction law to specialist help from electricians or plumbers who know how to bring old systems up to code. For years now, ASC has been collaborating with other local organizations, in particular with Rebiennale / R3B, which has been pushing for a circular economy approach to reusing waste materials from the Biennale, promoting an idea of social and environmental sustainability. A lot of the Rebiennale / R3B materials end up in the squats and are used for building furniture or doing small repair work.

MIRKO GATTI:

In addition to other occupied buildings, for example in Santa Marta, ASC has been squatting the Casette, a public housing estate on the island of Giudecca, since 2013. The Casette were built in the early 1940s by the local Istituto Autonomo Case Popolari (Autonomous Institute for Public Housing, or IACP). Today, they're owned by the Azienda Territoriale per l'Edilizia Residenziale della Provincia di Venezia (Housing Authority for the Province of Venice, or ATER). These are apartments with the most basic fittings. Chiara, you live in one of them. Can you tell us how the idea of squatting the Casette came about?

CHIARA BURATTI:

The Casette are nine small blocks, with three or four floors each. They're arranged in four rows, with all apartments facing an interior courtyard. They were officially named the Case Minime, or "Minimal Houses," but they've only ever been referred to as the Casette—little houses. Residents whose families have lived there for generations talk about the construction starting before the 1940s, and how their grandfathers came home from the Second World War and moved in with their families despite the buildings not being finished. They completed the works themselves. In a way, you could say they were already doing a kind of

FIG. 2
Out of 120 units, about 40 have stood empty for decades. They are considered uninhabitable because even minor maintenance works are not being carried out due to structural underfunding.

FIG. 3
In cooperation between members of ASC, residents, and the Berlin-based association ConstructLab, small interventions will be carried out as part of the German contribution to the Architecture Biennale 2023, repairing the social infrastructure of Casette to support the community in its struggle for the right to housing.

FIGS. 4–5
Since 2013, members of the grassroots organization Assemblea Sociale per la Casa—in cooperation with legal tenants and homeowners—have squatted some of the empty units and taken care of renovation works themselves and at their own expense. The residents collectively take care of the maintenance of common areas.

FIG.6
Assemblea Sociale per la Casa runs on a collaborative model, allowing for the sharing of skills and resources. A gazebo at the center of the courtyard is used as a place of conviviality, as well as for regular assemblies.

CONSTRUCTLAB PARTICIPATORY WORKSHOP AND URBAN INTERVENTION

The design-build collective ConstructLab emerged primarily out of a collaboration of five architects from the Parisian collective EXYZT, who squatted the French Pavilion at the Biennale Architettura 2006. Their experience with the Biennale and the activation of public space in Venice make them an ideal partner for participatory collaborations with the city's population, as well as for neighborhood care, repair, and maintenance. In Casette, a neighborhood on the island of Giudecca shaped by the local, welfare-oriented squatters' community centered around Assemblea Sociale per la Casa (ASC), ConstructLab are developing a gazebo in the outdoor space, a notice board, and several mobile carts containing either a kitchen, a printing workshop, or a tool kit. Their goal is to strengthen the collective infrastructure of ASC and the local residents, as well as to support them in their struggle for the right to the city and the right to housing.

autorecupero. The courtyard is public, open to anyone, but the blocks are enclosed by a low perimeter wall on three sides. Once you step through the entrance arch, it feels like you've entered somewhere halfway between a public space and a community space. But by the early 2000s, seventy years on, many flats were empty and falling apart. We're talking here about housing built during fascism, with poor quality materials, when Mussolini's policy of autarky, or self-sufficiency, was in full force and resources were scarce. For many years, units were not reassigned after original residents had left because ATER didn't want to pay the huge costs involved in making them habitable again. There are about 120 homes in the estate, around 40 of which have stood empty for decades. The others are mostly inhabited by residents assigned to their units a long time ago, who are elderly by now. Other units have been sold off by the administration over the years through right-to-buy programs, meaning that the current owners often inherited them from original occupants. Many of the families have lived in Giudecca for generations. When ASC became interested in the neighborhood, one of the first things to emerge was the frustration of long-term legal residents. Many of them brought up the lack of maintenance in common areas, which ATER no longer takes responsibility for. These grievances can often seem unimportant, like the failure to fix a leaky pipe or to change a light bulb in the stairwell, but for elderly residents these things aren't trivial at all. The first time we went to the Casette, the residents gave us a guided tour of the neighborhood. They pointed at the buildings and began to tell us about the state of abandonment: "There's four empty apartments here, six there, another one there. An empty one below me and another next door to me. I can't heat my home properly because I'm surrounded by empty apartments." Right away, there was clearly a tremendous willingness to engage with us on this topic, and so in 2013 we sprang into action. We squatted 18 apartments, and we did so publicly, even notifying the papers. We wanted to join forces with the residents and make a public condemnation. Our goal wasn't just to secure a roof over the heads of members of ASC, but—more importantly—to fight against the desolation of Venice, starting with securing networks of care and social support.

MIRKO GATTI:

How does one join Assemblea Sociale per la Casa?

CHIARA BURATTI:

Exactly as the name suggests: by coming to our assemblies. Historically, the political struggle for the right to housing originated in working-class neighborhoods—all of them, not just the Casette—in particular through public assemblies. Our first gathering in Giudecca had one of the biggest turnouts we've ever seen. We were over 100 people, including affected residents, members of ASC, and others who simply supported the cause and wanted to share their experiences. Many of the people who turn to us have been evicted for falling behind on rent, or because their fixed-term rental contracts with private landlords came to an end and now they're struggling to find housing they can afford. Many are on the list for public housing, but the waiting times are too long. Not, as you might think, because there is no housing, but because before the existing units can be assigned, they have to be renovated. ATER is chronically underfunded and is no longer able (or perhaps no longer willing) to foot the bill for renovation works. Since the 1990s, there's been a total disinvestment at the national level. As a result, local authorities, even those with the best of intentions, no longer have resources at their disposal. [For more information on the history of Italian housing policies, see the essay by Sarah Gainsforth in this issue.] Until a couple of decades ago, there used to be a shared sense that workers had a right to housing. But that's completely vanished as the process of deindustrialization moved forward. Nowadays, housing is seen first and foremost as a financial investment, like a piggy bank. Today's housing policies don't respond to the needs of citizens anymore, but to the interests of the free market. And, from the market's point of view, a citizen without any state-provided housing alternative is a highly lucrative business opportunity.

MIRKO GATTI:

In Venice, the Casette are not an isolated case. According to a survey conducted by the Osservatorio CIvicO sulla Casa e la Residenza (Civic Observatory on Housing and Residence, or OCIO), there are around 2,200 empty public housing units in the city.[1] This is a jaw-dropping figure, especially in a place where the influx of tourists has inflated rents beyond all proportion. Laura, when were all these public housing units built? And why are they now empty?

LAURA FREGOLENT:

In fact, the right to housing for the most disempowered societal groups is a concept strongly rooted in this city's history; it's a tradition that dates back to the times of the Republic of Venice. Since the Middle Ages, public housing has been a common instrument of social policy in the city. Starting in 1903, public housing in Italy was built by the local chapters of the IACP, which you already mentioned. After the Second World War, public housing construction was massively expanded by the INA-Casa program, which was eventually replaced by a public housing fund known as Gescal (Gestione Case per i Lavoratori, or Workers' Housing Management). This fund was abolished in 1998 as part of a series of measures to implement neoliberal policies which no longer considered providing housing to be a public responsibility but something best left to the market. But as I like to say, the market only cares about the market. You can't expect it to act like a welfare institution. And so, from the mid-1990s onward, the IACPs were replaced by a whole slew of public housing management companies at the regional and provincial levels. This means it's not about welfare institutions anymore but about profit-oriented companies, who behave accordingly. In Venice, the public housing stock is owned partly by the City of Venice and partly by ATER. Together, they control almost 11,000 public housing units, which is around 8 percent of the total housing stock in the city—and much higher than the national average. Multiple factors, both historical and social, have led to the abandonment of the public housing stock. Some of it is just bad management, but, as Chiara pointed out, we can't place all the blame on the individual managing bodies. Rather, this is the result of decades of structural disinvestment at the national level. Forty percent of Venice's existing public housing stock was built pre-1940 and is in desperate need of renovation. But the costs of renovation work in this city are sky high, essentially for logistical reasons. How are local authorities supposed to manage costly refurbishments of all these homes when they've been systematically underfunded? Too often, the answer to this question has been that they should sell some units to fund the refurbishment of others—a drastic solution completely devoid of long-term thinking. In this context, finding new creative forms of reactivating the existing public housing stock, such as the autorecupero proposed by Assemblea Sociale per la Casa, is all the more urgent.

MIRKO GATTI:

Even if ASC's motives are undeniably noble, squatting public property remains an illegal act. Are there any plans in Venice to institutionalize the autorecupero process, similar to what the International Building Exhibition achieved in Berlin?

LAURA FREGOLENT:

Yes, there have been attempts. The previous administration tried to incentivize it, but it didn't go well. The terms were too restrictive. In the name of ensuring safety standards, they would only allow selected companies to carry out renovation work. This was a departure from the idea of autorecupero in the literal sense of the word, and it didn't help with keeping the costs down. All costs had to be borne by the assigned tenant, that is by an economically disadvantaged person often not in the position to afford such specialized services. It was certainly an interesting initiative, but it should have been more flexible about housing allocation and financing, and allowed for more informal approaches, over longer periods of

time, perhaps organized through some kind of cooperative.
Another issue is the profound change in the makeup of Italian society over recent decades. Residential buildings, particularly in the post-war period, have been built with a certain kind of nuclear family in mind, made up of two parents and their children. But families have changed dramatically, and we all know this is no longer the norm. Lives are less linear and families are increasingly diverse, as are the people applying for public housing. There are traditional families, of course, but also elderly people, single mothers with children, and young people struggling to enter the job market. We've also seen a huge increase in that gray area of people who earn too much to qualify for public housing, yet not enough to afford rent at market rates. These are all groups with complex housing needs, to which the response has been far from adequate. Cooperative or shared living spaces could be one way to meet these new and emerging needs. Increasing the amount of spaces shared by multiple parties is also a great means for public administrations to save money, as they allow for cutting costs without compromising on the quality of design or materials. The whole way we conceptualize housing needs to be reinterpreted, as does the idea of what it means to *live* somewhere, to *inhabit* a place. In this sense, inhabitation is a vast cultural project.

MIRKO GATTI:

Chiara, what's the relationship like between ASC and public institutions?

CHIARA BURATTI:

For us, ATER is first and foremost a negotiating partner. That is also the reason why the occupations don't happen in secret. On the contrary: They are public, transparent, and are always accompanied by an offer to talk with the institutions. What we want is to sit down with them and discuss potential new models for provisioning and administrating housing. For example, we'd like cooperatives to be eligible for public housing, too. It's with this in mind that we self-report to the authorities. We disclose every occupation and pay a monthly minimum rent. These voluntary payments are accepted by ATER. In this way, even if the squatting is illegal, we've established a clear line of communication with the managing body. In the beginning, the discussions between ASC and the public administration were very productive. At one point, we almost reached a formal recognition of our autorecupero strategy. It all went up in smoke in 2014, when both ATER and the Venice city council were placed under the control of external commissioners after a series of corruption scandals. It was quite the paradox: We were the squatters, but they were the ones under investigation. ATER remained under external management until 2018, and for several years we had no point of contact. Between 2018 and 2020, the president of ATER was Raffaele Speranzon, currently a Senator for the right-wing extremist Fratelli d'Italia party. He was replaced at ATER by Fabio Nordio, from the right-wing Lega party, who in 2022 put up for sale no less then 983 public housing units.[2] Unsurprisingly, we've had some trouble getting the conversation restarted. But we're not giving up. Regardless of the political leanings of the administration, dialogue with the institutions is vital. In June 2017, after we occupied the regional headquarters of ATER, we managed to secure a meeting with the regional Councilor for Social Welfare, Manuela Lanzarin, who is also a member of the Lega party. But since then, it's been constant rejection. There's a total lack of political will to deal with these issues.

MIRKO GATTI:

The journalist Sarah Gainsforth would say it's not a lack of political will, but that in fact the housing issue has been tackled all too well—simply in ways that systematically undermine the right to housing. In her book *Abitare Stanca*, Gainsforth writes that "Italy is a country of property owners thanks to so-called affordable housing schemes, subsidies and tax benefits, as well as targeted public policy and funding … Private home-ownership has been used as an instrument to ease class struggles and tackle social inequalities that were increasingly threatening the interests of financial and economic elites; it has enabled the restoration of such interests and the financialization of the domestic sphere … From this perspective, one could say that housing policies have been successful."[3] Indeed, according to the latest estimates from the Italian National Institute of Statistics, 80% of Italians are homeowners, a figure significantly higher than in most other European countries.[4] Many Italians also own a second home, or even a third. In many cases, these are family homes passed down from generation to generation. In touristic cities, second homes are often relied on for income, and profits from these rentals have soared massively in recent years thanks to the arrival of digital platforms such as Airbnb. But in a country where wealth is increasingly created from property and labor is devalued, people who do not own a house become marginalized. Tourism, combined with widespread property ownership, increases inequality and paradoxically becomes a hurdle for upward social mobility. From this point of view, Venice is a dispiriting trailblazer. Everyone talks about the tourists in Venice, but perhaps not enough about the landlords. Laura, who are the owners of all these holiday homes on Airbnb? And what regulations are in place with regards to short-term rental platforms?

LAURA FREGOLENT:

Italy has a widespread and longstanding culture of private home ownership, in place since

FIG.7
In an initiative by another Venetian grassroots organization, Rebiennale/R3B, some of the materials left behind each year by the Biennale have been used for building furniture or doing small repairs inside the Casette's squatted apartments.

FIGS.8–11
Apartments squatted by Assemblea Sociale per la Casa with built-in furniture made from reused materials salvaged from the Biennale.

well before the neoliberal policies of the 1990s. Look for example at the notorious INA-Casa program we have already talked about; it was approved in 1949 and is one of the largest and most important affordable public housing schemes in Italian history. The scheme saw the construction of approximately 355,000 housing units in 14 years—a number inconceivable today. These were intended for rental, but the plan already provided tenants with the option to buy the homes they lived in over time. In Venice today, a lot of people rent out their homes or their second homes to tourists, it's true. But I think it's important to distinguish between small-scale landlords renting out a single unit, and large commercial landlords who buy up property after property and rent out hundreds of units, removing them from the residential housing market. Public authorities need to introduce rules to contain this phenomenon. Again, the market only cares about the market, in all respects. Therefore, the task of a public administration is to intervene in order to address the imbalances the market creates. Ultimately, the problem is that the public administration lacks a long-term vision; there still is no plan for Venice that isn't based almost entirely on exploiting the city as a touristic destination. Certain recent real estate transactions must be read in this light. For example, the sale of Palazzo Diedo to billionaire investor Nicolas Berggruen, who already owns the imposing Casa dei Tre Oci on Giudecca. Palazzo Diedo was previously a primary school, then a judicial office, and it will now become a private art foundation. Another example is the large-scale redevelopment of the Procuratie Vecchie on Saint Mark's Square, at the hands of the insurance and asset management provider Generali Group. The complex has recently been refurbished by David Chipperfield Architects and turned into a privately managed cultural space. And then there are the former Sanguinetti barracks on San Pietro di Castello, which were part of a convent before being turned into state-owned barracks. Nowadays, the complex—which also includes the church of Sant'Anna—is still home to eight families. But the global real estate investment group ARTEA wants to turn it into a hospitality complex that is specifically targeted at corporate clients, for business conferences and similar events, plans which would require the families to leave their homes. In all these cases, the city council has approved the change in use. We're talking about very different, very high-profile projects, and I don't mean here to criticize them individually. But if we zoom out to the city as a whole, it's clear that we can recognize an economic and cultural vision that hinges entirely on tourism and events. So, I sympathize with the individual Venetian landlord who rents out their family home to tourists in order to fund their

partigiani
NO
GRANDI NAVI
SYSTEM CHANGE, NOT CLIMATE CHANGE
FCK NZS

child's education, and I can also sympathize with the person who sells an inherited property, because those kinds of properties can be very difficult and expensive to maintain. But I certainly do not feel represented by a public administration whose short-sighted vision—and actions—seem hell-bent on the cultural exploitation and commodification of the city. Finally, to return to your question about short-term rentals: All tourist accommodation, including accommodation rented out through Airbnb, must be registered and display an identification number on the doorbell. So there are some regulations already in place, but what is lacking is a cap on the overall number of tourist rentals, and thus on the number of homes removed from the long-term residential housing market, especially through digital platforms. The Alta Tensione Abitativa (Housing High Tension) collective has proposed regulations that would go in this direction, limiting the number of short-term rentals in order to contain their negative impact on long-term housing.

MIRKO GATTI:

It is the city administration itself that is actively pursuing an economy based solely on cultural events and tourism. At the same time, the municipal council has adopted a new strategy supposed to tackle the excessive flow of visitors: Starting in mid-2023, non-residents will have to buy an entry ticket to access the city. They will have to download a QR code onto their phones and show it to law enforcement officers when asked. What do you think of this drastic measure?

LAURA FREGOLENT:

I'm against it. In some ways, the entry ticket is just a tax. The vaporetto ticket could also be seen as such, given that non-residents have to pay up to 10 euros for a single ride—in this sense, we can see it as tourists cross-financing public transport. I do understand that maintenance costs in this city are enormous, and we need to finance them somehow. But if this is the aim, I'd like the political authorities to intervene and say: "Let's introduce a tax to finance a specific municipal service," for example, providing public housing. But for a city to be closed off—meaning that those who cannot pay are excluded—this is the exact opposite of my idea of what a city should be.

CHIARA BURATTI:

I think the entry ticket reveals a clear contradiction. On the one hand, new neighborhoods entirely dedicated to hospitality are springing up around the railway station and on the mainland, attracting huge international investors; Treviso airport is signing new contracts with low-cost airlines. Meanwhile, on the other hand, the entry ticket is being touted as some great solution to the tragedy of mass tourism. But an entry ticket should be for museums, not cities. And it is there that the paradox becomes clear: The entry ticket was never meant as a solution to the problem of tourism, but as a way to capitalize on it! The ticket contributes to the very logic of commodification of the city that it pretends to counter. If there is a real will to save Venice from mass tourism, then we need to look for answers elsewhere. For example, in structural policies that guarantee economic and social stability to all local residents.

LAURA FREGOLENT:

... And here is where Assemblea Sociale per la Casa comes in. They aren't simply fighting for the right to housing, but for the right to inhabit the city. The right to inhabit Venice, a city that has always been open and that has never been afraid of cultural contamination or people passing through.

1 Figure compiled in July 2022 by the Osservatorio CIvicO sulla casa e la residenza (OCIO), based on Insula records provided by the municipal council group Verdi e Progressisti (Greens and Progressives), as well as ATER records provided by the regional group Il Veneto che Vogliamo (The Veneto We Want). Accessed March 30, 2023, ocio-venezia.medium.com/lo-stato-degli-alloggi-pubblici-non-assegnati-a-venezia-aggiornamento-2022-bee156b8db99.

2 Mitia Chiarin and Francesco Furlan, "Acquisto case Ater nel Veneziano, le dieci domande e risposte per saperne di più," *Nuova Venezia*, July 21, 2022, accessed March 30, 2023, nuovavenezia.gelocal.it/venezia/cronaca/2022/07/21/news/acquisto-case-ater-nel-veneziano-le-dieci-domande-e-risposte-per-saperne-di-piu-1.41592375.

3 Sarah Gainsforth, *Abitare Stanca* (Florence: Effequ, 2022), 15.

4 See Istituto Nazionale di Statistica, *Titolo di godimento dell'abitazione (in affitto o di proprietà)* (Type of property right associated with the housing unit (rented or owned)), accessed March 30, 2023, dati.istat.it/Index.aspx?DataSetCode=DCCV_TITGODABIT.

CAUTIOUSNESS AS A SPATIO-

Text:
Andrej Holm

FIG. 1
Squatters renovating the rear building of Bülowstraße 52 in Berlin's Schöneberg district in February 1981. The apartment building had been left to decay by its owner, the nonprofit housing association Neue Heimat, whose failure to provide maintenance had induced the tenants to move out.

POLITICAL PRINCIPLE

The mantra of new construction is often recited as the solution to the housing crisis, despite the challenges it poses for climate policy. But from a social and ecological perspective, the prevailing orientation toward new construction is leading toward a cul-de-sac. Looking back at history makes something obvious: Approaches to creating the city of tomorrow already exist. Berlin's squatters' movement of the 1980s and the city's program of "cautious urban regeneration" can be considered prime examples of how a city grown over centuries can use its resources mindfully. But the concept of "cautiousness" adopted by these movements extended far beyond a material, resource-efficient approach to urban renewal; its impact was achieved above all through the momentum of democratization processes and by prioritizing social issues.

Considering the variously intertwined social and ecological crises we are facing today, the demolition of apartments and buildings that are still usable has been discredited. The massive squandering of resources involved in disposing of existing building material, the additional soil sealing effected by new building projects, and the gray energy leveraged even for buildings with exemplary energy efficiency are all at odds with sensible climate policy goals. Critical architects are justified in demanding a new culture of retrofitting, one that shifts the focus of building activity toward strategies of conversion, maintenance, and the energy-efficient renovation of existing buildings, to the point where the construction of new buildings and the designation of new development areas would be severely restricted—or sometimes outright prohibited.

Seeking solutions in the existing building stock, however, is the opposite of commonplace housing policy strategies. In Germany, officials in most major cities as well as at the newly created Federal Ministry for Housing, Urban Development and Building see the answer to rising rents and housing scarcity in the massive expansion of new construction. Nationwide, 400,000 housing units are slated to be built annually, 20,000 of which in Berlin.[1] The goal of this building program is to alleviate the pressures of the rental market by expanding supply. However, as various rent policy activists and organizations have been arguing for years, rents in new buildings exert only a limited influence on rents in the overall housing market, and are almost always too expensive to alleviate the urgent, widespread social need for housing.[2]

In other realms of society, we are, albeit slowly, adopting strategies of degrowth: fewer flights, less energy, less driving, less meat. So why—in times of raw material shortages, supply chain issues, and rising interest rates, no less—would the best solution for housing, of all industries, be to encourage as much unchecked growth as possible by significantly expanding the construction market?

Typical housing policy strategies, framed within a growth-focused narrative of progress (as in the current governing coalition's slogan, "Dare More Progress"),[3] are tied to a neoliberal set of values that emphasize the ideology of ownership and an increasingly technocratic style of politics. In practice, the mantra of "Build, build, build!" represents a closing of ranks between political leaders who have no interest in challenging the market, and investors who hope to earn money by building apartments. Both the Federal Government and numerous cities bank their housing policy on forming alliances between housing companies and housing interest groups. In addition to representatives from the real estate and construction industries, groups such as tenant organizations, welfare associations, environmental advocates, as well as cooperative and religious housing providers are invited into consultations. Yet, despite the broad spectrum of interest groups represented, these alliances have not succeeded in providing any impetus for more socially and ecologically sustainable housing and building policies. While such consultations regularly yield reports with a range of sensible suggestions, the latter are seldom translated into binding agreements or programs.

From a climate and social policy perspective, the fixation on growth and the corresponding alignment of political decisions with the interests of private profit, as well as the reliance on alliances instead of democratically legitimized decisions represent a dead end. A look at Berlin's history of urban regeneration, on the other hand, demonstrates how resource-effective, socially oriented, and simultaneously democratically legitimate urban development can actually be brought about.

THE PROMISE OF MODERNIZATION AND THE POLITICS OF AREA REDEVELOPMENT

The idée fixe of new construction is by no means a new phenomenon. Particularly in the heyday of postwar Fordist urban development, massive building programs were implemented in industrialized nations across the globe, encompassing both the construction of single-family homes in suburban settlements and large-scale apartment construction within expansive housing estates. In the spirit of the Athens Charter, the functionally separated city was regarded as the ideal image of urban development and as the answer to the squalid living conditions of 19th-century industrial cities. The newly designed cities and settlements did not merely symbolize social modernization and the promise of prosperity associated with it; in their conjunction of mass production with mass consumption, they also lived up to the principles of Keynesian welfare economics. Single-family homes in US suburbs, structured around individual transportation, have become emblematic of the automotive city, but in Europe, too, an orientation toward new construction and a fixation on cars converged into guiding principles for urban development during the second half of the 20th century.[4]

FIG. 2
In a former children's sewing machine factory in the Wrangelkiez area of Berlin's Kreuzberg district, squatters use the building's own carpentry workshop to repair windows, doors, and support beams as well as for larger renovations such as the greening of the roof.

Fordist models shaped urban policy in West Berlin as well, although they ran into unusual circumstances due to its enclosure by the Berlin Wall, which set physical limits on suburbanization and urban expansion with the unusual geographical and political constellation it yielded. In East Berlin, urban planning in the postwar years focused on reconstruction and later, in the mode of socialist urban expansions, on the construction of large housing estates in the periphery. Instead, West Berlin's urban development policy from the 1960s onward hinged on the process euphemistically known as "Flächensanierung" [area redevelopment], which required tearing down thousands of turn-of-the-century apartment buildings and replacing them with new ones. Paradigmatic for this phase of demolition and redevelopment are neighborhoods like Rollbergviertel in the district of Neukölln or the redevelopment zone Brunnenstraße in the district of Wedding. Going hand in hand with a cultural devaluation of Berlin's historical working-class districts and planning priorities set on the automotive city, demolishing the city's old housing stock was not only regarded as an inevitable process, but as a grand promise of modernization.

But by the early 1970s, resistance to the large-scale demolition mandated by Berlin's redevelopment policies was growing. In reports and research papers published by experts, critical questions were leveled at prevailing redevelopment practices, highlighting negative aspects of the demolition of entire neighborhoods.[5] These critiques focused less on the aesthetic perspective of losing the historical urban fabric and instead on issues such as housing costs, the destruction of established social networks, and the socio-psychological consequences of disrupting emotional attachment to the built environment.

The critics took cues from similar developments in other countries and cities. Witha Sauter and others demonstrated through their studies of urban redevelopment in Stuttgart, for example, how moving into modern neighborhoods with newly built housing stock was linked to an enormous financial burden for renters.[6] Similarly, the work of Marc Fried and Chester Hartman, which looked at demolitions in major US cities to examine the social and psychological consequences of displacement, was invoked in the Berlin discussions and used to level a relatively far-reaching critique of the demolition plans developed by the Berlin government, known as the Senate.[7] Particularly in Kreuzberg, in the SO36 zip code area, a broad resistance to the city's redevelopment plans developed in the 1970s. Already designated as a redevelopment zone in 1963, a large share of the turn-of-the-century historical building stock was slated to be torn down and replaced by new buildings and a highway. After ownership was transferred to a redevelopment agency and the technical issues were clarified in the late 1960s, the first buildings began to be demolished around Ritterstraße, Prinzenstraße, and Wassertorplatz without consulting the affected residents.[8] However, the next phase of the "redevelopment," known as redevelopment zone Kreuzberg South (SKS), faced tough resistance. When, during a public panel discussion held within the framework of a competition for the redevelopment zone, 90 percent of the building stock was declared to be "unsuitable for renovation" and therefore ready to be demolished, the outrage of local residents boiled over.[9] To defuse the conflict, administrators organized further events and

FIG. 3
In February 1981, Kurdish-Turkish women and their children, who suffer multiple disadvantages on the housing market, squatted Kottbusser Straße 8 in Berlin's Kreuzberg district together with employees of the Treff- und Informationsort für Frauen aus der Türkei e.V. (Meeting and Information Association for Women from Turkey). The upper banner reads "Hakkimizi aldik" (We have asserted our rights ourselves).

permitted the formation of a council of affected residents. But the officials' goal of dampening protest by institutionalizing the conflict backfired spectacularly. Activists used the formal nature of the council to make further demands, generate press coverage, and call for meetings with responsible authorities, since the redevelopment agency's advisory services had little to offer them. The final report issued for the redevelopment zone in 1991 characterizes these times as follows:

"In 1970, GEWOBAG [the city-owned housing company; editor's note] set up an advisory office in Ritterstraße 111, where the remaining tenants were to be funneled toward replacement apartments. There was no opportunity to advocate for the modernization of their apartments and against demolition. Residents were also offered no opportunity to find an affordable apartment … in one of the area's existing historical buildings. Renters had to accept an apartment in one of the 'social' buildings offered them, alongside rent increases of up to 300–400%."[10]

To prepare for the area's redevelopment, buildings listed for demolition were systematically thinned of renters and often stood empty for years. Across Berlin, as part of the urban redevelopment program, more than 35,000 apartments were vacated by 1980. In Kreuzberg alone, an estimated 10,000 apartments stood empty.

As a sort of interim solution, apartment owners and property managers deliberately rented out apartments to families of Turkish origin—not only because, as "Gastarbeiter" [guest workers], they were expected to be staying only temporarily, but also in the hope of creating something akin to a white flight of German renters leaving the neighborhood. In the first years after the identification of the redevelopment areas, the number of migrants in Kreuzberg alone rose to over 25,000 (some 15 percent). The majority of these residents hailed from Turkey and experienced highly precarious housing conditions, since the buildings slated for demolition were no longer maintained even at the most basic level.

INSTANDBESETZUNG AS A CATALYST FOR CHANGE

Vacancy, displacement, continued neglect: The Kreuzberg district became a symbol for all the downsides of the promise of modernization behind Berlin's urban regeneration program—and increasingly a site of resistance. Emerging from the orbit of the extra-parliamentary opposition and the social unrest of the late 1960s, the "Professional Action Group for Regional Planning" of the left-wing association Republikanischer Klub (Republican Club) founded an "Office for Urban Regeneration and Social Work" in 1968 with the aim of formulating counter-strategies to the prevailing planning regime, keeping residents informed through a local publication with a print run of 10,000 called *WOHN-INFO* (Housing Information), and organizing counseling sessions.[11] But it was not only political activists who sought to organize resistance against demolition. Debate groups also emerged in church parishes to address the urban redevelopment plans and to host public discussion panels. Klaus Duntze, pastor of St. Martha's church on Glogauer Straße, offered insights into the precarious living conditions in his parish and its surrounding neighborhood with his 1972 book *Der Geist, der Städte baut* [The Spirit That Builds Cities], positioning himself squarely against top-down urban regeneration.[12] At his behest, the 1974 annual meeting of the Association of German Architects (BDA) took place at St. Martha's, turning the attention of the profession on Kreuzberg's exceptional situation.[13]

The municipal administration responded to the pressure from civil society and to the growing criticism of its redevelopment plans by expanding opportunities for participation and by incorporating affected residents into the formal structures of the redevelopment regime. Opportunities for "Civic Participation in the Preparation and Implementation of Urban Redevelopment Measures" were enshrined into law and increasingly used by district authorities and city administrators in charge of the redevelopment zones in Kreuzberg to manage the criticism levied at the planned schemes.[14]

Together with the parish, various officials initiated a competition to develop "Strategies for Kreuzberg," inviting residents and experts to develop "approaches to formulating new goals" and "feasible programmatic recommendations" aimed at improving living conditions, reducing existing social conflicts, and expanding citizen participation.[15]

Yet, extending representation to affected groups did not prevent the advocates of large-scale demolition from proceeding with their plans. In early May of 1977—in the middle of the ongoing competition—the demolition of a fire station in Reichenberger Straße was initiated, even though proposals had been drafted for the station to be converted into a neighborhood center. In reaction, teenagers occupied the building to give weight to their demands for preservation. Lobbying by the "Strategies for Kreuzberg" committee led to a temporary halt of the demolition work. But although an appeal to the demolition permit was still pending at Berlin's Higher Administrative Court, and although a meeting of the project commission was imminent (where the conversion proposal was supposed to have been considered), officials decided otherwise: On the morning before the meeting, the city council ordered the building to be demolished under heavy police protection.[16] The hastily enforced demolition also structurally weakened the "Strategies for Kreuzberg" committee. A later report from the group summarizes: "The conflict over the fire station led to deep mistrust between civil society representatives and project commission administrators."[17]

The citizen activist group SO36, which had been founded in the meantime along with other organized interest groups in the neighborhood, became increasingly determined to act independently to save their neighborhood from demolition, no longer banking on the government's proposals for "participation." In their campaign against vacancy in the neighborhood, activists from the group realized that neither appeals to building owners nor complaints to the district office would ever lead to buildings being rented out again, so in February 1979 they decided to publicly squat two apartments on Görlitzer Straße 74, protecting the buildings from demolition and forcing over 40 apartments to be rented out.[18] The term they used to describe their activism, "Instandbesetzung" [a portmanteau of "Instandsetzung," i.e., maintenance, and "Besetzung," i.e., squatting; editor's note], emphasized the restorative and caring approach included in their notion of occupation and proved effective both within the neighborhood and in media coverage. Seeking to increase the pressure of their protest against demolition and vacancy, in late November 1979, SO36 organized the squatting of another building, this time at Lübbener Straße 3. Their slogan, "Lieber Instandbesetzen als Kaputtbesitzen" (Better occupy and preserve than own and squander), became the movement's motto, connecting the desire to preserve historical building stock to the fundamental question of property ownership in a capitalist housing economy. Against this backdrop, Instandbesetzung can be understood as a practice that deliberately decouples a building's use from the property rights attached to it, as philosopher Daniel Loick describes in greater detail in *The Abuse of Property*: "The meaning of the squatters' call goes beyond its agitational use in concrete housing struggles; namely, it directly refutes the basic dogma of property theory, according to which the use of a thing presupposes ownership of it. The practice of repairing through squatting [Instandbesetzen] denies this connection, and, on the contrary, assumes that property is not a condition but rather an obstacle to use."[19]

Spurred on by the partial success of the squatting movement and emboldened by its positive coverage in the media, other groups began adopting the practice. In March 1979, a group of unemployed youth squatted a vacant industrial loft at Waldemarstraße 33, followed

FIG. 4
The increasingly criminalized squatters' "weapons": screws and screwdrivers, hammers and nails, nuts, caulk, fire extinguishers, respirators.

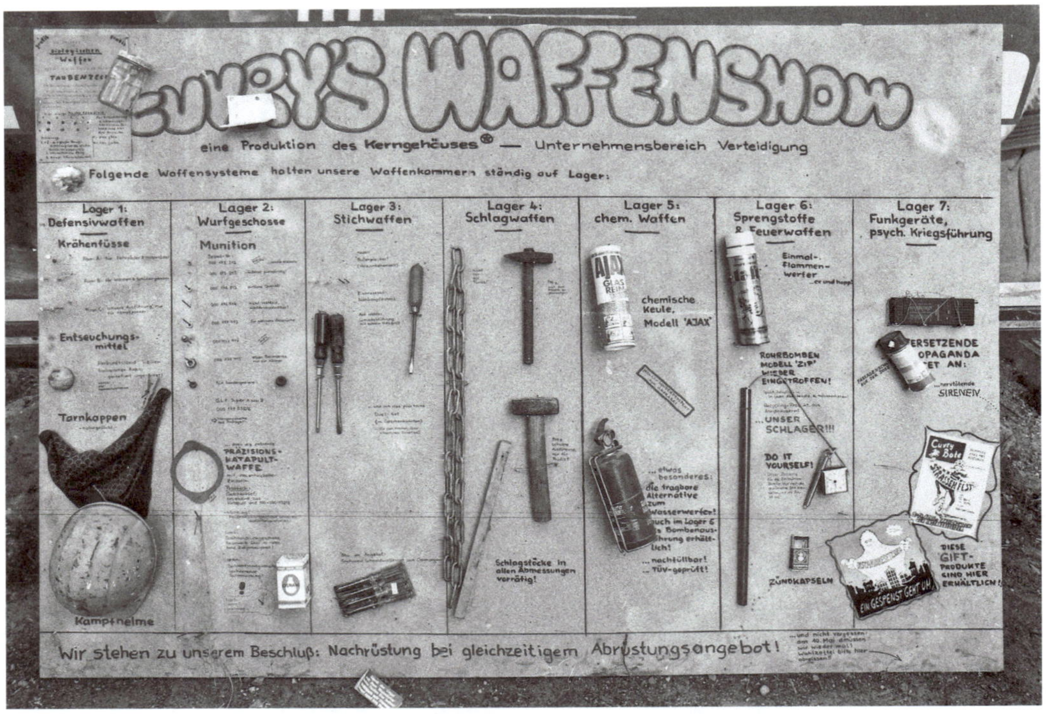

in September by a building at Leuschnerdamm 9. More occupations followed in early 1980, leading to the founding of the "Squatters' Council K 36," which helped squatters coordinate shared projects among individual buildings and organize mutual support for publicity work, negotiations with the city government, and reactions to pending evictions.[20] Throughout 1980, further buildings were occupied and the circle of participants and supporters in the race to save the historical building stock grew apace: A representative from the Social Democratic Party, Walter Momper, who would later go on to serve as Mayor of Berlin, supported a case of Instandbesetzung on Fichtestraße, while an occupation of two buildings on Forster Straße involved Turkish families for the first time.[21]

The way the squats were treated by property owners and officials, however, varied greatly. Whereas in some cases leases were signed, other buildings were cleared by the police. After one particularly controversial eviction in December 1980, a major street battle broke out between the police and members of the broader squatting scene. Around the same time, the Berlin Senate came under fire after it acted as guarantor for a risky loan taken out by real estate developer Dietrich Garski; when the latter defaulted, the city was suddenly liable for over 100 million Deutsche Mark. In early 1981, the governing coalition, made up of social democrats and free-market liberals collapsed as a result. The institutional legitimation crisis, compiled by the limited power of the interim city government that followed, spurred more building occupations. A further reason was the widespread assumption that the elbow room for squatting—as well as its legal recognition—would be diminished by the anticipated electoral victory of the conservative Christian

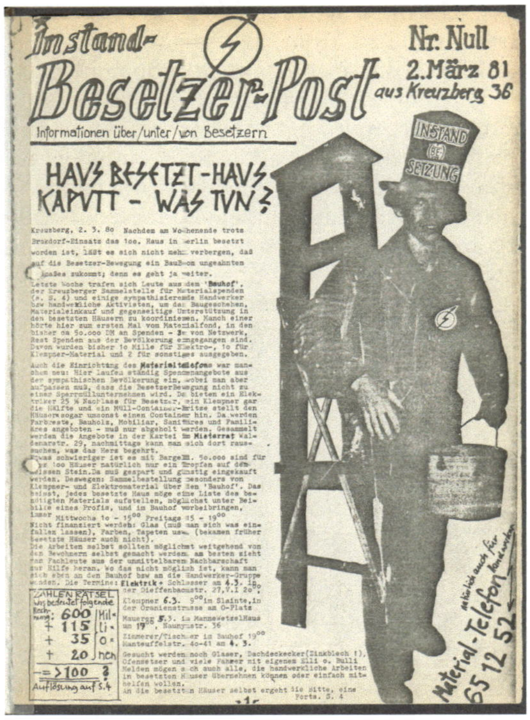
Instand-Besetzer-Post
Nr. Null
2. März 81
aus Kreuzberg 36
Informationen über/unter/von Besetzern
HAUS BESETZT-HAUS KAPUTT - WAS TUN?
Material-Telefon 65 12 52

FIG. 5
Instand-Besetzer-Post, no. 0, March 1981

As the movement's main medium of communication, the *Instand-Besetzer-Post* (mail for squatting and maintaining] provided information on renovation techniques and the housing struggle's recent developments. This issue announced a newly established telephone number for coordinating the donation of construction materials and referring tradespeople.

Democrats. By May 1981, the number of occupied buildings across Berlin had risen to 165, of which 80 were located in Kreuzberg alone. Despite later evictions, about 100 squats would obtain legal recognition, nearly all of which were repaired and modernized by the residents themselves with the aid of support programs facilitating self-building, based on German postwar laws encouraging the practice in the absence of institutional or personal economic means.[22]

In addition to preserving the urban fabric, one of the main goals for residents was implementing self-determined forms of living together. Self-administrated renovation work, cooperative housing typologies, the mixing of residential and working space, and in many cases collective contractual arrangements (for instance, cooperative or framework rental agreements reached through nonprofit associations) are among the ways of living that can be understood as reversals of the Fordist model of urban development. Instead of functional separation, standardization, and individuation, what unfurled in occupied and subsequently legalized buildings opened up possibilities for flexible use, diversity, and collectivity.

Parallel to the squats, "Strategies for Kreuzberg" also reached its conclusion, leading to 15 individual projects receiving financial backing from the city government to carry out renovation works approved by residents. The original demolition plans were not only rejected in the proposals issued at the end of the participatory process; they had become practically unimplementable due to the high degree of politicization surrounding the demolition schemes after the various occupations. Former supporters of area redevelopment were forced to admit that, in Kreuzberg, other approaches to urban regeneration needed to be sought.

FIG. 6
The Bauhof (builder's yard) in Manteuffelstraße 40/41, occupied in 1981, served as a storage and distribution hub for building materials and supplies, which were organized by means of a card index located at the tenant council's office.

THE INVENTION OF CAUTIOUSNESS

To consolidate this newly suggested path toward urban renewal without demolition in Kreuzberg, two redevelopment zones, namely SO36 and Luisenstadt, were selected as proof-of-concept areas and added to the program of the city's International Building Exhibition (commonly referred to as IBA '87) in the category "IBA Alt," focused on old housing stock (for more information on IBA '87, see the contribution by Gristoph Grafe and Tim Rieniets in this issue). That section's planning director, Hardt-Waltherr Hämer, played a crucial role in elaborating the concept of "cautious urban regeneration" for historical urban areas. He delineated twelve principles of urban development which harkened back to the demands of the citizen activist group "Strategies for Kreuzberg" and the Instandbesetzung movement, making their demands the formal basis for administrative action in redevelopment zones. Some of the principles[23] include:

"Renewal must be planned and realized—retaining building stock—with current residents and tradespeople."

"Planners should agree with residents and tradespeople about the aims of renewal measures, and technical and social planning should go hand in hand."

"Careful alteration of ground plans should also make new forms of living possible."

"Renewal of flats and houses should take place step by step and be gradually supplemented."

The cautious urban regeneration that became the hallmark of IBA Alt between its inception in 1981 and the fall of the Berlin Wall can be seen as a complete about-face in West Berlin's urban renewal policy. Instead of top-down redevelopment carried out in the interests of large housing companies and predicated on displacing residents, the cautious regeneration program was defined by extensive participation processes, prioritization of preservation measures, and with the interests of residents in mind.

The new paradigm of urban renewal can be characterized as a triangle of "structural cautiousness" (preserving built substance and gradual renewal), "social cautiousness" (caution vis-à-vis the social structure, i.e., an orientation toward residents' interests and an avoidance of displacement), and "procedural cautiousness" (comprehensive involvement of residents in planning processes).

In the course of Kreuzberg's urban renewal, many of the hopes vested in the process of cautious regeneration were ultimately fulfilled. A majority of the urban fabric was preserved, and participation processes gave a comparatively large degree of creative freedom to affected residents, groups from civil society, and block councils. All the while, the existing population was largely preserved, as later studies have demonstrated.[24] Ulla Terlinden cites the final report on the Kottbusser Tor redevelopment from the 1990s to illustrate how "a working-class population has largely reestablished itself there, corresponding to the Kreuzberg average as it existed before the regeneration."[25] The final study on Kreuzberg's redevelopment also analyzes the fluctuation rate to draw conclusions on housing satisfaction. In buildings "which were renovated and modernized with renter coordination and support, that is in consultation with tenants,"[26] the latter stayed in their units considerably longer than in other buildings. The highest degree of housing satisfaction was discovered in formerly squatted buildings, where residents, within the framework of subsidized self-building programs, were able to decide on renovation and modernization measures independently.

According to the final report, however, one thing remains unclear: "Whether this positive outcome can be maintained after the status as redevelopment area is lifted and the threat of private modernization and rising rents returns."[27] Berlin's urban renewal policy in the following years triggered a massive wave of gentrification in the former East. This deferred displacement pressures in Kreuzberg in the immediate aftermath of the subsidy program's expiration, but before long conflicts surrounding housing issues were back on the agenda. "Cautiousness" can therefore not be regarded in simple programmatic terms as an altered planning culture. Rather, it owes its success to massive interventions by the state, making available a broad palette of options for legal intervention, extensive subsidy programs, and a far-reaching suspension of private actors on the housing market.

MAINTENANCE: USING HISTORICAL EXPERIENCE FOR THE FUTURE

The history of cautious urban regeneration should not only be viewed as a professional toolbox for built fabric–preserving renovation strategies and as a democratic conception of planning, but rather as a *model of transforming urban policy* that can yield lessons for the social and ecological challenges facing us in

FIG.7

IBA Alt's pilot project for the so-called Block 103 integrated exemplary measures of ecological urban renewal into the renovation and maintenance of the buildings, such as gray water cleaning and reuse, solar panels, and facade greening.

S.T.E.R.N. (Gesellschaft der behutsamen Stadterneuerung Berlin), ed., *Schritt für Schritt – Behutsame Stadterneuerung in Kreuzberg: Eine Wanderausstellung,* Berlin 1990, 63.

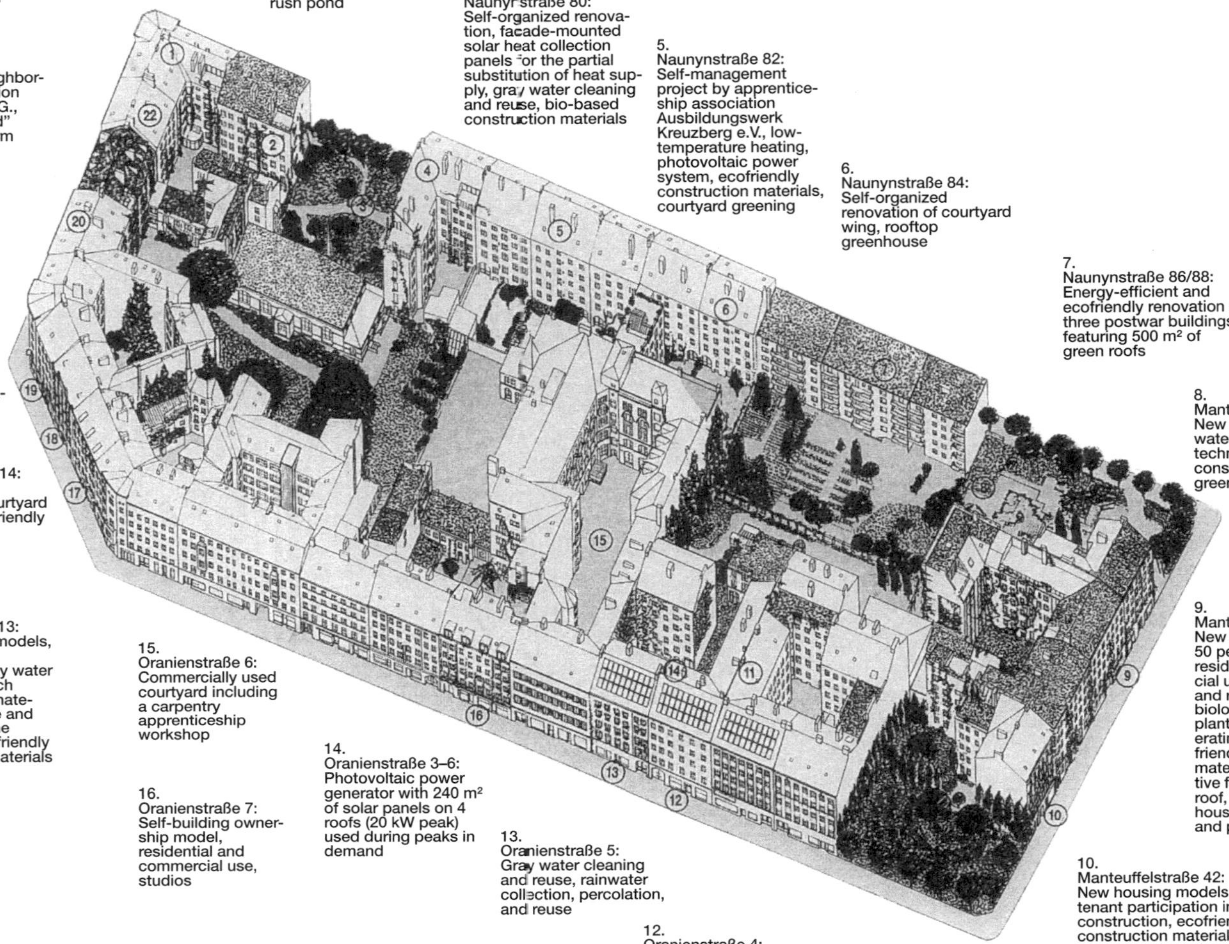

1 See Sozialdemokratische Partei Deutschlands (SPD), BÜNDNIS 90/Die Grünen und Freie Demokratische Partei (FDP), *Mehr Fortschritt wagen: Bündnis für Freiheit, Gerechtigkeit und Nachhaltigkeit. Koalitionsvertrag 2021–2025* (Berlin, 2021), 69; see also Presse- und Informationsamt des Landes Berlin, *Wohnungsneubau und bezahlbares Wohnen: 'Berlin schafft 16.500 Wohnungen trotz Krise,'* press release, December 14, 2022, accessed March 8, 2023, www.berlin.de/rbmskzl/aktuelles/pressemitteilungen/2022/pressemitteilung.1275218.php.

2 In Germany, the 13 million people (approx. 7.7 million households) at risk of poverty are provided with only little more than 1 million social housing units with fixed rents and occupancy requirements. Between 2007 and 2021, the required 10% share of social housing in new residential constructions, which accounted for an average of just under 25,000 completed social housing units per year, could not compensate for the nearly 70,000 units whose funding from earlier subsidy periods expired annually. See Pestel Institut, *Bauen und Wohnen in der Krise: Aktuelle Entwicklungen und Rückwirkungen auf Wohnungsbau und Wohnungsmärkte* (Hanover, 2023); see also Guthmann, *Berlin Immobilien Report 2023*, accessed March 8, 2023, www.guthmann.estate/de/marktreport/berlin/.

3 SPD et al., *Fortschritt* (see note 1), 1.

4 Christa Reicher and Anne Söfker-Rieniets, "Die Nachkriegsära und ihre Leitbilder," in *Stadtbaustein Wohnen: Lehr- und Grundlagenbuch*, eds. eid. (Wiesbaden: Springer Fachmedien, 2022), 31–35.

5 See *Sanierung: für wen? Gegen Sozialstaatsopportunismus und Konzernplanung*, ed. Büro für Stadtsanierung und soziale Arbeit Berlin-Kreuzberg (Berlin, 1971); see also *Sanierungsfolgen: Eine Wirkungsanalyse von Sanierungsmaßnahmen in Berlin*, eds. Heidede Becker and Jochen Schulz zur Wiesch (Stuttgart: Kohlhammer Deutscher Gemeindeverlag, 1982); see also Gruppe Aktion 507, *Manifest der Gruppe 507: Kommt! Seht! Diskutiert! Ausstellung zu den Bauwochen am Ernst-Reuter-Platz: Diagnose zum Bauen in West-Berlin* (Berlin, 1968).

6 See Wolfgang Ehrlinger et al., "'Sanierung' macht die Mieter pleite," *ARCH+* 29 (1976), 13–17.

7 See Marc Fried, "Grieving for a Lost Home: Psychological Costs of Relocation," in *Urban Renewal: The Record and Controversy,* ed. James Q. Wilson (Cambridge: MIT Press, 1966), 359–79; see also Chester Hartman, "The Limitations of Public Housing: Relocation Choices in a Working-Class Community," *Journal of the American Institute of Planners* 29, no. 4 (1963), 283–96.

8 See Jürgen Enkemann, "Alternativen zur Kahlschlagsanierung: In den 1960er und 1970er Jahren keimte Protest gegen die Stadtplanung auf," *MieterEcho* 384 (2016), 4–7.

9 See ibid., 5.

10 SPAS (Verein für Sozialplanung und angewandte Stadtforschung in Kreuzberg Nord e.V.), *Abschlussbericht der Sanierung Kottbusser Tor P I, P V, P VI (Sozialplanbericht)*, vol. 1b, *Sanierungsabschluß-untersuchung: Sozialplanbericht; Sanierungsgebiet Kottbusser Tor Planungseinheiten I, V und VI* (Berlin, 1991), 56.

11 See Rote Pressekorrespondenz, "Überbaustrategie: Stadtsanierung in Kreuzberg," *Rote Presse Korrespondenz* 1, no. 4 (March 15, 1969), 9.

12 See Klaus Duntze, *Der Geist, der Städte baut: Planquadrat, Wohnbereich, Heimat* (Stuttgart: Radius, 1972).

the 21st century. Then, as now, the point of departure is a fixation on demolition (then) or new construction (now), seemingly without alternatives. Criticism, doubts, and demands for a fundamental revision were ridiculed, ignored, or denigrated as "radical attitudes." Conversely, the radical nature of free-market ideology and the dogma of perpetual growth were readily ignored or considered to be immune to questioning. And in the same way that, in the 1970s, area redevelopment was seen as the only path to urban renewal, today new housing construction is being declared as the only effective answer to the housing crisis. The recently defeated government in Berlin's City Hall made up of social democrats, the Green Party, and socialists, signed a coalition agreement in 2021, declaring: "The coalition pledges to make new housing construction and conversion a top priority in the city."[28] Instead of seeing the orientation toward new construction as one possible means to an end, new construction becomes an end in itself, the government's raison d'état.

Like other mantras and unchallenged convictions, hegemonic perspectives on housing and urban renewal policy are relatively resistant to argument or facts pointing the other way. In the 1970s and 1980s, Berlin's break with prior assumptions was made possible by three conditions. First among them is the persistent intervention of protest groups that coalesced against the demolition plans and, through a broad spectrum of activist tactics, publicly articulated discontent and materially challenged prior assumptions (through mass occupation of vacated apartment buildings). Furthermore, professional discourse (through familiarity with experiences of preservationist urban renewal on an international level) communicated knowledge of possible and realizable alternatives. And lastly, rifts within existing interest groups (in favor of area redevelopment), caused by the de facto failure of previous plans, provided additional leverage.

FIG. 8
Bauausstellung Berlin GmbH, ed., *Bausteine zur Selbsthilfe: Badeinbau,* Berlin, 1984

The *Bausteine zur Selbsthilfe* (Elements of Self-Help) was a publication series (this volume focusing on installing bathrooms) guiding the self-organized renovation of old buildings. It was published by the urban renewal working group's self-help appointee in the context of IBA Alt.

From today's point of view the "cautiousness" embedded in cautious urban renewal is therefore interesting not only as an urban planning strategy for handling existing housing stock, but also as a political principle that aligns itself with the interests of residents and breaks with prevailing patterns of urban policy. Successfully shifting housing policy toward a more sustainable and democratic model of urban development would require a few things: a strengthening of protest groups, the elaboration of alternate development plans accompanied by professionals, and a public debate about the contradictions of contemporary strategies. Amidst growing social movements, shifts in professional approaches, and ongoing political crises, it is imperative to develop strategies to effectively prevent further demolition, to envision practical alternatives, and to counter the inertia of political forces unflinchingly hurtling down the road of perpetual capitalist growth.

13 See Christa Kamleithner, "Aneignung versus Planung: 'Strategien für Kreuzberg' und der Streit um die Ausrichtung der ARCH+, 1975–77," in *Dokumente der Architektur* (2021), accessed February 1, 2023, beta.dokumentederarchitektur.de/analysis/Aneignung-versus-Planung-Strategien-fr-Kreuzberg-und-der-Streit-um-die-Ausrichtung-der-ARCH-197577.
14 Urs Kohlbrenner, "Umbruch in den siebziger Jahren: Grundlage und Modelle der bewahrenden Stadterneuerung," in *Stadterneuerung Berlin: Erfahrungen, Beispiele, Perspektiven,* ed. Senatsverwaltung für Bau- und Wohnungswesen (Berlin, 1990), 45–56.
15 Böttcher et al., "'Strategien für Kreuzberg': Bericht der Vorprüfergruppe und Stellungnahme der Projektleitung," *ARCH+* 37 (1978), 64.
16 See Bernd Laurisch, *Kein Abriß unter dieser Nummer: 2 Jahre Instandbesetzung in der Cuvrystraße in Berlin-Kreuzberg* (Gießen: Anabas, 1981), 24; see also Bürgerinitiative Feuerwache/Schornstein, *'Unser' Baustadtrat Kliem wohnt nicht in Kreuzberg – aber wir!* (Berlin 1977).
17 Böttcher et al., "'Strategien für Kreuzberg'" (see note 15), 65.
18 See Laurisch, *Kein Abriss* (see note 16), 34.
19 Daniel Loick, *The Abuse of Property*, trans. Jacob Blumenfeld (Cambridge: MIT Press, forthcoming 2023).
20 See Jörg Klitscher, "Der Häuserkampf in Kreuzberg," *Berlinische Monatsschrift* 6 (2001), 150–54.
21 Ibid.; see Ausstellungskollektiv Kämpfende Hütten: *Kämpfende Hütten – Urbane Proteste in Berlin von 1872 bis heute*, exhibition brochure (Berlin, 2016), 17
22 See Andrej Holm and Armin Kuhn, "Häuserkampf und Stadterneuerung," *Blätter für deutsche und internationale Politik* 3, no. 10 (2010), 107–15.
23 "The twelve principles of careful urban renewal," originally published in Hardt-Waltherr Hämer, "Careful Urban Renewal," in *Urban Renewal Berlin: Experience, Examples, Prospects,* ed. Senatsverwaltung für Bau- und Wohnungswesen (Berlin, 1990), 64–65.
24 See Matthias Bernt, *Rübergeklappt: Die 'Behutsame Stadterneuerung' im Berlin der 90er Jahre* (Berlin: Schiler & Mücke, 2003).
25 SPAS, *Abschlußbericht* (see note 10), vol. 2, *Zusammenfassung der Ergebnisse und Empfehlungen: Städtebaubericht – Sozialplanbericht* (Berlin, 1991), 31, cit. Ulla Terlinden, *Gesellschaftliche Modernisierung durch Stadterneuerung? Eine historisch-empirische Analyse sozialen Wandels und staatlicher Zielsetzungen an Beispielen* (Berlin: Technische Universität Berlin, 1992), 205.
26 SPAS, *Abschlußbericht,* vol. 1b (see note 10), 129.
27 Ibid., 129.
28 Sozialdemokratische Partei Deutschlands (SPD) Landesverband Berlin, Bündnis 90/Die GRÜNEN Landesverband Berlin and DIE LINKE. Landesverband Berlin, *Zukunftshauptstadt Berlin: Sozial. Ökologisch. Vielfältig. Wirtschaftsstark. Koalitionsvertrag 2021–2026* (Berlin, 2021), 8.

KOTTI & CO

Design Practices Between Care, Allyship, and the Fight for the Right to the City

Tashy Endres and Sandy Kaltenborn
in conversation

FIG. 1
The Gecekondu was erected on the southern part of Kottbusser Tor square by the tenants' association Kotti & Co in 2012 on public land. The structure, while technically illegal, is tolerated by the district of Friedrichshain-Kreuzberg.

The neighborhood and tenants' association Kotti & Co, founded in 2011, is shaped by its many members from migrant communities, and is considered the cradle of a new movement called "Stadt von unten" [city from below], which centers on tenants' rights. Kotti & Co's activist practice derives from the idea of caring for the urban environment and defending the right to housing for the inhabitants at Kottbusser Tor square (affectionately called "Kotti" by locals), in Berlin's Friedrichshain-Kreuzberg district, who often face multiple kinds of marginalization simultaneously. Today, Kotti & Co plays an important role in urban policy discourse and the struggle for the socially minded and democratic provisioning of housing and against displacement and racism in the city. Tashy Endres (an active member of Kotti & Co from 2012 to 2017) and Sandy Kaltenborn (cofounder of Kotti & Co) reflect on twelve years of activism and on the group's protest strategies from a political, spatial, and design point of view. They also discuss the emancipatory potential of the underlying processes driving the formation of collectives and knowledge, while also critically addressing the role of institutions and professions in the project of comprehensive social transformation.

SANDY KALTENBORN:
If we look back on the history and political achievements of Kotti & Co from today's vantage point, what do you feel were the crucial successes?

TASHY ENDRES:
Our successes become apparent if we remember what the situation was like when we started: 12 years ago, rents started to rise dramatically, and when it came to social housing, the rent for over 50 percent of apartments was above the Berlin rent index. Global capital was increasingly flowing into the German real estate market in the wake of the 2008 financial crisis, massively intensifying speculative investments in housing in the city. Many people with low incomes were forced to cut back on basics such as food, health, or clothing to pay the skyrocketing rents. However, among the broader general public, there was virtually no debate about rent increases, social housing, or the right to the city. Even tenant associations told us there was nothing that could be done on the question of social housing. Today, it is safe to say that we have achieved just about everything we set out to do: The Employment Office now carries the cost of real rents for unemployed people living in social housing projects, rent increases in social housing throughout Berlin have been stopped (2015), and ownership of the social housing stock at Kottbusser Tor has been once again municipalized (2021). That has saved an awful lot of people from losing their homes. On the back of previous struggles and the experiences gained, we provided a lot of inspiration for the new movement on urban policymaking. Many of our threads were then woven further: As early as 2016, for example, we led a

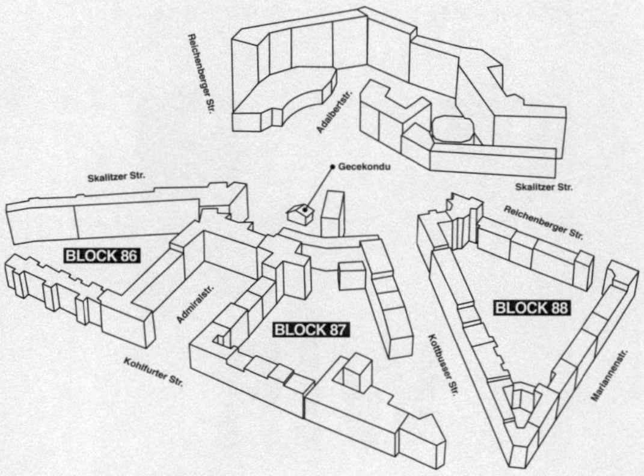

FIG. 2
1970s social housing blocks around Kottbusser Tor square

The majority of the buildings south of Kottbusser Tor was privatized when the city's largest housing agency GSW was sold off to an international consortium (made up of Goldman Sachs's Whitehall Street investment fund and Cerberus Capital Management) in 2004. The housing stock was acquired by Deutsche Wohnen SE in 2013 and finally re-municipalized in 2021.

campaign for the constitutionally permissible socialization of Deutsche Wohnen, a publicly traded corporation which was also the owner of the lion's share of the apartments at Kottbusser Tor. Derided back then, the question was put to the vote in a State referendum I co-initiated as the logical next step after Kotti & Co, "Deutsche Wohnen & Co enteignen" [Expropriate Deutsche Wohnen & Co], five years later—and the result was emphatic: In 2021, a majority of voters in Berlin decided in favor of expropriating private, profit-oriented housing companies of all housing stock exceeding 3,000 units to guarantee the availability of housing. It was not least the broad politicization of the topic, reaching deep into mainstream society, which ensured that Berlin's government, known as the Senate, transferred the social housing units on the southern end of Kottbusser Tor back into municipal ownership shortly before the referendum was to be held. The tables have turned; look who's smiling now.

SANDY KALTENBORN:
From the outset, we were forced to conceptualize our protest on a large scale, reaching over and above Kotti. The actual site-specific problems persuaded us to interrogate the political system of providing social housing in Germany. The conference called "Nichts läuft hier richtig" [Nothing's going right here], which we hosted in 2012 together with housing policy experts from Berlin's State parliament, helped us get a better understanding of how the underlying structure of social housing in Germany is anything but socially sustainable. It is in fact a system of "interim social use," with private investors and housing construction companies benefiting from government subsidies and tax breaks to build apartments

that they can rent out at a high price once the mandatory period of rent control, known as social obligation, has expired. Our core topics and demands—the return of social housing to municipal ownership, the permanent continuation of various forms of rent control for units build by private investors, the democratization of State-owned housing agencies, and later on the issue of expropriation—were therefore only the logical consequence of what had already taken place on the ground at Kotti in an exaggerated manner in terms of problems and needs. If we talk about successes, I also find it important to mention how, in our case, all manner of different knowledge spaces and practices came together at a very early date and went on to generate a creative protest design with its multifaceted tactics and strategies that went hand in hand with the site-specific conditions. Back then, there was strong interaction and cohesion between individual tenants who had lived here for generations, sometimes spread across different floors and often with a migration history dating back to the so-called "Gastarbeiter" [guest workers] period when Germany's booming postwar economy was heavily dependent on recruiting millions of foreign workers. As we were holding our first Kotti & Co assembly at Café Südblock on the southern end of the square, with our different bodies marked by so many different biographies and the corresponding notions of what it means to be in the world, it became clear that we were not hosting a traditional activist get-together. From the beginning, we were forced to be mindful of finding a language that had to be mediatorial, tentative, and inclusive. We created a space between ourselves that had us relating to one another with a curiosity and a mutually productive dependency that went beyond the issue of rents. Alongside that core topic, talks focused a lot on experiences of migration, racism, and other, more worldly and everyday matters. The shared (hi)stories about the Berlin squatters' movement of the 1980s from a perspective of migration gave us new viewpoints and an "informal knowledge" about the right to the city. We then gradually integrated this into our communicative outreach and distilled it into political language.

TASHY ENDRES:

I only joined Kotti & Co in 2012, during the squatting of Kottbusser Tor. How did you effectively structure the organization in the first few months as a tenants' organization?

SANDY KALTENBORN:

In our first year, we began with small public protests and occasional events, collected signatures, distributed flyers, and established links with political parties. We met once a week and enjoyed backyard parties together. All these activities were a source of invaluable experience as to how we functioned together as a group. Nevertheless, we were soon forced to recognize that nothing had moved substantially. It was the period of worldwide squatting of public spaces to create political pressure from the bottom up and with broad social backing: There was Tahrir Square in Cairo, the Movimiento 15-M in Spain, Occupy Wall Street, etc. On Whitsunday weekend in 2012, we hosted a street party directly on Kotti's southern plaza. Under the cover of the party, we squatted the square. We placed a platform made of stacked freight pallets on the floor, put a few benches and chairs around it, gathered there at 6 p.m., and said: "We'll stay here as long as it takes to solve the problem." This laid the groundwork for the space we called Gecekondu, which, in Turkish, refers to an informal settlement and literally means "built overnight." A structure erected between dusk and dawn on public land was protected under Ottoman law.

TASHY ENDRES:

When I joined you on the day of the sit-in, I was immediately won over by the fact that it was not a "traditional" protest. The public square was not occupied by and for a closed group. It was not some fear-inspiring place but an open space where people cared for one another. A samovar stood in the middle, and everyone was invited to have a cup of tea and chat. The neighborhood gathered, a perfect representation of its social stratification. I felt that the promise of a new kind of community was in the air; not one based on us all being the same, but one that took its roots in the fact that we are all different and that we can turn that difference into our strength. This act of squatting created a space for participation and belonging on many different levels: You belonged if you prepared tea, if you gave a concert, if you took on a day shift or a night shift in the Gecekondu, if you came along to the rally. But you also belonged by simply gaining the confidence to drop by with complicated letters and helping one another work out the actual meaning behind the German legalese. Belonging, now that is something we do not frequently offer one another in a city … you don't become a part of this neighborhood and belong to it by virtue of a passport or a postal address; you belong by accepting it, respectfully listening to others, accepting and extending invitations, giving and receiving care. For all the conflicts that arose, that perspective of mutual care was always at the center of our protest. With the Gecekondu practice, knowledge and people who are often marginalized in Germany symbolically and literally seized the space they were entitled to, alongside their right to the city. The Turkish concept was key, but it was not a particular right for only a few, as we all joined up to create the Gecekondu—so, on the contrary, it actually demonstrated in its own way: "We are all here to stay!"

FIG. 3
In collaboration with political, scientific, and tenancy law experts, Kotti & Co was able to show, based on a building on Kohlfurter Straße, that the social housing projects have already been amortized multiple times over. Profits, however, have been privatized.

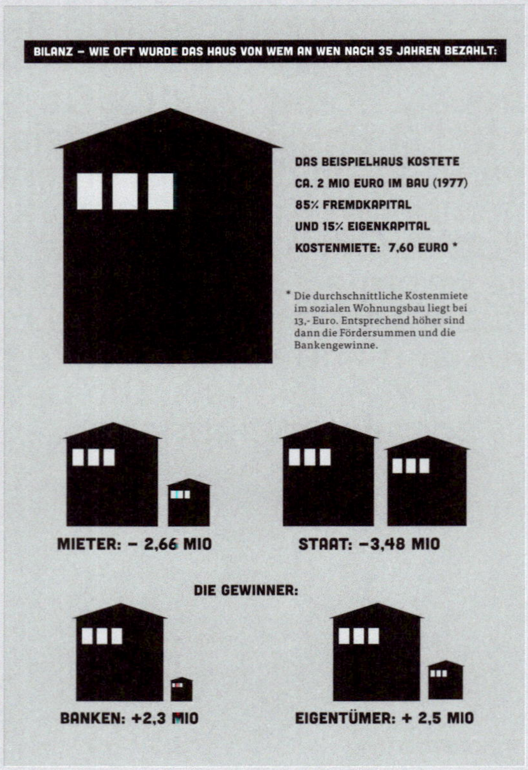

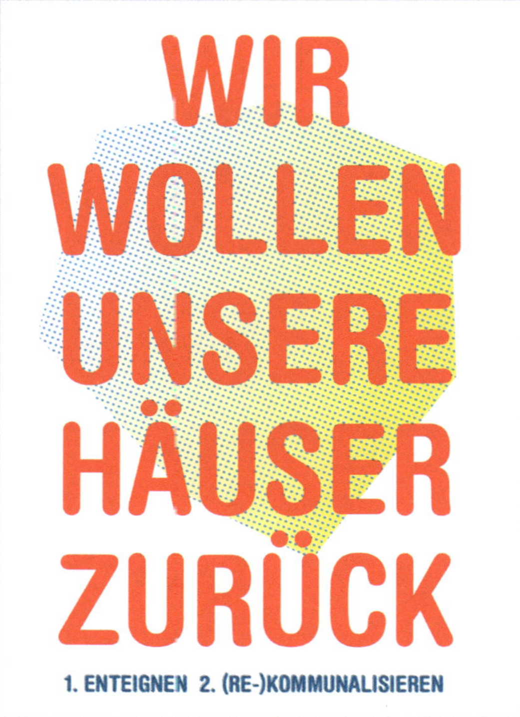

FIG. 4
In the run-up to the 2016 Berlin State election, Kotti & Co initiated a small campaign aimed at re-municipalizing the social housing blocks around Kottbusser Tor. The campaign subsided soon after the election, but was taken up by activists two years later and overwhelmingly approved by voters in a 2021 statewide referendum called Deutsche Wohnen & Co enteignen (Expropriate Deutsche Wohnen & Co).

FIG. 5
The initial sit-in in 2012

In their speech at the Gecekondu, founding members Jale Öztekin and Fatma Cakmak outline Kotti & Co's demands: a rent freeze for social housing, covering of real rents in social housing units by the Employment Office, a conference focusing on long-term solutions to the social housing sector's problems, and a recommunalization of the once privatized buildings around Kottbusser Tor.

SANDY KALTENBORN:
With this message as its core tenet, the squatting of the square was essentially a political act. But alongside the political protest we sought to express through the sit-in, everyone had to work to make certain the protest functioned and persisted. Making tea, disposing of garbage, cleaning, painting posters, hanging up banners, transporting things, etc. There was always something that needed to be done and which in the traditional sense was more a matter of reproduction work than protest activities. From the very outset, we emphasized that every activity was of equal importance. The everyday world was therefore at home in our protest, in the sit-in, and thus in our understanding of politics. The protest was a collective violation of the rules, a transgression. In a sense, everyone who gathered there became an ally. This strengthened the feeling of solidarity and, moreover, the leap out of everyday life somehow rearranged the logics of spacetime. It was a lot of work, but escaping our work and everyday stress was also very fruitful. The passing of time was different in this public space unburdened by any prior format. Because everyone had different ideas about how all the different things should look, and with everyone offering to give a hand, this spirit got translated into a space with an inviting feeling. This was neither purely activist nor academic knowledge, but instead a mixture in which a lot of informal, migrant, and also subaltern knowledge could be articulated. And I believe that this basic arrangement gave rise to what we once dubbed "multilayer protest," meaning different practices, activities and organizing strategies with which, in subsequent years, we attempted to increase the pressure on politicians on all conceivable levels and in different areas of society.

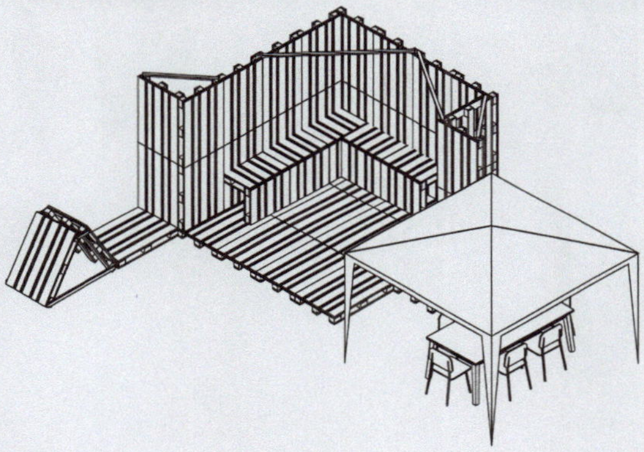

FIG. 6
The Gecekondu's base structure made from shipping pallets: It extended the neighborhood's living rooms into the streets and acted as a base camp for a 24/7 protest held in shifts. It also was a place for neighbors to socialize, have tea, and help with expanding the structure.

TASHY ENDRES:
I think it is important to go into some of the details about the role of the Gecekondu, as it almost always formed the spatial point of origin for all these processes of (self-)organizing: It was here that we came together as a neighborhood; it was here that we organized all sorts of things, from Halay dances against high rents and symphony concerts to Hip Hop battles; it was here that our 50 rallies started and ended; it was here that we welcomed innumerable activist groups from Berlin and all over the world with whom we had established links; and it was here that we offered free advice on tenancy laws and social welfare rights for the neighbors. That is how we were always up to date on the latest strategies by landlords and the Employment Office. Starting out from the Gecekondu, we organized neighborhood campaigns on the horrendous fixed costs and maintenance problems of apartment buildings to overcome the mutually-isolating logic of tenancy laws. Thanks to our community organizing practices, we were able to establish a network of contact persons in the various buildings. At a smaller level, this assumption of responsibility for the buildings preempted the democratic self-administration structures on which the return of buildings to municipal ownership hinged—and for which we campaigned on a more macroscopic level devising specific models based on participatory studies in the neighborhood. With these, as well as with our advisory work on tenancy laws and on social welfare rights, we were able to compile exact data on the real rent burden. This data allowed us to successfully campaign for the area around Kotti to be placed under statutory milieu protection by district authorities, a designation entailing

high hurdles for changing the size, amenities, and ownership models of housing units so as to protect the existing tenants and to limit speculative real estate transactions. The data also applied pressure on the Senate Department of Social Services and the Employment Office to take on the real rents for social housing. Years after having arranged the conference on social housing held at the Berlin State parliament, we were invited to take part in a Senate Committee of Experts on reforming social housing. And even if the brief for that Senate Committee pretty much echoed our description of the problems formulated long before, it was clear to us that the stitched-up proposals it put forward were not solutions. For that reason, we returned to Kotti and used the data from the Committee as background information for the 2015 State referendum on rent caps, for which we joined up with a broad alliance of tenants' associations to draft a law on the provisioning of social housing in Berlin. This pressure then led to a law capping rent increases for all social housing in Berlin, and steps to democratize the state-owned housing associations (e.g., by strengthening the tenants' councils and creating a public-law institution for housing supply, called Wohnraumversorgung Berlin or WVB). At the same time, we cooperated with numerous cultural institutions in the neighborhood, across Berlin, and internationally, and did an incredible amount of public relations work to influence the discourse around social housing, the right to the city, and against racism and gentrification. It was both necessary and fascinating to organize politically with people on all these levels—and sometimes well beyond the point of exhaustion for each and every one of us. From time to time, we had to take a break; and, chatting with neighbors over a cup of tea in the Gecekondu, we were reminded exactly why all of this was worth doing.

FIG.7
Second extension: The Gecekondu is enlarged with a makeshift container and reclaimed windows, enabling a continuation of the protest during the sit-in's first winter.

SANDY KALTENBORN:
How do you reflect on the Gecekondu and the processes of spatial production from an architectural perspective?

TASHY ENDRES:
What seems to me to be most worthy of emphasis is that it was our collective use which shaped the Gecekondu, and that is an important part of why it became this kind of engine of belonging. For the day on which we occupied the square, Stefan Endewardt, an architect and friend of ours, had designed a simple and unfinished structure made of freight pallets: a podium with two walls and two benches. It constituted an infrastructure, reduced to its load-bearing functions, open and unfinished, so that the neighbors could take it up and inscribe their needs, ideas, and acts of care into it. To keep us from getting wet, someone set up a huge parasol bearing the logo of Schultheiss, a Berlin brewery; because we needed more space, someone placed a couple of tents alongside it; because we wanted to serve tea, someone put up a cable running from the print shop through the tree to us so we could power the samovar and some fairy lights; and because people wanted to proudly show their neighbors how much the press reported on us, soon an entire wall was covered with newspaper clippings. Some activities were well coordinated in advance, others just followed the principle that, "if you want to do something, do it; and if you want to build something, build it." With each new day, the Gecekondu looked a little different. It could morph from a public stage for passionate speeches to an intimate living room for vulnerable chats between people who, until moments earlier, had been strangers. It was a design shaped by all of us and, in that sense, anarcho-democratic architecture. At the same time, it demonstrated very publicly what was at stake: our precious coexistence. That was more powerful and symbolic than any political speech. And it clearly demonstrated: We are not going to wait until you act, we're taking things into our own hands!

FIG.8
The Gecekondu's interior hosts a multitude of formal and informal gatherings, events, and parties, as well as free counseling on tenancy and social welfare rights.

SANDY KALTENBORN:
When the Gecekondu was converted for the approaching winter, the building—and with it the established processes—changed once again. How?

TASHY ENDRES:
In the summer, the Gecekondu with its two walls was an open structure, which made it easy for people to sit down and become part of the group. At some point, it simply got too cold to sit outdoors and we needed to convert things in a major way. A single container was

FIG. 9
Third extension: In line with the Gecekondu's beginnings as an open structure, the roof is expanded to reach out above the sidewalk. Additionally, a new facade consisting of reclaimed balcony doors is installed.

FIG. 10
The Gecekondu is open again for celebrations after its third extension, hosting festivities such as Iftar (daily fast breaking) during the month of Ramadan.

provisionally placed next to the Gecekondu. Various design ideas were floated and because I did not want to stymie those efforts, I initially kept silent about my being an architect. I had become part of the core group, but not because of my architectural background. When materializing the ideas proved to be more difficult, at some point I drafted a design proposal for how we could integrate the container and close the Gecekondu using a load-bearing structure and a facade made of recycled windows, while keeping it open and inviting. At first, everyone welcomed the proposal and put a lot of energy into carrying out the plan. But one week later, when those of us in the core group stood in the new Gecekondu, some were disappointed that we were only really able to heat the container but not the greenhouse-like structure made of the reused windows. It became clear that the classical media of the architectural field—floor plans, collages and discussions—had not sufficed to enable us to collectively understand the future space. As a group, we needed a 1:1-scale experience to develop the next steps in the design process. That is something that tends not to happen in most "participatory" planning processes, but it was precisely the precondition for us managing to balance our differences in the way we approach space. All of that also confronted me with my own architectural presumptions: I had previously worked for Lacaton & Vassal in Paris and had adopted their approach of creating large, greenhouse-like transparent volumes that can be opened and which enclose smaller, heat-insulated units. However, other people in the core group wanted more of a regular house, a unified space that can be heated like a living room. Ahmet Tuncer, who is also a member of the core group and had a lot of experience in interior construction to share from working on many different construction sites, suggested insulating everything. And as a result, a large part of the transparent skin of the building gave way to 30 centimeters of Styrofoam. Knowledge from academia and knowledge from the construction world do not often meet as equals when it comes to design issues. And this productive and exciting interaction gave rise to quite a unique building: The Gecekondu is not the easily-cleaned, anonymous multipurpose hall of tolerance in which anyone can do as they like as long as they don't leave a trace and do not constrain the options of the other users. Instead, the Gecekondu is an expression of relationships—of negotiations, conflict, different forms of knowledge, patience, of middle grounds overlapping each other.

SANDY KALTENBORN:
How has that influenced your self-perception as an architect?

TASHY ENDRES:
This real-world experience became one of the starting points for my research and teaching on educational approaches for future architects that are critical of discrimination, thereby fundamentally rethinking architecture. We cannot erase or reverse power relationships like racism or gendered and classist divisions that assign us different places in society simply by acting differently on a small scale. They are inscribed into property relations, building codes, and planning processes, but also into our biographies, our bodies, our (aesthetic) ideas, ways of behaving, or into what we would perhaps naively term "intuition"—and impact the way space is produced and used on all levels.
If they want to be able to contribute to material changes in these power dynamics, architects in particular, as part of the dominant groups in society, first have to unlearn a massive amount of things they have been brought up to perceive as "normal" or have learned to regard as the "norm" in their architecture studies. The construction process surrounding the Gecekondu showed me once again that often, unlearning the professional role we are trained to play in academia is necessary for architects to "participate" in construction processes that shift the real power divide in terms of both method and outcome. These processes of (un)learning are essential for an empowered architectural practice that is critical of discrimination. And they turn the question of participation on its head. Perhaps, Sherry Arnstein's famous Ladder of Citizen Participation works the other way around: Could architects use it to climb down from their ivory tower of purported expertise and learn to participate in the political organizing processes of their neighbors? I am curious about your view on this in relation to issues of the visual design and communication strategies of Kotti & Co, both areas where you played a central role.

SANDY KALTENBORN:
Let me begin with a small example: One of the first visual messages we put out was my adaptation of Milton Glaser's "I ♥ NY" to read "I ♥ Kotti," a small 10 by 10 centimeters sticker. This formally low-threshold declaration of love should be read against the backdrop of the prevailing negative image of Kottbusser Tor nurtured by the media back then: Suddenly, a marginalized, under-represented, and structurally poor neighborhood was professing its love of a place that, mere moments ago, had been read as an unsafe predicament for the city. This speech act constituted the neighborhood as a group for the first time and rendered it publicly visible. The "tourism postcard" with its charming photos of Kotti and the words "Greetings from Kottbusser Tor" pursued a similar communication strategy: It is not the Brandenburg Gate or the Berlin Palace that are favorably coded on these postcards, but instead this highly complex urban space with all its social and political ruptures. And only at second sight, in a much smaller font, could you read the message "stop soaring rents." This was quite different from how social struggles usually communicate and are talked about, with the opposition, the struggle, and the demands taking center stage. The sticker was later accompanied by a banner with the same formal language, with the difference that now instead of "I" there was a "We". The protests gathered thousands of participants with "I ♥ Kotti" stickers on their jackets marching behind a big "We ♥ Kotti" banner. It was, if you will, my attempt to negotiate the relationship between the individual and the political collective on the small scale of a communication design layout. The price you pay for being part of a political collective is often the latent subjugation of the individual to the collective's norms—which was exactly what we didn't want to happen. Our constant key issues were therefore: How can an emancipatory meta-narrative be constructed for an urban society that is diverse, but ultimately very fragmented? Irrespective of the formal language and media format, how do you always communicate in an inclusive, poetic, and open manner without papering over the differences? In other words, how do you design something that respects diversity and does not create new forms of exclusion through aesthetic distinction? That is why the design ran analogously to the open, fragmentary aspect of the Gecekondu and our group in general.

TASHY ENDRES:
To what extent did the close interaction with the people at Kotti & Co influence your professionally trained methods and also how you perceive your practice as a communication designer?

SANDY KALTENBORN:
That can be easily visualized using a different example: At first, I gave the posters and leaflets for the more than 50 noise protests a colorful, joyful, and pugnacious touch. Yet, it quickly became clear that many of the users from our neighborhood, whose everyday reality receives only scarce representation in the media, mostly gazed at photos of the prior protests shown on the flyers. Along the lines of: "Look—I took part!" This observation inspired me to redesign the back of the protest announcements as a kind of family album. Had I not been to the Gecekondu daily, I would never have noticed or gotten the idea. From an outside perspective, the social complexity and function of this "photo album" is hardly

FIG. 11
"I ♥ Kotti," adhesive label, 98 × 98 mm

This adaptation of Milton Glaser's "I ♥ NY" was produced and distributed more than 200,000 times in the early years of the protest.

FIG. 12
Postcard, Kotti & Co

FIG. 13
Kotti & Co has organized more than 50 rallies, most of which had the Gecekondu as their starting and ending point. Neighbors often brought pots, wooden spoons, and whistles to noisily manifest their protest.

FIG. 14
Housing projects south of Kottbusser Tor

The mural was created in 2012 in collaboration with the Argentine group Pirqas al Sur and teenagers from the neighborhood.

FIG. 15
Kotti-Info: Informational newsletter in German and Turkish covering topics such as tenancy rights, organizing strategies, and assistance programs, alongside everyday events around Kottbusser Tor. Published twice a year, it is distributed free of charge to 2,000 households in the neighborhood.

legible. On the pictures, you simply see some people at a rally. I consider this a basic problem in the reception of designed artifacts: The context, conditions of production, and social uses are unintelligible. But in my opinion, that is precisely where the potential of their design becomes clear, in particular if you have a socio-political objective. Media are, after all, far more than simple carriers of information. The "Gecekondu experimental method" poses fundamental questions as to what defines design professions, be it design proper or architecture. An inaccurate grasp of the profession can constrict the practice. I was less interested in what I thought to be well designed or even "beautiful" in professional terms, and more in how to design amidst the heterogeneous social framework. And if you follow this train of thought to its logical end, you will find that the traditional professional understanding of what constitutes design and suitable media for conveying meaning rest on a very reduced notion of communication. For example, looking back I would say our tea kettle, the samovar, was our strongest social medium. The way I see things, the fact that we placed it where we did can be read as applied communication design.

TASHY ENDRES:

To conclude, I would find it interesting to reflect together on what actually happens with the Gecekondu and our political praxis when they become the subject of an architecture publication, a project, or an exhibition. What is the relationship between socio-political organizing and the world of culture and academia?

SANDY KALTENBORN:

Over the past 12 years we have often had this kind of experience where we collaborated with institutions whose knowledge was located in academia and who were not directly part of our political struggle. We did so to get our political demands out into as many parts of society as possible. This also amounts to a transfer of cultural, social, and political knowledge or capital toward other scenes, other contexts. I therefore think that you need to be clear from the outset that these scenes and their related institutions have an intrinsic logic and goals that differ from the logic of protest. For us it was a matter of gaining more power in favor of direct political change while the other side focused on conveying knowledge and fostering discourse. Now that may seem trivial. But you can construe the whole thing as transactional, meaning the transfer of protest knowledge, street wisdom, and cultural capital into the institutions, and, in return, visibility and representation. It usually worked well when the institutions also supported things that could not neatly be absorbed in the projects. In other words: When they began to selflessly redistribute resources. It seems key to me that you repeatedly revisit the different origins and interests of the two sides and negotiate them transparently. Even if that is more easily said than done.

TASHY ENDRES:

In addition to these different points of departure and interests to which you refer, there are also different senses of urgency and temporal rationales: For us it was about surviving as a neighborhood and changing the embedded material and structural power relationships. We said that we would stay until our rents were lowered and the problems of social housing were solved. Institutions tend not to have that commitment, and often operate in a project-based logic of switching from one topic to another in a tightly scheduled attention economy. What if an institution said they would now dedicate themselves to the right to the city, to antiracism, or to climate justice for the next 10 or 20 years? In any case, institutions must be measured up against whether they depict our praxis and knowledge as interesting ends in themselves, as an aesthetic surface, or worse, as social exoticism—or in a way that makes them allies to a social project of transformation. This includes the issue of whom the institutions make the knowledge produced by social movements available to. Often it is commodified in the outfit's operating logic and placed in formats that are socially very exclusive. Be it through the language and the way it addresses certain groups, a required level of formal education, or access fees … We are, through this conversation for example, also part of that: Because we already possess a lot of cultural capital, we are able to translate our experiences at Kotti & Co into relatively inaccessible language and research or publication projects, from which we extract even more cultural capital, intentionally or not—that is something that most of our fellow activists at Kotti cannot do.

SANDY KALTENBORN:

Yes, the problem remains that the knowledge only structurally flows in one direction—and the formatting of the project can undermine any more sustained allyship with social movements. As you said, the right to the city was not some project hypothesis that we sought to explore in abstract terms, but boiled down to the question whether our neighbors would be forced out of their homes or not, whether the mailboxes would bear the same names three years down the line, whether the poor people would retain their right to the city center, period. From my viewpoint, it is exciting and interesting that many of these societal policy issues that progressive institutions explore in abstract terms at times personally affect their very own staff. With all the collaborations that we have had through the years with cultural institutions, universities, theaters, etc., the most interesting personal conversations with project managers were those that did not focus on the particular project's products. Not because the projects themselves were boring, not at all, but because a desire for authentic allyship and bonding in achieving socio-political outcomes emerged in the personal interaction, while the conditions of production only allowed for limited changes to the boundary lines of the institutional setting. A possible step in the right direction might be to pay more attention to this dynamic and turn it into a launch pad for future collaborations.

TASHY ENDRES:

The question that we—and many institutions—are now facing is how institutions can (un)learn structural power relationships and what a transformative understanding of "professionalism" could look like?

SANDY KALTENBORN:

I believe that with the Gecekondu, Kotti & Co has shown how open-ended experiments must be designed if they want to tackle issues affecting society and democracy—that is what social protests are at heart. The issues of design we have sketched here, of communication, of language, of the appropriate media and distribution strategies—including the spaces and contexts in which they are received—are all key. And only to a very limited extent can we base this practice on the traditional canon of our professions, even if we label it as "social design." To this end, we need at least two things: First, as you said, to practically unlearn things and, second, to immerse ourselves in socio-political debates. And by that, I mean insert ourselves into the conflict, take a side, put our own authorship into context, and, to a certain degree, make ourselves productively dependent on others.

BELLEVUE DI MONACO

Whose City (Center)? The of a Housing and Cultural Center

Text:
Christian Ganzer and Denijen Pauljević
for Bellevue di Monaco

FIG. 1
Housing and cultural center Bellevue di Monaco

Protests in 2012 saved the ensemble of three buildings at Müllerstraße 2–6 in Munich's Glockenbachviertel district, and the soccer field to the left of the striking 1950s building, from demolition.

USES
Housing and cultural center for refugees and local residents; counseling on migration and asylum issues, on the labor market, and on housing for refugees; advice for female refugees; women's café; intercultural conflict counseling; language partnerships and courses; sewing and bicycle workshops; learning and homework assistance; seminars; readings; running group; boxing; choir; poetry and rap workshop; dance, theater, and photo workshop; film screenings, concerts, and panel discussions; studios; café; sports field

SIZE
8,000 m²

MANAGEMENT
Sozialgenossenschaft Bellevue di Monaco eG

LEASEHOLD LANDLORD
City of Munich

ARCHITECTURE
Hirner & Riehl Architekten und Stadtplaner PartG mbB BDA

FOUNDED
2016, completed 2018 (rooftop sports field in 2021)

LOCATION
Munich

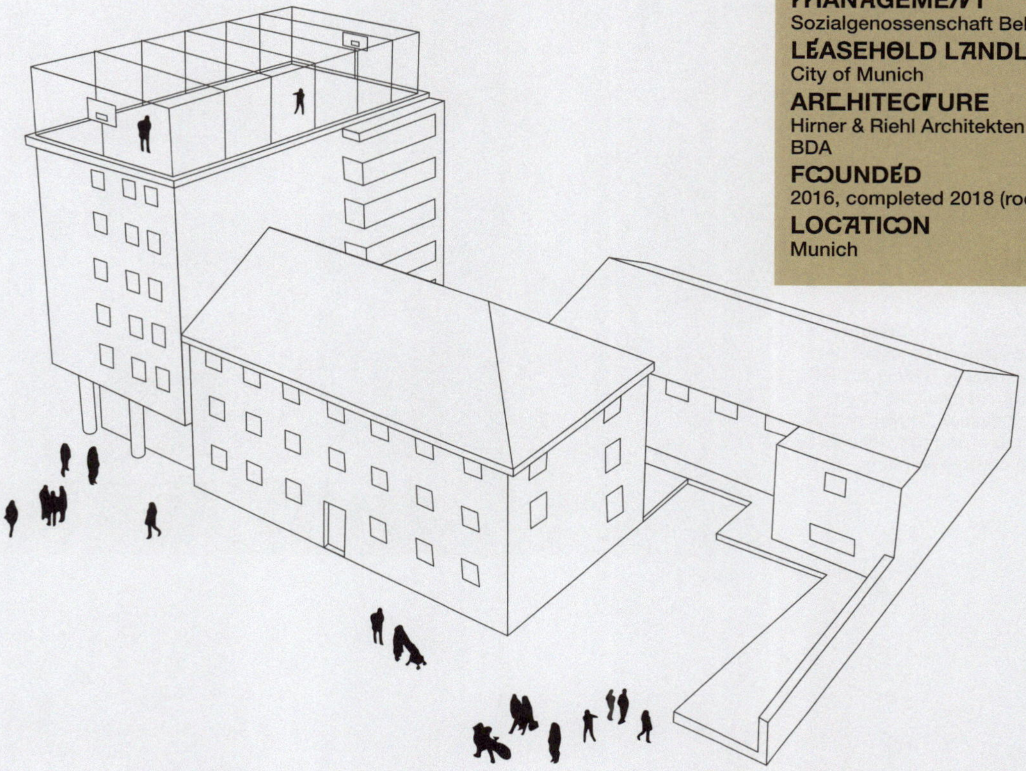

FIG. 2
Since 2016, the social cooperative Bellevue di Monaco has been managing the complex: the building at the intersection of Corneliusstraße and Müllerstraße forms a courtyard with two more buildings.

Bellevue di Monaco is a refugee housing project and cultural center opened in 2016 in the heart of Munich and run by a social cooperative founded for that purpose. The ensemble consists of three buildings grouped around an inner courtyard in the Glockenbachviertel neighborhood. The building on the corner of Corneliusstraße and Müllerstraße features a public café run in cooperation with refugees, housing in the five stories above, and a spectacular sports field on the roof. In addition to an adjacent three-story residential building, a third structure in the back houses counseling facilities, as well as room for educational, cultural, and recreational activities. From the outset, the project's programmatic approach has significantly contributed to shifting the issue of displacement and migration from Munich's outskirts (where most refugee accommodations are located in abandoned barracks and commercial buildings) to the heart of (urban) society. Today, Bellevue di Monaco—the name is a tongue-in-cheek reference to language used by luxury real estate developers, Monaco being the Italian name for Munich—is a well-established part of the city and a socially inclusive location for participation and encounters between Munich's citizens and newly arrived residents. From the very beginning, the project faced political hurdles and resistance that could only be overcome with tenacious efforts by people battling to claim the right to the city.

The project's politicization began with a resolution by the Munich city council in 2012 to tear down the largely vacant buildings on Müllerstraße 2–6, which were communally owned. At that time, rents in major cities were skyrocketing. This only intensified following the 2008 financial crisis with the growing privatization of municipal and communal properties and global financial capital increasingly forcing its way into the housing markets. Against this backdrop, the question of "To whom does the city (actually) belong?" gained momentum in Munich's debates on urban policy. The debate was exacerbated by high real estate prices in the contiguous Glockenbachviertel and Gärtnerplatzviertel neighborhoods, which were among the highest in Germany in the early 2010s. In 2011, for example, a condominium in the 56-meter-high luxury residential tower The Seven, one block over from Bellevue di Monaco, was sold for more than 14 million euros—the highest sales price per square meter ever recorded in Germany at that time. Before this high-rise was turned into luxury condominiums, it housed the municipal heating plant. The latter was sold to a group of investors by Munich's public utility company in 2007. In retrospect, the sale is considered by many to be a disgrace. The decision to tear down the municipally owned ensemble of buildings at Müllerstrasse 2–6 therefore came at a time of heightened tensions, especially as demolition

FIG. 3
A weeklong "guerrilla renovation" by activists in March 2013 pushed the city council to renovate the remaining apartments at Müllerstraße 6 by October of the same year and make them available to an independent youth welfare organization. However, this was only intended as an interim use, and the city initially would not budge from its demolition plans.

of the three buildings would also have spelled the loss of one of the few remaining public city center playgrounds located on the site, which is used by the adjacent childcare center. This prompted parents and educators to organize a protest march through the neighborhood, joined by hundreds of people. The small soccer field was not only the march's destination; it was also the beginning of a new debate on the future of Munich's city center.

During this protest campaign, citizens began focusing on the three buildings which now make up Bellevue di Monaco. The city administration justified the slated demolition by claiming that the buildings were beyond rescue by modernization. The ensemble was

FIGS. 4–5
Bathroom and kitchen of the apartment after the guerrilla renovation

The guerrilla renovation of a 40-square-meter apartment at Müllerstraße 6 by Goldgrund activists cost 2,500 euros. According to their estimates, renovating the entire building would cost 80 percent less than a new construction.

not heritage-listed because changes had been made to its interiors, a peculiar choice given its interesting architectural history. The striking building on the corner of Corneliusstraße and Müllerstraße with its tall, fully glazed ground floor dedicated to retail is one of the few surviving downtown examples of utilitarian architecture from the 1950s, designed by architects Georg and Christian Kronenbitter. The building next to it was first built in 1828 in what was then the city's main suburb after the city walls had been razed. Later, additional stories were added, and in the 19th century it was used as a bathhouse. At the time of the protests, the rear courtyard building was being used commercially and the main store

FIG.6
During the renovation, the Munich-based organization Culture Kitchen prepared lunches daily for volunteers and workers.

FIG.7
The second phase of modernization began in September 2016 by establishing the site office so as to carry out the refurbishment while simultaneously using some sections of the buildings. This offered the advantages of partially using the buildings before construction ended as well as being able to flexibly adapt the spatial program and later uses.

had an interim tenant. The apartments largely stood vacant, some of them empty for 15 years, which the citizens felt was scandalous given the acute housing shortage in Munich.

Supported by the fictitious real estate organization Goldgrund, which had made a name for itself in Munich with artistic interventions in the public realm on issues relating to housing and urban policy, the neighbors, parents of children in the childcare center, and other citizens gained access to the building at Müllerstraße 6 and secretly renovated one of the vacant apartments over the course of a week: They sanded down and painted window frames, renewed the bathroom's tile joints, replaced the old flooring with parquet, gave the walls a fresh coat of paint, and decluttered, cleaned, and refurbished the apartment. Goldgrund then uploaded a video of the guerrilla renovation, which showed the activists dressed as gorillas, to YouTube: *Müllerstraße 6—Hier renovieren wir für die Stadt München!* (Müllerstrasse 6—we're renovating for the City of Munich!) with a song by the band Moop Mama. The clip not only went viral on the internet but also led to the city's mayor at the time, Christian Ude, a Social Democrat who had begun his career as a lawyer defending tenants, to come over from City Hall on foot to see the renovation with his own eyes. He thereafter instructed the administration to modernize the building swiftly and cost-effectively in line with the example set by the guerrilla renovation, at least securing its interim use.

The guerrilla renovation—a form of squatting and maintaining vacant buildings known in German as *Instandbesetzung* [a portmanteau of "Instandsetzung," i.e., maintenance, and "Besetzung," i.e. squatting; editor's note]—had shown the city administration real alternatives to the prevailing imperative of tearing down and building anew. The activists sensed that they had struck a nerve with those in power. Until this point, the city council's governing coalition of Social Democrats and Greens had considered themselves "good guys" and had undoubtedly tried to help tenants through various instruments such as awarding certain areas preservation status and implementing the so-called Munich model, which supported middle-income families and households in finding housing. Nevertheless, the administration dug in its feet and stuck with its plans to build as much new housing as possible, insisting that modernizing the three buildings made no sense in terms of energy consumption levels—whereupon the activists had an expert provide an energy consumption report. When the administration claimed the buildings were in danger of collapsing, they hired an independent civil engineer (and informed a TV crew from the local Bayerischer Rundfunk channel to publicize the opposing opinion). Expert opinions were solicited on sustainable urban development, embodied energy, and heritage protection—but to no avail. The city refused to budge from its plans and argued that maintaining the existing buildings would involve "considerable expenses." No mention was made of the seven million euros the demolition and new building would cost. At the end of 2013, the negotiations finally ended in a compromise whereby the soccer field and the 1950s building would be preserved and the two other buildings designated for demolition.

A few months later, in the summer of 2014, the discussions took yet another turn. The civil war in Syria led to a growing number of refugees arriving in Munich, and arrival centers began to be overwhelmed. The city sent out an internal circular searching for "any space with four walls and a roof." Nationwide, people formulated responses to the dramatic situation, including the concept initially developed by Goldgrund for Bellevue di Monaco. The project's idea was strongly supported by civic society—among other things due to mass rallies against the rise of right-wing extremism organized by an alliance of people affiliated with Bellevue di Monaco under the title "Platz da?! Flüchtlinge sind willkommen! Gemeinsam gegen Pegida, Rassismus und Hetze" [Make room/make way?! Refugees welcome. Standing together against Pegida, racism, and hate speech; Pegida is an islamophobic and far-right political movement founded in Germany in October 2014; editor's note].

Finally, in January 2015, the Munich city council and the new mayor Dieter Reiter, a Social Democrat, performed an about-face on the demolition plans and opened all three existing buildings on Müllerstraße to accommodate refugees. The informal alliance was institutionalized in the social cooperative Bellevue di Monaco eG, which applied to manage the project through an EU-wide tender by the city administration. The legal structure makes it possible to raise the capital required for renovation and conversion works through membership contributions without being profit-oriented. As a form of organized civic self-help, the social cooperative's statutes stipulate a nonprofit orientation and dedication to the creation and expansion of (infra)structures based on solidarity with people who are not necessarily members of the cooperative themselves. All decisions are taken democratically because, irrespective of the scale of a person's monetary contribution, every member's vote counts equally. The organization must report to its members and to the cooperative association, which ensures complete transparency.

In April 2016, 15 months after the city council's resolution, the social cooperative was awarded the project and was assigned

the buildings under a 40-year leasehold arrangement. In addition to housing about 50 refugees, Bellevue di Monaco has made an important contribution as a platform for interaction and networking between Munich's citizens and newly arrived residents across different generations. Several social welfare organizations as well as over 300 volunteers—including many people who personally had to flee their home countries—provide counseling and education programs, as well as cultural and recreational activities, such as help with homework, language courses, counseling on asylum and migration law, and open-house meetings at Bellevue di Monaco—all of which have low thresholds. In this way, Bellevue di Monaco builds bridges for refugees, enabling them to gain a foothold in Munich: through sports and dance events, sewing and bicycle repair workshops, seminars, concerts, readings, movie screenings, discussion groups, and theater projects, not to mention the collaboratively run café and other spaces to work and join forces on projects. As an investment in a broad cultural and social program rather than an expensive new building, it is a prime example of how converting an existing building for new uses should be favored over demolition, as a more cost-effective and ecologically sustainable alternative for creating spaces of commoning, protection, and interaction.

FIG.8
The ramp to the site's former underground parking lot is now an open-air stage in the courtyard. It serves as a meeting point for residents and neighbors and hosts the social cooperative's public events.

FIG. 9
Bellevue di Monaco offers a varied cultural and educational program for residents and visitors. The upcycling fashion label Bellevue Couture started as a nonprofit sewing project for refugee women run by the social cooperative. Discarded fabric scraps are processed into handmade one-of-a-kind pieces—bags, baskets, pillows, etc.—which are sold on site.

FIG. 10
The café is managed together with refugees and hosts various counseling services as well as concerts, readings, and film screenings.

FIG. 11
The café's original aluminum-and-brass shop window facade was refurbished and broken window panes were replaced.

FIG. 12
The public café on the ground floor opened in 2018. The furniture is the result of an in-house workshop at Bellevue di Monaco.

FIG.13
The redevelopment concept aimed at providing apprenticeships for refugees involved in the construction process, in cooperation with local trades businesses.

THE REFURBISHMENT

Bellevue di Monaco contracted Munich-based architecture practice Hirner & Riehl to handle the refurbishment. Out of six shortlisted candidates, the studio won thanks to its insistence on pragmatism in dealing with the existing buildings, flexibility in responding to the structure's physical state, and an architectural strategy based on minimal interventions. The architecture practice presented neither a finished design nor proposals for reconfiguring the floor plans (these were to be finalized in consultation with the cooperative), and instead developed a methodology intended to secure and highlight the existing buildings' qualities rather than excessively changing them. The heterogeneous ensemble of existing buildings was to be complemented by unifying, functional elements, with the tight budget of 1.7 million euros going primarily into the labor required to repair existing architectural elements rather than the purchase of new industrial products. The principle was to treat what was in place "cautiously," in this way conserving resources.

Text:
Matthias Marschner for
Hirner & Riehl
Architekten
und Stadtplaner

A key element of the concept involved persuading local trades companies during the construction phase to involve refugees in the renovation works and in part also to offer them officially recognized apprenticeships. The process whereby Bellevue di Monaco's social cooperative supervised the selection of possible candidates proved to be quite elaborate, as certain preconditions had to be met in terms of basic education, knowledge of the German language, and residence status for them to be considered for an apprenticeship in the first place. During a six-week certified internship, the companies and the refugees tested how well they worked together. In some cases, this culminated in hirings or apprenticeships.

The social cooperative, which was still in its infancy, immediately needed a place to begin working; it used the momentum with the help of the many volunteers who provisionally

FIG. 14
The renovation included a restoration of the existing windows, an adjustment of fixtures and handles, new weatherproof sealing, as well as repairs and a partial relocation of existing interior doors.

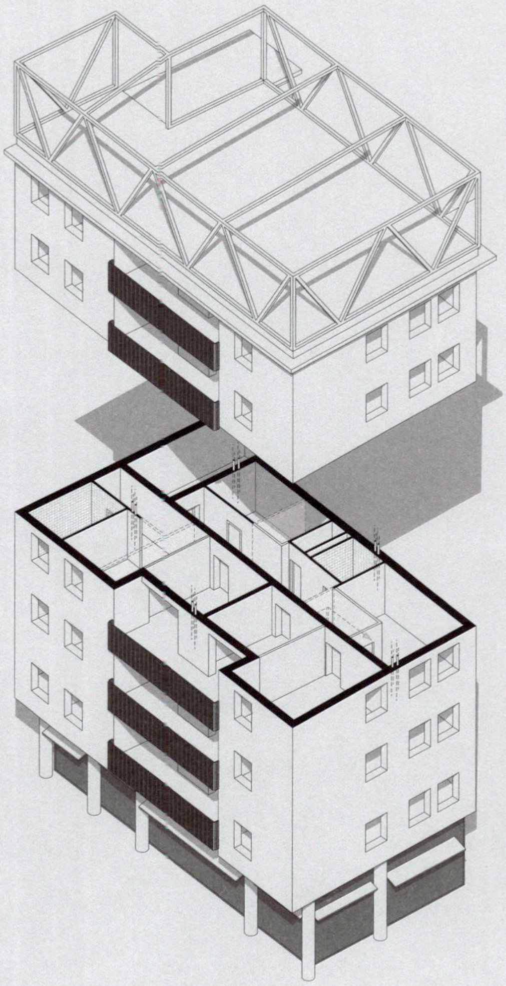

FIG. 15
Axonometry of the renovated building on the corner of Müllerstraße and Corneliusstraße, with a horizontal section through the third floor apartments.

FIG. 16
On each floor, the one- and two-room apartments located in the 1950s residential building were merged to form new shared flats for refugee youths.

FIG. 17
The building mostly uses the same radiators and installation lines, which were repaired or replaced only where necessary.

FIG. 18
The apartments' bathtubs and toilets were largely preserved. Only individual broken tiles, pipes, and wiring were replaced.

FIG. 19
The 1950s building's terrazzo flooring only needed thorough cleaning. However, the rear wing's staircase necessitated more repairs. The railings were repainted and the handrails were sanded down and received a new protective coating.

FIG. 20
On the balcony, only the weathered wooden balustrades had to be replaced, with new elements made of anodized aluminum. The windows were kept, and the facade received a fresh coat of paint.

refurbished the building—into which the cooperative promptly moved. The renovation during ongoing usage proved challenging. The construction happened in four stages, with the advantage of enabling the spatial program and uses to be optimized along the way. The interventions into the buildings' layouts and infrastructure were minimal.

There was no blueprint for this kind of overall refurbishment—at least not beyond a restoration in line with heritage regulations. A large number of different windows and doors were restored, removed for upgrading in terms of heat, fire, or noise insulation, and then reinstalled. Old terrazzo flooring and bathroom tiles were mended, and a decrepit wooden staircase was touched up. An individual solution had to be found for each construction element, often resulting in intensive feedback loops with the tradespeople. Time and again, decisions had to be made on site as to whether the work required to preserve a structural element was unjustifiably disproportionate. The cautious approach helped to keep the construction costs comparatively low, at 720 euros per square meter. Preserving the buildings' piping proved especially arduous. Specialist planners refused to get involved, which led to a protracted search for suitable companies who were up to handling the work without the usual prior planning by specialists. In the building dating from the 1950s, the heating pipes were largely retained in their original state, as otherwise a lot of the original fit-out would have needed expensive replacement.

FIG. 21
Since its opening in October 2020, the sports field on the roof, managed by the nonprofit local organization buntkicktgut, can be used free of charge by everyone living in Munich.

In a very short time span, the formerly vacant buildings were transformed into a vibrant location. In the building at the intersection of Corneliusstraße and Müllerstraße, four flat-shares for four young adults each now rise above the café. The adjacent building hosts nine apartments, of which seven are reserved for families and single parents with a history of migration. In the rear courtyard building, two floors were fitted out as event spaces and offices, and in the courtyard an open-air auditorium leading down to the basement was created by converting the former ramp to an underground parking garage. Because every available square centimeter was soon put to use, the idea of creating a football field on the roof of the 1950s building quickly evolved. It was foreseeable that the special approval process for this feature would be lengthy—and would set a precedent in Munich—which is why a decision was made to use the procedure of a subsequent permit and postpone this measure until after the other construction stages. This final section was completed in 2021, two and a half years after Bellevue di Monaco's official inauguration. The project's success is due in part to the cooperative's clear decision-making structure, which enabled it to respond swiftly to all the questions that arose daily during construction work. But above all, the project exists in its current form because the cooperative itself was willing to take the risk and venture down this unusual path.

Assemblea Sociale per la Casa (ASC)
(founded 1998) is a grassroots organization active in Venice, advocating for housing rights, providing legal and material support to tenants who have received an eviction notice, and promoting the upkeep of abandoned public housing through collaborative self-help programs, which offer Venetians a real alternative to fleeing the city's soaring rents.

Marco Baravalle
is a researcher, activist, and curator. He is a member of S.a.L.E. Docks, a collective and self-managed space for visual arts and activism in Venice founded in 2007. Baravalle is part of the IRI (Institute of Radical Imagination) and research fellow at Università Iuav di Venezia, and author of *L'autunno caldo del curatore: Arte, neoliberismo, pandemia* (2021) and coeditor of *Art for UBI (manifesto)* (2022).

Chiara Buratti
(born 1988) is an anthropologist, social scientist and political activist. She has lived in Venice since 2011, where she is a prominent activist with several grassroots organizations. Among these are the Italian base trade union Associazione per i Diritti dei Lavoratori (ADL Cobas) and Assemblea Sociale per la Casa (ASC). The latter campaigns for the right to housing in Venice by providing legal support to those excluded from the private rental market, as well as material support to residential communities who wish to take care of the maintenance of decaying publicly owned dwellings.

Ludovico Centis
(born 1980) is Assistant Professor of Urbanism at UniTS, Università di Trieste. His research focuses on the ways in which individuals and institutions, as well as desires and power, shape cities and landscapes. Recent books include *The Lake of Venice: A Scenario for Venice and Its Lagoon* (2022, coauthored with Lorenzo Fabian), *They Must Have Enjoyed Building Here: Reyner Banham and Buffalo* (2021), and *A Parallel of Ruins and Landscapes* (2019).

Concular
(founded 2020) sees itself as a platform and a network whose mission is to facilitate the closing of material cycles in the construction sector. The founders have been dealing with the topic of a circular economy since 2012 and have been running the online platform restado.de ever since. Concular has 35 employees and is involved in numerous construction projects in Austria, Germany, and Switzerland. Their main task is to compute and digitize construction resources, broker the transfer of materials, and provide guidance on how to reduce emissions, waste, and disposal costs.

ConstructLab
(founded 2012) is a platform for artistic research, constructive experimentation, and interdisciplinary design. Their projects—encompassing temporary and permanent architectures—combine design and fabrication with participatory processes. The focus is on cooperation with local communities and the know-how of each individual. Team ConstructLab in Venice: Alexander Römer, architect and carpenter, Berlin; Peter Zuiderwijk, graphic designer, The Hague; Patrick Hubmann, designer and carpenter, Porto. Support: Claudia Ribeiro, costume designer, Porto.

Die Zusammenarbeiter
(founded 2009), initiated by Christian Schöningh in Berlin, combines program development, process engineering and architecture for community-oriented groups and resource-efficient buildings. In the spirit of its open network concept, the office regularly initiates interdisciplinary cooperations on a project-by-project basis.

Maria Eichhorn
is an artist based in Berlin. In 2022, she was the artist responsible for the German Pavilion at the 59th Venice Art Biennale. Among others, Eichhorn participated in documenta 14 in Athens and Kassel (2017), Documenta11 in Kassel (2002), and the Venice Art Biennale (2015). Her publications include *Relocating a Structure* (2022); *Hannah Arendt: Jewish Cultural Reconstruction Field Reports, Memoranda, Etc.* (2021); *Film Lexicon of Sexual Practices / Prohibited Imports* (2019); and *Catalogue Raisonné* (2017). In 2017, she initiated the website www.rosevallandinstitut.org.

Tashy Endres
studied architecture and political science. She has worked at Decolonizing Architecture, Lacaton & Vassal, and as a research assistant at UdK Berlin, among others. Her teaching and research focus on urban political economy and intersectional anti-discrimination education for architects. She has been a political activist for twenty years, including with the Landless Workers Movement in Buenos Aires, Occupy Wall Street in New York, as well as Kotti & Co and Deutsche Wohnen & Co enteignen in Berlin. She is currently setting up a training and retreat center for regenerative and transformative organizing.

Anne Femmer
(born 1984) is an architect and co-founder of SUMMACUMFEMMER Architekt*innen in Leipzig. She has worked at a variety of international offices during and after her studies at TU Dresden and ETH Zurich, including with Adolf Krischanitz in Vienna, Go Hasegawa in Tokyo, von Ballmoos Krucker in Zurich, and architecten de vylder vinck taillieu in Ghent. From 2015 to 2018, she was a design assistant at ETH Zurich with Christian Kerez and Jan de Vylder. In 2019, she was a visiting professor at TU Munich and at the Integral Architecture chair at TU Graz from 2020 to 2022. Since 2022, she has been a visiting professor at UdK Berlin. She is a co-curator of *Open for Maintenance*, the German contribution to the 18th Venice Architecture Biennale (2023).

Laura Fregolent
(born 1966) is a professor and co-ordinator of the Urban and Regional Planning bachelor's program at Università IUAV di Venezia. Her research focuses on urban and territorial transformations connected, in particular, with issues of housing and the conflicts generated by projects of urban renewal, at both an environmental and a social level. Fregolent's work also investigates the relationship between data, urban policy, and the democratization of planning tools, with particular reference to the context of Venice and the Veneto region.

Hélène Frichot
(born 1970) is Professor of Architecture and Philosophy and Director of the Bachelor of Design at the University of Melbourne, Australia. Her research fosters creative practice methodologies and develops concept-tools and theories that draw on feminist new materialism, the post-humanities, environmental humanities, and affect theory. Recent publications include *Dirty Theory: Troubling Architecture* (2019), *Creative Ecologies: Theorizing the Practice of Architecture* (2018) and *How to Make Yourself a Feminist Design Power Tool* (2016).

Sarah Gainsforth
(born 1980) is an independent researcher and freelance writer. She writes for Italian media *L'Essenziale* and *Internazionale*, among others. Her work focuses on urban planning, housing, social inequalities, gentrification, and tourism. She is the author of *Airbnb Città Merce: Storie di resistenza alla gentrificazione digitale* (2019, shortlisted for the Premio Napoli 2020), *Oltre il turismo: Esiste un turismo sostenibile?* (2020), *Abitare Stanca: La casa, un racconto politico* (2022), and *Cameriera* (2022).

Mirko Gatti

(born 1987) is a freelance architect and has been an editor, project manager, and curator at ARCH+ since 2014, where he worked, among other projects, on *An Atlas of Commoning* and *1989–2019: Politics of Space in the New Berlin*. He studied architecture in Milan, completed an M.A. at Goldsmiths, University of London, and was a research fellow at ETH Zurich. While his interest in architecture encompasses such fields as critical theory and political activism, his approach remains highly practical.

Franziska Gödicke

(born 1998) studied architecture at Bauhaus-Universität Weimar and Università Iuav di Venezia. She has been part of the editorial team at ARCH+ since July 2021. As a freelance writer, her essays have appeared in publications such as ETH Zurich's *trans Magazin*. In January 2022, she joined the collaborative architectural practice b+ in Berlin. In workshops and guest critiques at venues such as the AA London, RWTH Aachen, and the University of Cambridge, she focuses on questions of care, repair, and maintenance, with a particular emphasis on post-socialist structures in East Germany. She is a co-curator of *Open for Maintenance*, the German contribution to the 18th Venice Architecture Biennale (2023).

Christoph Grafe

(born 1964) is an architect, curator, and author who lives and works in Amsterdam, London, and Wuppertal. He is Professor for Architecture History and Theory at the University of Wuppertal and had taught in Delft, Antwerp, Milan, and Hassel. From 2011 to 2017, he was director of the Flanders Architecture Institute in Antwerp. In 2014, he published the book *People's Palaces: Architecture, Culture and Democracy in Post-Western Europe*. He is a member of the editorial teams of *OASE* and *Eselsohren*.

Juliane Greb

(born 1985) is an architect and has been leading her own office in Ghent since 2015. Parallel to her studies at RWTH Aachen and AHO Oslo, she worked in the editorial team of ARCH+. After finishing her studies, she worked at architecten de vylder vinck taillieu in Ghent, where she was responsible for realizing a number of experimental residential buildings as a project manager. Subsequently, she worked on a freelance basis for osar architects in Antwerp. In recent years, she has taught at UAntwerp and TU Delft, and is currently a visiting professor at PBSA Düsseldorf. She is a co-curator of *Open for Maintenance*, the German contribution to the 18th Venice Architecture Biennale (2023).

Aimi Hamraie

is Associate Professor of Medicine, Health, and Society and American Studies at Vanderbilt University in Nashville. Hamraie's research on disability culture and accessibility draws on the fields of critical disability studies, architectural and urban theory, and science and technology studies. Their design as director of the Critical Design Lab focuses on using a disability culture framework for approaching media and technology. Hamraie is the author of *Building Access: Universal Design and the Politics of Disability* (2017). They are also a public member of the U.S. Access Board and a 2022 United Artists Fellow in Media.

Haus der Materialisierung – Center for Climate-friendly Resource Usage

is an association of various initiatives and institutions that research, practice, and work in the fields of sustainable management and climate-friendly resource usage. Haus der Materialisierung is part of the pioneer project Haus der Statistik, which is under development by Koop5 near Berlin's Alexanderplatz since 2018. Participants work in a self-organized manner, as freelancers or (partially) funded in various forms of associations and business models. Since the summer of 2021, the headquarters of the Center for Climate-friendly Resource Usage, developed as part of a city-wide campaign dubbed "Re-Use Berlin," are located at Haus der Materialisierung under the direction of Kunst-Stoffe Berlin.

Christian Hiller

(born 1975) is a media scholar, editor, and curator. He has managed exhibitions, event series, publications, and research projects for institutions such as the Stiftung Bauhaus Dessau, the Haus der Kulturen der Welt in Berlin, and ARCH+. He has curated international exhibitions such as *bauhaus. film* (SESC São Paulo, among others), *Mensch-Raum-Maschine* (Bauhaus Dessau, MMCA Seoul, among others), and *Encounters with Southeast Asian Modernism / Contested Modernities* (Gudskul Jakarta, Goethe Institut Myanmar, NTU CCA Singapore, and others). With ARCH+, he has curated projects including *projekt bauhaus* (2015–19), *An Atlas of Commoning* (2018), and *Cohabitation* (2021). He is a co-curator of *Open for Maintenance*, the German contribution to the 18th Venice Architecture Biennale (2023).

Hirner & Riehl Architekten und Stadtplaner

(founded 1990) has the aim of developing buildings that are sustainable from a formal, functional, and ecological point of view, by taking up and strengthening what already exists and thus prolonging the history of the site they work on. In the field of innovative timber construction, Hirner & Riehl Architekten und Stadtplaner have been among the pioneers and leading offices in Bavaria since 2001. The office is based in Munich and employs more than 40 people. In addition to new educational buildings, the focus of their praxis is on the renovation and conversion of historical building complexes.

Andrej Holm

works as a social scientist with a focus on urban and regional sociology at the Humboldt University in Berlin. His numerous publications deal with urban politics in neoliberalism and the associated processes of revaluation and displacement. Taking center stage in his work is the referral to urban social movements. In addition to academia and activism, Holm regularly advises administrations, political parties, and associations on questions of housing policy.

Institute of Radical Imagination (IRI)

is a think tank involving political scientists, economists, lawyers, architects, hackers, activists, artists, and curators to share knowledge with the aim of defining and implementing zones of post-capitalism in southern Europe and the Mediterranean. IRI works nomadically across the nodes of the network—Madrid, Athens, Istanbul, Cairo, Palestine, Naples—and connects with other nodes in the Global South. A hybrid between a research center, a refuge for artists, a museum, and a policy-making body, IRI is an intellectual logistical infrastructure operating across arts, academia, and activist networks, generating ideas that respond to specific needs on the ground.

Sandy Kaltenborn

is a cofounder of the activist group Kotti & Co and the nonprofit association Kotti-Coop in Berlin. He studied communication design at the Kunsthochschule Berlin-Weißensee and has headed the office image-shift | visuelle Kommunikation & andere Missverständnisse. Since its inception, the office has worked at the intersection of art, culture, educational institutions, and social movements. Kaltenborn has been teaching graphic and communication design in the field of political activism, both in Germany and abroad.

Kotti & Co

(founded 2011) is a tenants' rights activist group. In 2012, as a means of protest, they erected a wooden house overnight at

Kottbusser Tor in Berlin's Kreuzberg district. Kotti & Co has since developed into one of Berlin's major players in the struggles for social and public housing, for the democratization of urban developments, and against racism and displacement from the perspective of the history of migration. Kotti & Co pushed through a Berlin-wide freeze on rent increases in social housing and, in 2021, the remunicipalization of the social housing blocks at Kottbusser Tor. In 2015, they initiated the first Berlin referendum on rents and are among those who envisioned the referendum "Deutsche Wohnen & Co enteignen."

Petter Krag
(born 1978) is an architect, photographer, and partner at Büro Juliane Greb since 2017. After his studies in photography at the Oslo Fotokunstskole and six years working as a freelance photographer, he studied architecture at AHO Oslo. He has collaborated with artists on a variety of publications and exhibitions, and worked at international architecture offices including Christian Kerez in Zurich and architecten de vylder vinck taillieu in Ghent. He is a co-curator of *Open for Maintenance*, the German contribution to the 18th Venice Architecture Biennale (2023).

LXSY Architekten
(founded 2015) is a Berlin-based architecture office initiated by Kim Le Roux and Margit Sichrovsky. Beyond architecture, their concerns span the positive social, cultural, and ecological impacts the discipline can have on the built environment. As architects, they deal with the question of how society wants to live and work together in the future. LXSY see resource-efficient circular planning and construction as keys to sustainable change. In their view, the built environment is the material repository of the future. They were recipients of the German Design Award 2017 and the Iconic Award 2019.

Melissa Angela Alemaz Makele
(born 1989) is an editor at ARCH+. She studied architecture and art history at KIT Karlsruhe and was a guest student at HfG Karlsruhe. After her studies, she worked at firms including Atelier BowWow and Studio Velocity in Japan. In 2022, she was a Berlin Stipend recipient at Akademie der Künste in Berlin. She is a co-curator of *Open for Maintenance*, the German contribution to the 18th Venice Architecture Biennale (2023).

Matthias Marschner
(born 1967) is an architect and partner at Hirner & Riehl Architekten und Stadtplaner since 2016. In his practice, he is committed to social and ecological construction. He has been involved in the project Bellevue di Monaco since the early days of the protest movement.

Vittoria Martini
(born 1975) is an independent art historian living in Italy. Her research focuses on the institutional, geopolitical, and curatorial history of the Venice Biennale as a lens through which to read the various inconsistencies and urgencies of contemporaneity. Over the years, the study of the Venice Biennale from this perspective has led her to work with artists presenting critical projects, such as Antoni Muntadas (Spanish Pavilion, 2005), Alfredo Jaar (Chilean Pavilion, 2013), and Maria Eichhorn (German Pavilion, 2022 and 2023). She recently published *Thomas Hirschhorn: The Bijlmer Spinoza-Festival. The Ambassador's Diary* (Hatje Cantz, 2023) and "The Giardini: Status of the Property," in Maria Eichhorn, *Relocating a Structure*, the catalog of the German contribution to the Venice Art Biennale 2022 (Verlag der Buchhandlung Walther und Franz König, 2022).

Shannon Mattern
(born 1976) is the Penn Presidential Compact Professor of Media Studies and History of Art at the University of Pennsylvania in Philadelphia. Before that, she served for nearly two decades as a Professor of Media Studies and Anthropology at The New School in New York. Mattern's research and teaching focus on media architectures, information infrastructures, and urban technologies. Her books include *A City Is Not a Computer* (2021), *Code and Clay, Data and Dirt: Five Thousand Years of Urban Media* (2017), *Deep Mapping the Media City* (2015), and *The New Downtown Library: Designing with Communities* (2007). Mattern is President of the Metropolitan New York Library Council Board.

Anh-Linh Ngo
(born 1974) is an architectural theorist, curator, and editor-in-chief of ARCH+. He regularly curates exhibitions and research projects with ARCH+, including *projekt bauhaus* (2015–19), *Cohabitation* (2021), and *The Great Repair* (2023). From 2010 to 2016, he was a member of the art advisory council at the Institut für Auslandsbeziehungen (ifa), for which he developed and co-curated the traveling exhibitions *An Atlas of Commoning* (2018) and *Post-Oil City* (2009). He is currently a member of the board of trustees of IBA 2027 StadtRegion Stuttgart, the board of trustees of the Akademie Schloss Solitude, and the Goethe Institut's advisory council. Since 2022, he has been a member of the Akademie der Künste Berlin. He is a co-curator of *Open for Maintenance*, the German contribution to the 18th Venice Architecture Biennale (2023).

Johannes Odenthal
(born 1956) studied Art History and Archeology in Cologne, Bonn, and Paris. Until 2022, he was Director of Programming of the Akademie der Künste Berlin. From 1997 to 2006 he was artistic director of the dance, music, and theater departments at the Haus der Kulturen der Welt in Berlin. He is an editor of, among others, *Into the Open: Nele Hertling, New Spaces for Art* (2022), *Ismael Ivo: I believe in the body* (2022), *The Century of Dance: A Reader* (2019) and author of *Dance Body Politics: Texts on Contemporary Dance History* (2012). Odenthal was a co-editor of *Positionen*, a series of publications on international art scenes published by Steidl from 2009 to 2013.

Rebiennale / R3B
(founded 2008) is a loose coalition of citizens, students, architects, artists, and political activists in Venice committed to the reuse of waste materials from the Biennale. Over the years, the group's desire to be more closely involved in the planning and production of installations and exhibitions grew stronger. Out of this impetus, in 2019, the initiative founded the professional woodworking company R3B, short for Reuse, Recycle, Rebuild – Biennale. Today, Rebiennale consists of seven trained craftspeople with a vast inventory of equipment and machinery and an extensive network of committed activists.

Tim Rieniets
(born 1972) studied architecture and works as a city planner. Since 2018, he has been a Professor for Urban and Spatial Development at Leibniz Universität Hannover. From 2013 to 2018, he was head of the state initiative StadtBauKultur NRW. He was co-curator of the exhibition *urbainable – stadthaltig: Positions on the European City for the 21st Century* (2020) at the Akademie der Künste Berlin and of the Rotterdam Architecture Biennale (2009/10). Publications coedited by Rieniets include: *Umbaukultur: Für eine Architektur des Veränderns* (2020), *The City as Resource* (2016), *Atlas of Shrinking Cities* (2006), and *City of Collision* (2006).

Rosa Loo
is a collective of authors that came together for the article "IncLoo*sive Architecture" featured in this issue. The text examines the socio-spatial, ecological, and architectural dimensions of toilets and sanitary infrastructure from different perspectives. Rosa Loo are Sabine

Bongers-Römer, Katharina Ciax, and Martine Kayser (klo:lektiv); Sina Kamala Kaufmann (writer); Stefan Karlowsky and Ariane Krause (IGZ, Leibniz-Institut für Gemüse- und Zierpflanzenbau e. V.; Ariane Krause also zirkulierBAR, KanTe and NetSan); Johanna Moser (architect); Michel Riechmann (Eawag, Valoo, NetSan); and Eleftheria Xenikaki (KanTe):

Sabine Bongers-Römer

(born 1992) analyzed in her master's thesis how (semi-)public toilets are provided by different municipalities in Germany. She is part of the six-member feminist group klo:lektiv, whose mission is to raise awareness about the topic of toilets and sanitary infrastructure in public and scientific discourse. She is currently a research assistant at TU Dortmund, where she conducts research on the values behind planning and spatial practice.

Katharina Ciax

(born 1994) is a sociologist and part of the six-member feminist group klo:lektiv. Ciax's research focuses on the exclusionary character of urban spaces, using toilets as an example, as well as on the technological, social, and affective practices of appropriation of marginalized bodies. She currently works as a research assistant at the University of Jena investigating atmospheres of urban securitization and militarization.

Martine Kayser

(born 1988) is a social geographer dealing with toilets in (semi-)public spaces and part of the feminist collective klo:lektiv. Her main interest lies in developing and establishing inclusive and sustainable sanitation solutions together with different stakeholders. This also means taking into account social power structures and socio-spatial conditions in the design, provisioning, management, and access to sanitary infrastructure.

Sina Kamala Kaufmann

is a writer. In 2019, she published a collection of stories under the tile *Bright Matter*. Beside this, she is co-editor of Extinction Rebellion's civil disobedience resistance handbook, *Wann wenn nicht wir** (2019).

Stefan Karlowsky

(born 1986) is a biochemist with a soft spot for environmental science and material cycles. His research at the Leibniz-Institut für Gemüse- und Zierpflanzenbau (IGZ) e. V. focuses on sustainable cultivation methods, and as co-coordinator of the EU project "P2GreeN" (Horizon Europe) he deals with the transformation of European sanitary system towards a nutrient-based circular economy.

Ariane Krause

(born 1982) is an industrial engineer with a focus on the sanitary and nutrient transition as part of a circular economy. In scientific experiments and system analyses, she demonstrated the effects, potentials and risks of using recycled fertilizers made from sanitary waste in urban and rural farming. At the Leibniz-Institut für Gemüse- und Zierpflanzenbau (IGZ) e. V., she coordinates the REGION.innovativ project zirkulierBAR (BMBF), which operates a laboratory for circular value creation with dry toilets in the city of Eberswalde. Krause is also a member of the Kollektiv für angepasste Technik Berlin (KanTe) and Netzwerk für nachhaltige Sanitärsysteme e. V. (NetSan).

Johanna Moser

(born 1980) is an architect whose work focuses on the conversion of existing buildings and the development of solutions for architecture to become a place of resource regeneration. She collaborates with Kollektiv für angepasste Technik Berlin (KanTe) and Third Skin Architects, among others.

Michel Riechmann

(born 1988) is an environmental engineer. His research at the Swiss Federal Institute of Aquatic Science and Technology (Eawag) focuses on the development of technologies for the recovery of nutrients from urine. He is also strategically involved in the Circular Sanitation Network Switzerland (VaLoo), in its German equivalent NetSan, and in the expert committee for resource-oriented sanitation systems at the German Association for Water, Wastewater and Waste (DWA).

Eleftheria Xenikaki

(born 1980) works as a freelance architect in the design workgroup of Kollektiv für angepasste Technik Berlin (KanTe), where she is primarily interested in barrier-free design, participatory and cooperative planning, and ecological architecture.

Giovanna Silva

(born 1980) lives and works in Milan. She is the founder and editor-in-chief of *Humboldt Books* and cofounder of *San Rocco*. She teaches photography at NABA Nuova Accademia di Belle Arti Milan, Università Iuav di Venezia, and ISIA Urbino. Her photography books have been published by Mousse, Hatje Cantz, and Nero, among others. Her work has been shown, among others, at the 10th and 14th Venice Architecture Biennale, MACRO in Rome, Triennale di Milano, FRAC Orléans, C/O Berlin, the Rabat Biennale, and the Italian Cultural Institute in New York.

Sozialgenossenschaft Bellevue di Monaco eG

(founded 2015) is a social cooperative which started as a civic alliance with the goal of establishing a residential and cultural center for migrants and refugees in the center of Munich. After months of debate about urban vacancies in 2014, and after the protests against the German identitarian movement Pegida [Patriotic Europeans Against the Islamisation of the West], around the turn of the year 2014/15, activists were able to obtain approval by the city government to lease three buildings in the city center. The cooperative currently has more than 750 members.

Eva Stricker

(born 1980) is a freelance architect and author based in Zurich. Since 2018, her research has been focused on questions of circular construction at the Zurich University of Applied Sciences (ZHAW). Since 2022, she has also been teaching at RPTU Kaiserslautern-Landau. She is a co-editor of the book *Bauteile wiederverwenden: Ein Kompendium zum zirkulären Bauen* (Park Books, 2021).

Florian Summa

(born 1982) is an architect and co-founder of SUMMACUMFEMMER Architects in Leipzig. After his studies at RWTH Aachen and ETH Zurich, he worked for five years at Caruso St John Architects in London and Zurich. From 2015 to 2018, he was a design assistant at ETH Zurich with Adam Caruso. In 2019, he taught at TU Munich. From 2020 to 2022, he was a visiting professor at the Integral Architecture chair at TU Graz. Since 2022, he has been a visiting professor at UdK Berlin. He is a co-curator of *Open for Maintenance*, the German contribution to the 18th Venice Architecture Biennale (2023).

TRNSFRM eG

(founded 2018) is a Berlin-based, cooperatively organized construction company dedicated to dealing with real estate differently. At the core of their work is the idea of defending the commons through a practice of building that focuses on social and cultural uses, as well as affordable and communal living. To this end, as a cooperative, they support, take on, and realize construction projects that enable resource-efficient, circular, and socially equitable real estate development.

Françoise Vergès

is an author, decolonial, antiracist activist, and feminist. She is cofounder of the collective Decolonize the Arts (2015–20) and curates performances with artists and activists. Her recent publications include *A Feminist Theory of Violence* (2022), *De la violence coloniale dans l'espace public* (2021), *A Decolonial Feminism* (2021) and *Programme de désordre absolu: Décoloniser le musée* (2023).

La Biennale di Venezia

18. Mostra Internazionale di Architettura

Partecipazioni Nazionali

swiss arts council

prohelvetia

Neighbours

Karin Sander
Philip Ursprung
Biennale Architettura 2023
Swiss Pavilion

Cover image: © ARCH+ SUMMACUMFEMMER BÜRO JULIANE GREB
Inside cover flap: © Giovanna Silva
Contents page: © ARCH+ SUMMACUMFEMMER BÜRO JULIANE GREB
Chapter introductions Caring / Repairing / Maintaining (Through Squatting): © ARCH+ SUMMACUMFEMMER BÜRO JULIANE GREB

MAINTENANCE AND REMODELING

Essay Hélène Frichot
Fig. 1 © Mierle Laderman Ukeles. Courtesy of the artist and Ronald Feldman Gallery
Fig. 2 © Ila Bêka and Louise Lemoine
Fig. 3 © Courtesy of the artists and Manchester Art Gallery. Photo: Alan Seabright
Fig. 4 © documenta archiv. Photo: Nils Klinger

Essay Christoph Grafe, Tim Rieniets
Fig. 1 © Bernd Bess
Fig. 2 © Christoph Grafe
Fig. 3 © Marc Petitjean
Fig. 4 Courtesy of Assemble
Fig. 5 © Philippe Ruault
Figs. 6–7 © Delphine Mathy
Fig. 8 © Andreas Meichsner

CARING

Photo essay Giovanna Silva
Figs. 1–11 © Giovanna Silva

Essay Ludovico Centis
Fig. 1 © Archivio Veritas / Museo dell'Acqua di Venezia
Fig. 2 Courtesy of the author. Source: Lorenzo Fabian, Ludovico Centis, *The Lake of Venice: A Scenario for Venice and Its Lagoon* (Conegliano: Anteferma, 2022)
Fig. 3 Source: Archivio di Stato di Venezia, *Savi ed Esecutori alle Acque, Disegni, Diversi*, 109
Fig. 4 Source: Benedetto Bordone, *Isolario*, 1528
Fig. 5 © Ministero delle Infrastrutture e dei Trasporti. Provveditorato Interregionale alle opere pubbliche per il Veneto, Trentino Alto Adige e Friuli Venezia Giulia. Concessionario Consorzio Venezia Nuova
Fig. 6 © Ludovico Centis

Essay Marco Baravalle
Figs. 1–3 Courtesy of Farout Festival Base

Essay Françoise Vergès
Fig. 1 Courtesy of the artist and of the Fabric Workshop and Museum. Photo: Carlos Avendaño
Fig. 2 © Courtesy of the Gordon Parks Foundation. Photo: Gordon Parks
Fig. 3 © Justice for Cleaners Goldsmiths
Fig. 4 Photo: Padmapriya
Fig. 5 © Black Quantum Futurism

Essay Rosa Loo
Figs. 2–3 © Industrial Design program, HGK Basel, Luisa Tschumi and Leonie Roth
Fig. 4 © finizio – Future Sanitation
Fig. 5 © Coopérative Équilibre
Fig. 6 © EOOS NEXT
Fig. 7 © ARCH+ SUMMACUMFEMMER BÜRO JULIANE GREB

Essay Aimi Hamraie
Fig. 1 © picture alliance / AP Photo / Jeff Markowitz
Fig. 2 PD-US. Source: Harry H. Laughlin: *The Second International Exhibition of Eugenics*, exhib. cat. (New York: American Museum of Natural History, 1921) 89
Fig. 3 © Judy A. Crookes, Henry Dreyfuss Associates
Figs. 4–6 © University of Illinois
Fig. 7 © ARCH+ SUMMACUMFEMMER BÜRO JULIANE GREB

REPAIRING

Essay Johannes Odenthal
Figs. 1–3 © ARCH+ SUMMACUMFEMMER BÜRO JULIANE GREB

Essay Vittoria Martini
Fig. 1 Photo: Giovanni Pellegrini. Photo editing: Alexander Romey
Fig. 2 Drawing: Arno Löbbecke. Photo: Jens Ziehe
Figs. 3–6 Photo: Jens Ziehe
Figs. 7–10 © ARCH+ SUMMACUMFEMMER BÜRO JULIANE GREB

Practice Rebiennale / R3B and Concular
Figs. 1–6 © ARCH+ SUMMACUMFEMMER BÜRO JULIANE GREB

Essay Eva Stricker
Fig. 1 © Martin Pawley
Fig. 2 Photo: Giuseppe Micciché
Fig. 3 © Seiler Linhart Architekten. Photo: Rasmus Norlander
Fig. 4 © Roland Bernath
Fig. 5 © baubüro in situ ag. Photo: Martin Zeller
Fig. 6 © Simon Jüttner

Practice CRCLR House
Fig. 1 © Die Zusammenarbeiter
Figs. 2, 14–17 Photo: Andreas Trogisch
Fig. 3 Photo: Angela Elbing
Figs. 4, 7, 8, 10–13 © Studio Bowie
Fig. 5 © Die Zusammenarbeiter and LXSY Architekten
Fig. 6 © Die Zusammenarbeiter. Drawing: Benedikt Kurz
Fig. 9 © LXSY Architekten

Practice Haus der Materialisierung
Fig. 1 © Studio Patric Dreier
Fig. 2 © Nils Koenning
Figs. 3–4 © Erik Göngrich
Figs. 5–6, 8–10 © Raquel Gómez Delgado
Fig. 7 © Paolo Gatto

MAINTAINING (THROUGH SQUATTING)

Essay Sarah Gainsforth
Fig. 1 © Eredi di Luigi Ghirri. Courtesy of Mai 36 Galerie, Zurich
Fig. 2 © Alessandro Guida / paesaggisensibili
Fig. 3 © Architectural Press Archive / RIBA Collections
Figs. 4–5 © Alessandro Guida / paesaggisensibili

Practice Assemblea Sociale per la Casa
Figs. 1–11 © Giovanna Silva

Essay Andrej Holm
Figs. 1–2 Photo: Arnim Stauth
Fig. 3 Photo: Kemal Kurt
Fig. 4 © Michael Kipp / Umbruch Bildarchiv
Fig. 5 © Instand-Besetzer-Post
Fig. 6 Courtesy of Käthe Kruse
Figs. 7–8 © S.T.E.R.N. GmbH

Practice Kotti & Co
Figs. 1, 5, 7–10, 14 © Sandy Kaltenborn
Fig. 2 © image-shift / Athena Javanmardi
Figs. 3–4 © Drawing: image-shift / Sandy Kaltenborn
Fig. 6 © CAD drawing: Stefan Endewardt 2012
Figs. 11–12 © image-shift / Sandy Kaltenborn
Fig. 13 © Christian Ditsch
Fig. 15 © image-shift / Athena Javanmardi & Sandy Kaltenborn

Practice Bellevue di Monaco
Fig. 1 © REGUPOL. Photo: Tom Bauer
Figs. 2, 15–16, 20 © Hirner & Riehl Architekten und Stadtplaner
Figs. 3–5 © Ziska Thalhammer
Figs. 6–7 © Andrea Huber
Fig. 8 © Ulrike Myrzik
Figs. 9, 11, 14, 17–19 © Gila Sonderwald
Fig. 10 © Moritz Grebner
Fig. 12 © Regina Recht
Fig. 13 © Patrick Wild
Fig. 21 © Frank Schroth

La Biennale di Venezia
18. Mostra Internazionale di Architettura
Partecipazioni Nazionali

Open for Maintenance – Wegen Umbau geöffnet
German Pavilion
18th International Architecture Exhibition
La Biennale di Venezia

Duration: May 20 to November 26, 2023
Pavilion Opening: May 19, 2023

Curatorial team
ARCH+ / SUMMACUMFEMMER /
BÜRO JULIANE GREB:
Anne Femmer, Franziska Gödicke, Juliane Greb, Christian Hiller, Petter Krag, Melissa Makele, Anh-Linh Ngo, Florian Summa

Website: openformaintenance.net
Instagram: @germanpavilionvenice

Commissioned by

Federal Ministry for Housing, Urban Development and Building

Team
Elke Doppelbauer, operations / invitation management
Nora Dünser, managing editor exhibition catalog
Mirko Gatti, research associate
Anna Hugot, curatorial staff
Sascha Kellermann, events
Beatrice Koch, curatorial staff
Daniel Kuhnert, editorial staff
Arno Löbbecke, director
Victor Lortie, editorial staff
Vittorio Romieri, curatorial staff
Barbara Schindler, communications / marketing
Finn Steffens, editorial staff

Translations
Mirko Gatti (EN–IT), Victor Lortie (GER–EN)

Visual identity
Stan Hema, Berlin:
Peer Hempel, André van Rueth, Daniela Vogel

Prepress
max-color, Berlin

Public relations
Bureau N, Berlin: Inga Krumme, Silke Neumann, Caroline Wolf

Contact architects
cfk architetti, Venice:
Clemens Kusch, Martin Weigert

Participants

Arbeitsgruppe Sanitärwende [Project group sanitary revolution] with Eawag – Swiss Federal Institute of Aquatic Science and Technology with Michel Riechmann; finizio – Future Sanitation with Florian Augustin, Tom Kühne; KanTe – Kollektiv für angepasste Technik with Sina Kamala, Ariane Krause, Johanna Moser, Eleftheria Xenikaki; klo:lektiv with Sabine Bongers-Römer, Katharina Ciax, Martine Kayser; Leibniz Institute of Vegetable and Ornamental Crops (IGZ) with Ariane Krause, Stefan Karlowsky; urin*all with Leonie Roth, Luisa Tschumi; German Toilet Organization; NetSan; VaLoo; ZirkulierBAR; as well as Agriluska with Luca Vallese; IDRO Group Srl

Assemblea Sociale per la Casa, Venice

Sozialgenossenschaft Bellevue di Monaco eG, with Hirner & Riehl Architekten und Stadtplaner PartG mbB BDA, Munich

Centro Sociale Rivolta, Venice

ConstructLab, Berlin
with Patrick Hubmann, Alexander Römer, Peter Zuiderwijk

CRCLR House, Berlin
with Concular with Lore Ameel, Serdar Gökay Küçuk, Annabelle von Reutern, Rebekka Steinlein; Die Zusammenarbeiter & TRNSFRM eG with Christian Schöningh; Impact Hub Berlin with Sascha Stremming; LXSY Architekten with Kim Le Roux, Margit Sichrovsky
Project group Trivial Circuit
with LXSY Architekten with Kim Le Roux, Margit Sichrovsky, Christine Andreas; Impact Hub Berlin with Sascha Stremming; Concular with Annabelle von Reutern; graphic design: Marie-Louise Greb; text: Axel Sichrovsky

Maria Eichhorn, Berlin

Giorgio de Finis, RIF, Museo delle Periferie, Rome

FORWARD DANCE COMPANY by LOFFT – DAS THEATER, Leipzig
with Pável Aguilar, Mouafak Aldoabl, Elsa Artmann, Renan Alves Manhães, Anna Boblest, Gustavo Fijalkow, Alice Giuliani, Giulia Marcotullio, Friederike Otte, Alfred Quarshie, Tamara Rettenmund, Alessandro Schiattarella, Alissa Sebri, Lisa Zocher

Haus der Materialisierung – Center for Climate-Friendly Resource Usage, as part of the Haus der Statistik pilot project at Alexanderplatz, Berlin
with BAUFACHFRAU Berlin e. V. with Andrea Hüttche, Jutta Ziegler; Berliner Stadtmission with Sofie Göppl Leon; FahrArt Atelier with Benjamin Känel; Kostümkollektiv with Katrin Wittig; Kunst-Stoffe e. V. with Jan-Micha Gamer, Rhea Gleba; MaterialWerk UG with Corinna Vosse; Mitkunstzentrale with Rahel Jakob, Julie Teuber, Nora Wilhelm; mrtz Forschungswerkstatt with Moritz Wermelskirch; Ort-schafft-Material with Jannis Schiefer, Elena Stranges; stefan is doing things with Stefan Klopfer; STREETWARE saved item with Alice Fassina; Studio Patric Dreier; ZUsammenKUNFT Berlin eG with Kim Gundlach, Andrea Hofmann

Institute of Radical Imagination, Naples
with Marco Baravalle, Emanuele Braga, Gabriella Riccio; in collaboration with Anna Rispoli and S.a.L.E. Docks, Venice

Kotti & Co, Berlin
with Tashy Endres, Sandy Kaltenborn

Laboratorio Occupato Morion, Venice

Rebiennale / R3B, Venice
with Giulio Grillo, Tommaso Cacciari, Davide Mozzato, Mirko Pedrotti, Matteo Pavan, Alessandro Dus, Alessandra Tirel, Alice Montioli, Jacopo Povelato, Alice Bazzoli

SerenDPT, Venice
with Gianluca Corò, Marco Bertoldi, Luca Giuman, Sarah Puccio, Aurora del Sordo

Giovanna Silva, Venice / Milan
with Angelo Boriolo (Boris), Milan

Responsible for the incorporated work
Relocating a Structure
Ellen Strittmatter,
Commissioner of the German Pavilion 2022
Yilmaz Dziewior,
Curator of the German Pavilion 2022
Maria Eichhorn,
Artist of the German Pavilion 2022

EXHIBITION CATALOG

This publication is part of the exhibition *Open for Maintenance – Wegen Umbau geöffnet*, the German contribution to the 18th International Architecture Exhibition—La Biennale di Venezia curated by ARCH+ / SUMMACUMFEMMER / BÜRO JULIANE GREB.

ARCH+
Journal for Architecture and Urbanism

Publishers
ARCH+ / Spector Books

Publishers of ARCH+
Nikolaus Kuhnert, Anh-Linh Ngo

Advisory board
Arno Brandlhuber, Beatriz Colomina, Philipp Oswalt, Stephan Trüby, Georg Vrachliotis, Mark Wigley, Karin Wilhelm

Editor-in-chief
Anh-Linh Ngo*

Managing director
Arno Löbbecke

Editorial team
Nora Dünser*, Mirko Gatti*, Franziska Gödicke*, Christian Hiller*, Felix Hofmann, Sascha Kellermann, Markus Krieger*, Victor Lortie*, Melissa Makele* (project lead), Alex Nehmer*

In cooperation with
Anne Femmer*, SUMMACUMFEMMER, Leipzig
Juliane Greb*, BÜRO JULIANE GREB, Ghent
Petter Krag*, BÜRO JULIANE GREB, Ghent
Florian Summa*, SUMMACUMFEMMER, Leipzig

Managing editor
Nora Dünser*

Editorial assistants
Daniel Kuhnert*, Finn Steffens*

* Editorial team for this publication

Art direction
Stan Hema, Berlin

Design
Sara Božić, Peer Hempel, André van Rueth, Daniel Vandré

Project manager for Stan Hema
Niki Moreira

Copy editor
Victor Lortie

Translations
GER–EN: Petra + Jeremy Gaines (pp. 1, 28–37, 76–85, 110–115, 124–135, 136–147, 180–189, 190–199);
Daniel Kuhnert (pp. 42–53),
Victor Lortie (pp. 2–4, 38–41, 94–97, 148–151, 200–203, 206–208, features no. 117);
Rob Madole (pp. 98–101, 116–123, 172–179)
IT–EN: Natascha Bruce (pp. 62–67, 158–171);
Johanna Bishop (pp. 102–109)

Proofreading
James Copeland

Head of research and exhibition projects
Christian Hiller

Head of communications and marketing
Barbara Schindler

Head of operations
Elke Doppelbauer

Head of events
Sascha Kellermann

Publishing assistant
Friederike Kiko

Ambassadors
Martin Luce, Christine Rüb

Prepress
max-color, Berlin

Printing
Medialis Offsetdruck GmbH, Berlin

Image credits
ARCH+ has made every effort to notify all copyright holders. Any person or institution wishing to make a copyright claim is requested to contact the editors.

Copyright
This work is subject to copyright. All rights are reserved, whether the whole or part of the material is concerned, specifically the rights of translation, reprinting, reuse of illustrations, recitation, broadcasting, reproduction on microfilms, or in other ways, including storage in databases. For any kind of use, permission from the copyright owner must be obtained.

ARCH+ features
Initiating partner

SSS SIEDLE

The Experimental Scholarship Program for young architectural researchers is funded by X-A Experimental gGmbH

EXPERIMENTAL

Advertising
marketing@archplus.net
archplus.net/en/mediakit

ARCH+ Verlag GmbH
Friedrichstraße 23a
10969 Berlin
Tel +49 30 340 467 17
verlag@archplus.net
Managing Directors:
Nikolaus Kuhnert, Anh-Linh Ngo

ARCH+ gGmbH (nonprofit limited liability company)
ggmbh@archplus.net
Managing director: Arno Löbbecke

Donation account
GLS Bank
IBAN: DE47 4306 0967 1229 2768 01
BIC: GENODEM1GLS
archplus.net/en/nonprofit

Distribution
Spector Books
Harkortstraße 10
04107 Leipzig
www.spectorbooks.com

Germany, Austria: GVA, Gemeinsame Verlagsauslieferung Göttingen GmbH & Co. KG, www.gva-verlage.de
Switzerland: AVA Verlagsauslieferung AG, www.ava.ch
France, Belgium: Interart Paris, www.interart.fr
UK: Central Books Ltd, www.centralbooks.com
USA, Canada, Central and South America, Africa: ARTBOOK/D.A.P., www.artbook.com
South Korea: The Book Society, www.thebooksociety.org
Japan: twelvebooks, www.twelve-books.com
Australia, New Zealand: Perimeter Distribution, www.perimeterdistribution.com

Subscriptions
German issues only:
archplus.net/abo

Direct orders
of English ARCH+ issues:
archplus.net/en/shop/issues
vertrieb@archplus.net

ISBN 978-3-95905-703-5 (Spector Books)
ISBN 978-3-931435-78-3 (ARCH+)

© 2023 ARCH+ Verlag GmbH, the authors, and translators
© 2023 Spector Books, Leipzig

First edition: 2023
Printed in Germany

Program partner
For the duration of the Biennale, the Goethe-Institut, as a program partner of the German Pavilion, will take up topics such as inclusion, care work, and urban practices in artistic and performative projects, as part of the programmatic series *Performing Architecture.*

PERFORMING ARCHITECTURE | GOETHE INSTITUT

Workshop program
The workshop program *Maintenance 1:1* by ARCH+ / SUMMACUMFEMMER / BÜRO JULIANE GREB in cooperation with the Sto-Foundation and AIT-Dialog, will be carried out in the context of the *Venice Biennale Lab* series. Participants will include higher education institutions, vocational training schools, and organizations from Venice and beyond.

Sto Stiftung

AIT DIALOG

Cooperation partner
Rebiennale/R3B has years of experience and expertise in reusing materials from the Biennale. As part of *Open for Maintenance*, they assisted the curatorial team in organizing and collecting the material and carried out the construction of the new ramp in front of the German Pavilion. In addition, they will participate in the workshop program for the duration of the Architecture Biennale.

rebiennale | R3B

The "Berliner Stadtinitiativen" series of workshops and events is funded by

Senatsverwaltung für Stadtentwicklung, Bauen und Wohnen | BERLIN

Technical and scientific supervision
Federal Ministry for Housing, Urban Development and Building: Anne Keßler, Stephan Mayer
Federal Institute for Research on Building, Urban Affairs and Spatial Development: Dr. Olaf Asendorf

Acknowledgements
We are particularly indebted to the following people and institutions:
Goethe-Institut: Joachim Bernauer, Elisa Costa, Rosina Franzè, Christina Hasenau, Antonella Perin, Chiara Sermoneta, Susanne Traub, Karin Varga
ifa: Dorothea Grassmann, Jochen Hetterich, Friederike Klussmann, Ellen Strittmatter, Gitte Zschoch
Sto-Foundation: Ralf Pasel, Till Stahlbusch, Ingeborg Totzke
as well as: Pasquale Ambrogio, Marius Babias, Marco Baravalle, Leonardo Basso, Fabiola Bazzo, Alice Bazzoli, Barbara Bergau, Niccolò Bocenti, Lukas Boss, Francesca Borghini, Chiara Buratti, Peter Cachola Schmal, Tommaso Cacciari, Marta Canino, Daniela Canorro, Elena Carraro, Shanti Colombo, Silvia Compagnin, Benedikt Duhoux, Alessandro Dus, Yilmaz Dziewior, Maria Eichhorn, Yngvild Faeroy, Christian Ganzer, Olaf Grawert, Giulio Grillo, Agata Guerrini, Till Hofmann, Luis Klocke, Anja Kreß, Nicolai Kuppel, Filippo Lunian, Matthias Mai, Benita von Maltzahn, Matthias Marschner, Valentina Montagnaro, Reiner Nagel, Denijen Pauljević, Nina Peters, Fred Plassmann, Jacopo Povelato, Leonie Radine, Anna Ramazzotto, Francesco Renzoni, Claudia Ribeiro, Felix Schaller, Carl-Stephan Schweer, Giovanna Silva, Marta Sottoriva, Tommaso Tagliabue, Ruggero Tallon, Marcus Thieme, Federica Toninello, Deniz Turgut, Martina Vergnano

Sponsors and supporters
The German contribution to the 18th Venice Architecture Biennale applies the resource-efficient but labor-intensive principles of reuse and circularity, involving many actors from civil society, researchers, and cultural practitioners. Without the support and trust of a large number of sponsors, corporate partners, and supporters, the project would not have materialized in this form. We would like to express our special thanks to the main sponsor Volkswagen Group, the Berlin Senate Department for Urban Development, Building and Housing, the corporate partners Albrecht Jung GmbH & Co. KG, Equitone, VHV x Hand schafft Wert, our sponsors Agrob Buchtal GmbH, Heidehof Stiftung, n.b.k., as well as our Friends Euroboden Architekturkultur and New Tendency, in addition to our program partner Goethe-Institut and the Sto-Foundation for their extraordinary support.

Main sponsor

VOLKSWAGEN GROUP

With kind support from
BRLO GmbH
caspar.
competitionline Verlags GmbH
HAROLD'S Lederwaren GmbH
J.MAYER.H und Partners, Architects mbB
JOANES Stiftung
mai public relations GmbH
ROBERTNEUN™
Martin Schnitzer und Hannes Dölker, Schnitzer& GmbH

Contributions in kind
BESSEY Tool GmbH & Co. KG
Bindulin-Werk H.L.Schönleber GmbH
Brüder Mannesmann AG
Cleaneroo GmbH
Deutsche Werkstätten Hellerau GmbH
E.C. Emmerich Werkzeugfabrik GmbH & Co. KG
FAMAG-Werkzeugfabrik GmbH & Co. KG
Festool GmbH
HEDI GmbH
hedue GmbH
IDRO Group S.R.L.
Kirschen Werkzeuge GmbH & Co. KG
Kvadrat
Mesko-Pinsel GmbH
PROXXON S.A.
Simpson Strong-Tie GmbH
ANDREAS STIHL AG & Co. KG
ULMIA GmbH
Werkzeug Weber GmbH & Co. KG

Legal advice
Carl-Stephan Schweer, Raue PartmbB

Corporate partners

JUNG

Hand schafft Wert × VHV Versicherungen

EQUITONE
Fibre cement facade materials

Sponsors

AGROB BUCHTAL

Heidehof Stiftung

n.b.k.

Friends

Euroboden Architekturkultur

NEW TENDENCY